TECHNIQUES OF SUBVERSION
IN MODERN LITERATURE

UNIVERSITY OF FLORIDA

PRESS/GAINESVILLE

M. KEITH BOOKER

TECHNIQUES OF SUBVERSION IN MODERN LITERATURE

TRANSGRESSION, ABJECTION, AND THE CARNIVALESQUE

Library of Congress Cataloging-in-Publication Data

Booker, M. Keith.
  Techniques of subversion in modern
  literature : transgression, abjection, and the
  carnivalesque / M. Keith Booker.
  p.   cm.
  Includes bibliographical references and index.
  ISBN 0-8130-1065-9
  1. English literature—20th century—History and
criticism.   2. American literature—20th century—
History and criticism.   3. Literature and society—
History—20th century.   4. Social problems in
literature.   5. Carnival in literature.   I. Title.
PR478.S57B66   1991
820.9'355—dc20   91-15888

The University of Florida Press is a member of the
University Presses of Florida, the scholarly publishing
agency of the State University System of Florida. Books
are selected for publication by faculty editorial
committees at each of Florida's nine public universities:
Florida A & M University (Tallahassee), Florida Atlantic
University (Boca Raton), Florida International University
(Miami), Florida State University (Tallahassee), University
of Central Florida (Orlando), University of Florida
(Gainesville), University of North Florida (Jacksonville),
University of South Florida (Tampa), and University of
West Florida (Pensacola).
  Orders for books published by all member presses
should be addressed to: University Presses of Florida,
15 Northwest 15th Street, Gainesville, FL 32611.

FOR DUBRAVKA

CONTENTS

ACKNOWLEDGMENTS

Numerous individuals read all or part of the manuscript and offered valuable suggestions for improvement, including Cheryl Herr of the University of Iowa and Marsha Bryant, Caryl Flinn, Anne Jones, Brian Richardson, Malini Schueller, and Al Shoaf, all of the University of Florida. Alistair Duckworth also belongs in this latter group, but deserves special mention for his encouragement to me in developing this manuscript and for his help in bringing it to fruition. Similarly, I would like to offer special thanks to Beth Schwartz for her valuable comments on Virginia Woolf and for originally bringing the work of Angela Carter to my attention. Finally, I would like to acknowledge most of all the contributions of my old mentor Brandy Kershner, who not only read all of the manuscript (most of it more than once), but offered inestimable support and encouragement throughout my stay at Florida.

Chapter 1 was originally published as "Postmodernism in Medieval England: Chaucer, Pynchon, Joyce, and the Poetics of Fission" in *Exemplaria* II.2 (1990): 563–94. Chapter 2 was originally published as "Beauty and the Beast: Dualism as Despotism in the Fiction of Salman Rushdie" in *ELH* 57 (1990): 977–97. Chapter 3 was originally published as "The Dynamics of Literary Transgression in Gilbert Sorrentino's *Mulligan Stew*" in *Essays in Literature* 17 (1990): 111–30. Chapter 4 was originally published as "What We Have Instead of God: Sexuality, Textuality, and Infinity in *The French Lieutenant's Woman*" in *Novel* 24 (1991). I would like to offer my thanks to these journals and their editors for permission to reprint these essays here in revised form.

Whenever you see a board up with "Trespassers will be prosecuted," trespass at once.

VIRGINIA WOOLF

IS LITERARY TRANSGRESSION
STUPID STUFF?

INTRODUCTION

According to one of the central myths of Judeo-Christian culture, human existence as we know it began in a fundamental act of transgression, in the expulsion of Adam and Eve from the Garden after their violation of God's ordinance against the eating of the forbidden fruit. But, as Adam tells Dante in *Paradiso* XXVI, it was not the fruit itself that was significant in this primal transgression: "the cause of my long exile did not lie / within the act of tasting of the tree, / but solely in my trespass of the boundary" (lines 115–17). Dante's Adam further emphasizes the symbolic nature of this primal breaching of God's law by suggesting that the resultant fall from grace was largely a linguistic one, that the confusion of languages usually associated with the Tower of Babel in fact dated all the way back to the Original Sin:

The tongue I spoke was all extinct before
the men of Nimrod set their minds upon
the unaccomplishable task; for never
    has any thing produced by human reason
been everlasting—following the heavens,
men seek the new, they shift their predilections.
    That man should speak at all is nature's act,

but how you speak—in this tongue or that—
she leaves to you and to your preference.

(lines 124–32)

Since the original Fall, human language has been characterized by a divinely imposed gap between signifier and signified
that leads to the proliferation of multiple tongues, as no language has claim to direct representation of reality. But it is God's
will that language be this way, and Dante, trusting that God's
will is good, eschews the ostensible linguistic stability offered
by Latin as the official language and writes his poem in the
vernacular. Stated otherwise, if the Incarnation renders the Fall a
fortunate one (as Dante believed), then it must render the arbitrariness and mutability of vernacular language fortunate as
well. Dante takes advantage of this good fortune to construct a
poem the richness of which is made possible by the very polysemy of vernacular language.

This essential relationship between poetry and the fallen condition of human language can also be discerned in the work of
that other great poet of the Fall, John Milton. In one of the most
curious phenomena of Western literature, Milton sets out to
"justify God's ways to man," then gives us *Paradise Lost*, a
poem whose most memorable element is the courage and gran-
deur of that archtransgressor, Satan. At first glance (given the
popular notion of Milton as devout Christian poet), this apparent privileging of Satan would seem inadvertent. Yet Milton's
thinking was profoundly transgressive. He was a fiercely anti-
clerical, radical heretic and a committed political revolutionary.
Indeed, as Christopher Hill points out, much of Milton's fascination with the story of the Fall comes about because he saw the
fallen state of mankind as the only explanation for the failure of
the Puritan Revolution (345–53). There were, then, certain parallels between the abortive heavenly coup of Satan and the failed
secular revolt of Cromwell. But, like Dante, Milton also saw
strong linguistic implications in the fortunate Fall. R. A. Shoaf
notes the way in which to Milton poetic tropes such as metaphor are only possible due to the mutability of language resulting from the Fall. In fact, poetry itself is only possible in a
postlapsarian world: "Thus Milton traces poetry back to an origin in the Fall—an origin, that is, in confusion" (*Milton* 67).

To both Dante and Milton transgression is a necessary prerequisite to poetry. Richard Kearney, in his survey of the history of the human imagination, goes even farther. He suggests that imagination itself is possible only after the Original Sin. Moreover, he notes that this perception is not limited to Judeo-Christian culture, as the birth of the imagination in Hellenic myth can be traced to Prometheus's transgressive bestowal of fire upon humanity. In both Hebraic and Hellenic traditions, "imagination is characterized by an act of rebellion against the divine order of things . . . while it empowers man to imitate God, it does so by means of an unlawful act" (80).

Transgression and creativity have been inextricably linked throughout the history of Western culture. And since at least the time of the Russian Formalists, it has been common to suggest that the transgression of boundaries is an essential feature of literariness. But the Russian Formalists were principally concerned with the ways in which literature violated the expectations brought about by the dominant conventions of literature itself. Their critics, such as Mikhail Bakhtin, have argued that the Formalist treatment of literature as a "closed, purely literary series" (Bakhtin and Medvedev 159), prevents the exploration of the truly important transgressive energies of literature, which are directed not at other literature but at dominant institutions and ideologies in the real world of politics and history. There is exciting potential in this suggestion that literature can in fact have a genuine political impact, and it is no accident that Bakhtin has risen to such prominence in contemporary literary criticism, where history and politics have become privileged terms and where adjectives of boundary crossing like "hybrid," "interdisciplinary," and "multigeneric" reign supreme.

Amidst this hubbub, the notion that literature can be genuinely transgressive in a political sense has risen from anathema to apotheosis, a development that is, in general, to be applauded. However, given the apparent ease with which transgression has been adopted as an "official" mode of literary discourse in recent years, one might legitimately ask what it is that is being transgressed against in "transgressive" literature. Many of the works that have been acclaimed as politically effective in this century have been so difficult and complex that only professional scholars seem to be able to recognize their radical potential, while these scholars themselves tend to work within a heavily institutionalized university environment that has itself—especially in

North America—proved remarkably ill-suited as a locus for political action.

Clearly, the question of transgression in literature is difficult and complex, dealing with the function and purpose of literature, the impact of ideas upon institutions, and the interactions between culture and politics. This situation is made all the more arduous by the difficulty in even defining transgression. After all, even the most transgressive works of literature do not in general immediately send their readers into the streets carrying banners and shouting slogans. Transgressive literature works more subtly, by gradually chipping away at certain modes of thinking that contribute to the perpetuation of oppressive political structures. As a result it is virtually impossible to document the actual political power of literature; about the only hard evidence we have of such a power is the terror with which totalitarian regimes have traditionally regarded literary works that they deemed dangerous.

Despite such difficulties, there seems to be a growing conviction among literary scholars that literature can serve legitimate and useful purposes that go far beyond mere entertainment. Literature itself has made such suggestions for quite some time. One of the important poems in the early development of modern poetry is a interesting piece by A. E. Housman intriguingly entitled "Terence, This Is Stupid Stuff." In the poem, a happy-go-lucky tavern dweller chides the poet Terence for including unpleasant and troubling images in his poetry. Poetry, argues this worthy, should be amusing and gay: Terence should "pipe a tune to dance to" instead of his melancholy rhymes.

Terence's reply amounts to the formulation of a theory of the poetic and its purpose. He argues that poetry has far more important things to do than stimulate gaiety. After all, he explains in a memorable couplet, "malt does more than Milton can / To justify God's ways to man." It is, according to Terence, the function of poetry to be troubling, to present images of painful reality. Invoking the example of Mithridates, the mythical king who drank small doses of toxin to build an immunity against the day his enemies would seek to poison him in earnest, Terence argues that the fictional painful images presented in poetry prepare us to deal more readily with real pain when it comes along.

Housman/Terence is making this proposal in the waning years of the nineteenth century, at the very dawning of the modern age in literature, and the modern writers who followed him seem to have taken his advice to heart. There is certainly no shortage of troubling images in modern literature, whether they involve Virginia Woolf's Septimus Smith falling to his death impaled upon fence railings or Thomas Pynchon's apocalyptic 00000 rocket falling upon the heads of us all. But what does Housman's adumbration of the Mithridatic function of literature have to say about the implications of such troubling fictions? For those of us who are interested in finding a genuinely subversive political potential in works of literature, Housman's poem might suggest that transgressive fictions can provide images that will inspire and equip us to effect transgressions in the real world. But one could also interpret the poem in the opposite way. Perhaps such fictions simply help us to tolerate injustices, sublimating our transgressive impulses into literature while pursuing a course of political quietism in the real world.

In this study I examine the work of a number of authors, ranging from Petronius, the ancient Roman, to contemporary postmodernists such as Salman Rushdie and Angela Carter, all of whom share a tendency to break rules, transgress boundaries, destabilize hierarchies, and question authority of various kinds in their work. My point is not that such literary transgressions occur; no one doubts that they do. The important question is how these transgressions function and whether they matter in the real sense of contributing to genuine social change. I have relied on a number of recent theoretical discourses to provide frameworks for my exploration of the dynamics of literary transgressions, including especially the notions of the carnival as put forth by Mikhail Bakhtin and of abjection as put forth by Julia Kristeva.

One of the methods I use to identify the transgressive energies of various texts is to seek elements in those texts that relate to Bakhtin's description of the carnivalesque spirit or to the tradition of Menippean satire, the genre that Bakhtin finds to be so thoroughly infused with the carnivalesque. The Bakhtinian concepts of carnival and of dialogism do, in fact, provide an extremely useful starting point for my readings of these texts. The notion of carnival, however, suffers from the same doubleness as Housman's suggestion of a Mithridatic function of literature. Despite the significance of the carnival as an arena for the staging of subversive energies, one must not forget that the carnival itself is in fact a sanctioned form of "subversion" whose very purpose is to sublimate and defuse the social tensions that might lead to genuine subversion—a sort of opiate of the masses. Terry Eagleton is only one of many who have pointed out this fact: "Carnival, after all, is a *licensed* affair in every sense, a permissible rupture of hegemony, a contained popular blow-off as disturbing and relatively ineffectual as a revolutionary work of art" (148, Eagleton's emphasis). Eagleton's critique is particularly relevant here because it calls into question both the validity of the carnival as a symbol of subversion and the political force of works of art in general.

The notion that a certain amount of authorized transgression can actually enhance the power of authoritarian regimes is one that literary works have themselves sometimes explored. In Italo Calvino's *If on a winter's night a traveler*, the Director General of the State Police Archives in the dictatorship of Ircania seems to acknowledge the power of transgressive literature when he complains that even his efficient organization cannot control what happens during the act of reading:

> this is the limit that even the most omnipotent police force cannot
> broach. We can prevent reading: but in the decree that forbids
> reading there will be still read something of the truth that we
> would wish never to be read . . . . (240, Calvino's ellipsis)

Yet even in Ircania a modicum of transgressive literature is tolerated, because the state needs objects against which to "justify constantly the existence of its repressive apparatus" (236). This kind of toleration of transgression is openly expressed in Samuel R. Delany's science-fiction novel, *Triton*, in which the small settlement on Neptune's moon includes within its confines an "unlicensed sector," where all official laws are suspended. But in this zone of authorized transgression, unofficial laws arise instead, preventing anarchy. Moreover, law enforcement officials are among those given carte blanche in this sector, where they can thus pursue criminals with unlimited violence and vigor. These unlicensed sectors are provided by the official government precisely to allow potentially dangerous energies to play themselves out, a strategy that contributes to the remarkable ability of Triton's pluralistic power structure to withstand

and absorb transgressions of all kinds. It is, we are told, a "politically low-volatile society" (148).

Eagleton relates his comment on the carnival to "the mutual complicity of law and liberation, power and desire, that has become a dominant theme of contemporary post-Marxist pessimism" (149). As far as revolutionary works of art are concerned, such pessimism seems justified. While some critics of postmodernism believe it to be the most transgressive current in contemporary art, others have argued that the movement is not transgressive at all, but in reality acts to reinforce the very norms it purports to oppose. For example, Gerald Graff has argued that postmodernism's exposure of the fictionality of what we conceive to be reality is not transgressive, but conservative of the current social norm. He suggests that postmodernism's "conventions of reflexivity and anti-realism are themselves mimetic of the kind of unreal reality that modern reality has become. But 'unreality' in this sense is not a fiction but the element in which we live" (180). Probably most important among such criticisms is Fredric Jameson's critique of the complicity between postmodernism and the values of late consumer capitalism, a complicity "which consistently affirms the identity of postmodernism with capitalism in its latest systematic mutation" ("Marxism and Postmodernism" 373).

Linda Hutcheon has responded to such critics as Jameson in works like *A Poetics of Postmodernism* and *The Politics of Postmodernism*. Her argument centers on the importance of parody in postmodernist art and suggests that while it is true that the voice of dominant culture sounds in postmodernist works, that voice is continually placed in dialogue with more subversive and transgressive voices. Thus, in a reversal of the situation of Calvino's Police Director, who feels that oppression must have something to oppress, Hutcheon argues that postmodernist works include dominant ideologies because transgression must have something to transgress against.

Hutcheon's subtle and interesting arguments are informed by a variety of theoretical resources, including Bakhtin. It is not entirely coincidental, then, that Hutcheon's model of the "paradoxical" and "duplicitous" nature of postmodernist parody gives it some of the dual character of the Bakhtinian carnival. This duality becomes even more complex in our contemporary cultural climate, where it is increasingly difficult to tell the good guys from the bad guys. According to Bakhtin much of the subversive force of carnivalesque literature derives from the intermingling of elements of official "high" culture with the "low" culture arising from folk sources; folk culture is associated with liberation and emancipation while official culture is associated with repression and tyranny. But in today's high-tech mass-media society one might argue that mass culture is no longer determined by the "folk," but instead by programming decisions made in corporate boardrooms. Such perceptions led Adorno and the Frankfurt School to a position on culture almost diametrically opposed to that of Bakhtin, in which they suggested that the mind-numbing effects of mass culture reinforced the status quo, while some (though not all) radically experimental "high" modernist art contained a genuine subversive potential.

By now, however, the modernist works that Adorno admired have largely become institutionalized as "great works," and the transgressive projects of experimental art seem to have become increasingly ineffectual. Matei Calinescu notes the way in which avant-garde art was crippled as a subversive force in the 1960s because the bourgeois society that it sought to disrupt simply appropriated it as a popular entertainment:

The avant-garde, whose limited popularity had long rested exclusively on scandal, all of a sudden became one of the major cultural myths of the 1960s. Its offensive, insulting rhetoric came to be regarded as merely amusing, and its apocalyptic outcries were changed into comfortable and innocuous clichés. Ironically, the avant-garde found itself failing through a stupendous, involuntary success. (120–21)

The plight of avant-garde art in the 1960s is emblematic of the remarkable ability shown by bourgeois society throughout its history to absorb and appropriate whatever subversive energies are directed against it. Since the 1960s, for example, the prevailing society has shown its Nietzschean "plastic power" in the rapid academic institutionalization of such potentially subversive critical approaches as Marxism, feminism, and deconstruction. Such subversive critical languages have virtually become the official mode of discourse in the academy (where it has become almost totally unacceptable not to sound subversive), while the academy itself has remained remarkably unchanged.

Calinescu points to another instance of this kind of appropriation when he suggests that "avant-garde" has by now been relegated to the status of an "advertising catchword." Indeed, both "high art" and subversion have become thoroughly inscribed in mass culture in the past few decades. MTV, the music video network, continually broadcasts a message of youthful rebellion against the tired old values of corporate America—sandwiched between commercial messages from the American corporate giants who underwrite these broadcasts. And as I am writing this introduction the American fast-food conglomerate Burger King is proudly announcing its transgressions against the norm with a multi-million-dollar advertising campaign featuring the slogan "Sometimes You've Gotta Break the Rules."

This appropriation of transgressive rhetoric by the dominant forces of bourgeois culture is complicated even further by certain prevailing cultural myths of individual defiance of authority. Everyone, it seems, would like to think of herself as boldly going where no one has gone before. Even Garrett Deasy, the antediluvian schoolmaster in Joyce's *Ulysses*, proudly proclaims to Stephen Dedalus that "I have rebel blood in me" (26). If there is a central founding myth of bourgeois society, it is the legend of the independent, rebellious individual; one might even view Milton's Satan as the prototypical bourgeois hero. In America such myths seem particularly strong, probably because of the formative impact of a particularly individualistic brand of Protestantism on American thought and because most of our national myths arose during a nineteenth century dominated by Romanticism. Thus the central American image of heroism is one of the rebellious individual, a sort of Byron of the Wild West. But nothing could be more conventional or conformist than this highly stylized (and strictly apolitical) notion of transgression, as witnessed by the fact that the major avatar of this figure in our recent history has been none other than that tough-talking, straight-shooting hombre Ronald Reagan, who parlayed a fierce opposition to Big Government into the leadership of the Biggest Government of them all.

No wonder that advocates of radical change are feeling pessimistic these days. But this is not to say that genuine transgression is impossible, only that it is difficult and that (in terms of literature) we should examine ostensibly transgressive works very closely for hidden complicities with the powers-that-be. This sort of examination has formed a central part of the three most transgressive critical movements of recent years. Marxist criticism has long been centrally concerned with the exposure of the false consciousness embedded in the ideologies of various works; feminist criticism has revealed the prevalence of gender discrimination in many of our "great works"; and deconstruction has demonstrated the logocentric thought that lies at the heart of so much of our literary/philosophical tradition.

These sorts of critiques are valuable, even vital, and we have learned a great deal from them. However, a more affirmative strain in all three of these movements has emphasized the elements of literary works that appear to understand and attack the evils of capitalism, sexism, and logocentrism. These positive assessments are valuable as well, though they have all shown a disturbing tendency to become prescriptive and normative, eventually leading back to negative critiques of works that do not conform to the newly prescribed norms.

Given the difficulty with which works of art achieve any kind of authentic transgression in our modern cultural climate, perhaps the time has come for "transgressive" critics to take a more affirmative stance toward artworks, to help them along, as it were, by reading them in a manner that highlights and emphasizes transgressive elements. Perhaps it is time to focus on the ways in which works are subversive, rather than on the ways they aren't, even if critics have to supply additional transgressive energies of their own to supplement those of the work.

Several projects in recent years have already proposed such transgressive modes of reading. In deconstruction, the emphasis placed by Paul de Man and others on the way in which many texts tend to deconstruct themselves is certainly a start. One might point out that texts have a curious way of effectively deconstructing themselves only after a sufficiently subtle reader has pointed out the ways in which they do so, but this discovery only highlights the role of the reader and critic in activating the subversive potential of a text. In Marxist criticism, the importance of the reader in effecting literary transgression has been strongly emphasized in the work of Tony Bennett:

The task which faces Marxist criticism is not that of reflecting or of bringing to light the politics which is already there, as a latent presence within the text which has but to be made manifest. It is that of *actively politicizing* the text, of *making its politics for it*, by producing a new position for it within the field of cultural relations and, thereby, new forms of use and effectivity within the broader social process. (167–68, Bennett's emphases)

But perhaps the most extensive examples of transgressive reading have arisen in feminist criticism. Feminist critics, perceiving themselves as outside a male-dominated tradition, have mounted a number of effective assaults on the ramparts of that tradition. For example, Judith Fetterley has argued that American literature has traditionally been strictly a man's world, positing a male position for the reader that females had no choice but to occupy if they were to be able to read at all. Fetterley's project is to oppose this tendency, reading as a woman despite the demands of texts that she do otherwise, and therefore revealing the invidious ideologies of gender that inform those texts. She argues a highly subversive potential for her project: "To expose and question that complex of ideas and mythologies about women and men which exist in our society and are confirmed in our literature is to make the system of power embodied in the literature open not only to discussion but even to change" (xx).

It is important to note that Fetterley is perfectly willing to admit that texts written by male writers can be of positive use to feminist readers. Other feminist critics (especially in Great Britain and America) have concentrated on women writers, seeking to reveal the positive transgressive energies embodied in women's texts that have largely been ignored by the patriarchal literary establishment. Still others (especially in France) have concentrated on studies of subversive alternative modes of "feminine" expression (whether employed by men or women) in their attempts to liberate the transgressive energies of literature.

The work of a number of poststructuralist, Marxist, and feminist thinkers greatly informs my work here, although I have attempted to avoid identification with any one critical approach. As Jim Collins repeatedly stresses in his recent book *Uncommon Cultures*, dominant culture is itself multiple; what

Collins refers to as "heretical activity" must be pursued on various fronts. There are many kinds of oppression, and while different oppressive ideologies may have many things in common, they also vary in important ways. The real-world emancipatory struggles against oppression based on class, gender, race, religion, and so on may be very differently oriented, and reading strategies intended to support these struggles may require different orientations as well. Moreover, in attempting to formulate strategies of transgressive reading, we must maintain a self-critical awareness of possible alternative strategies, lest transgressions become mere proscription and one mode of domination simply be replaced by another. There is a social worker in Delany's *Triton* who explains to a troubled teenager in that society of sexual heteroglossia that "anything, to the exclusion of everything else, is a perversion" (304).

This insight, though meant to apply specifically to sexuality, is strongly in accord with Bakhtin's insistence on the dangers of monologism and on the ultimate tyranny implied in the privileging of any one point of view above all others. However, it also interestingly indicates the dangers of unrestrained pluralism, because that, too, would be a "perversion." It is also true that any attempt to take multiple political stances is in danger of degenerating into the taking of no stance at all. It is here that the specific targeting of transgressive energies once more comes to the fore: plural strategies of subversion can only be effective if employed against specific targets, rather than being employed merely for the sake of pluralism itself.

In this study I present a number of examples of the reading strategies one might use to release the transgressive energies of particular texts. I approach these texts from a number of perspectives, including Marxist, feminist, and poststructuralist ones. By doing so I employ a very general notion of transgression as the disruption of hierarchies, taxonomies, or limiting systems of all kinds. Nevertheless, I do not valorize transgression for the mere sake of transgression, but will suggest that literary transgression has genuine political force only when it is carried out against a highly specific target. In literature, at least, a rebel without a cause is no rebel at all.

If there is a common thread in the kinds of transgressions that I examine in this study it is the very simple idea that political oppression can only exist in the presence of some distinction between the oppressor and the oppressed. Systems of classification and categorization will therefore loom large in this study, and the strategies by which dominant groups seek to define dominated groups as Other (and as inferior, undesirable, etc.) will be a constant object of inquiry. It is for this reason that the notion of the carnival is so important to my readings here, because the carnival is above all a place in which such hierarchical distinctions break down. In particular, the carnivalesque emphasis on the physical aspects of human existence, on things like sex and excrement and death, has great transgressive potential. These aspects of life are common to us all, male or female, white or black, capitalist or worker, king or peasant. As a result, they reveal the basic commonality of human experience and the fundamental factitiousness of all systems of rationalization for the exclusion or oppression of particular marginal groups. At the same time, the numerous stark contrasts typically found in carnivalesque texts prevent this dynamic from leading to a mere effacement of difference.

Because of the problems noted above, however, I employ the notion of "carnival" in a strictly metaphorical sense. This use of the carnival is somewhat more general than that of Bakhtin, and is much closer to the view espoused by Peter Stallybrass and Allon White, who generalize the Bakhtinian "carnival" into their notion of "transgression," which involves a violation of the rules of hierarchies in any of a number of areas, including literary genres and conventions, psychic forms, the human body, geographical space, and social order. Stallybrass and White suggest, moreover, that a transgression in any one of these categories of hierarchies has important consequences in the others as well. In their opinion, then, "the idea of carnival as an analytic category can only be fruitful if it is displaced into the broader concept of symbolic inversion and transgression" (18).

Stallybrass and White particularly emphasize the way in which oppressed, marginal groups are systematically identified with aspects of existence (death, excrement, etc.) that are deemed unpleasant by the dominant group, which in turn seeks to distance itself from such facts of life through oppression and rejection of the group with which those facts are identified. This process is one of which modern authors such as Thomas Pynchon have shown a profound understanding. For example, in *Gravity's Rainbow* Pynchon neatly summarizes the tendency of white dominant culture to associate excrement with death, and to associate both with dark colors in a dynamic that provides support for racism. The flushing of excrement out of sight down sparkling white ceramic toilets thus becomes a metaphor for the exclusion of blacks from full participation in white society:

Shit, now, is the color white folks are afraid of. Shit is the presence of death, not some abstract-arty character with a scythe but the stiff and rotting corpse itself inside the whiteman's warm and private own asshole, which is getting pretty intimate. That's what that white toilet's for. You see many brown toilets? Nope, toilet's the color of gravestones, classical columns of mausoleums, that white porcelain's the very emblem of Odorless and Official Death. Shinola shoeshine polish happens to be the color of Shit. Shoeshine boy Malcolm's in the toilet slappin' on the Shinola, working off whiteman's penance on his sin of being born the color of Shit 'n' Shinola. (688)[1]

Such reminders of the darker side of human existence constantly lurk in the margins of Pynchon's texts, and are closely related to what Julia Kristeva has described in *Powers of Horror* as the "abject." Indeed, abjection and the carnivalesque represent two different (potentially transgressive) reminders of the aspects of life that dominant culture systematically seeks to repress. Abjection and the carnivalesque are two sides of the same coin, two different expressions of the animal and mortal side of humanity: in the first case, we are reminded that we are animals and therefore must die; in the second, we are reminded that we are animals and therefore might as well live while we can. In either case the reminders so provided are common to us all and therefore tend to deconstruct all systems of social hierarchy.

In essays on authors such as Geoffrey Chaucer, Thomas Pynchon, James Joyce, Salman Rushdie, Gilbert Sorrentino, John Fowles, Virginia Woolf, and Monique Wittig, I explore various strategies for reading texts to highlight the transgressive, boundary-crossing energies embodied in them. The topics of the carnival and of the abject are present if marginal in all of these essays; they come to the fore in my final essay on Djuna Barnes and Angela Carter. In all of these essays I particularly seek to explain exactly how and why the text being read is (or is not) effectively transgressive. It is important to keep in mind, however, that in cases of literary transgression, much of the transgressive energy must come from the reader. I outline reading strategies that are designed to identify and accentuate the transgressive potential in various works, but different strategies yield different results, and no one strategy is ever the "right" one to use in a particular case.

Any number of texts could have been chosen to illustrate my points, and at this point I should probably explain why I chose the texts I did and why my own book is organized the way it is. First, in keeping with the theme of the transgression of category boundaries, I wanted a diverse set of texts that would defy neat categorization. I wanted a group of authors that many readers might be surprised to find together in one critical book. So the authors and works I chose constitute a mixture of gender, genre, style, nationality, and political orientation. Note, for example, that the authors included in my chapter titles include one medieval Englishman, one male Irish "modernist," one female British "modernist," one American female "modernist," and a variety of contemporary authors including one British female, one French lesbian female, one Indian-British male, one British male, and two male Americans.

I particularly chose the work of Chaucer to begin my book because I wanted to render problematic any neat identification between transgressive literature and the postmodern, though the two categories are highly correlated. For some time I wavered between Chaucer and Shakespeare for use in this temporal transgression, but finally settled on Chaucer because of the clear way in which his work effected a confrontation between the kinds of transgression associated with the Bakhtinian concepts of carnival and polyphony and those associated with the Derridean concepts of polysemy and free-play of the signifier.[2] Chaucer's work, despite its different historical context, enters nicely into contemporary theoretical dialogues, as well as showing some interesting similarities to the work of modern authors such as Joyce and Pynchon.

I chose Salman Rushdie as one of my authors largely because of his inherently transgressive cultural position. Rushdie is neither an Indian writer nor a British writer; his work falls into (and refuses to fall into) both categories, and it is the hybrid character of his background that is more important than either individual element. Moreover, Rushdie, as a Muslim apostate, bears a transgressive relationship to his own religious background, similar to that occupied by Joyce relative to Catholicism, except that Rushdie's dialogue with Islam is more complex due to the marginality of Islam itself in Indian culture. As a result Rushdie tends to have particularly well-focused targets in his transgressive work. I placed him directly after Chaucer because I realize the parallels that I draw between Chaucer and modern authors are in danger of obscuring the importance of specific positioning within a well-defined social, political, and historical context, while the importance of specific positionality in Rushdie's work is especially clear. Also, the element of Rushdie's work on which I focus—his attacks on dualistic thinking—follows nicely on the subversion of taxonomies and categories that I discuss in the Chaucer chapter.

I chose to look next at Gilbert Sorrentino because I felt that my discussions of Chaucer and Rushdie were beginning to make transgression sound all too easy. All one had to do was write in an unorthodox fashion, challenge a few received ideas, and effective transgression would be achieved. While it is my goal to focus on positive transgressive aspects in the works I read, I feel it is important to discuss possible ways in which a text might fail to achieve transgression. Sorrentino's book is stylistically brilliant. It's also one of the most enjoyable and hilarious texts I've ever read. But it strikes me as unsatisfying on a political level and as failing to achieve any genuine transgressions. I wanted to explore the reasons that Sorrentino's work strikes me in this way, and to compare it with the works of other authors (such as Joyce, Pynchon, Perec, O'Brien, etc.) whose work does strike me as being effectively transgressive.

I follow Sorrentino with a chapter on John Fowles because, on the surface, Sorrentino's work is the most formally sophisticated of any of the works I study here, while Fowles's is probably the least. Yet I find considerably more transgressive potential in Fowles's book, which in itself raises some interesting questions. *The French Lieutenant's Woman* has been dismissed by many as "mere" popular literature, thus allowing me to explore the issue of "high" versus "low" culture, and perhaps to problematize that distinction. The particular subject matter of Fowles's book also raises some important issues for transgressive readers, such as history, sexuality, and gender. Further, Fowles's book indicates the importance of transgressive reading because it ultimately fails to make a successful feminist statement, while at the same time raising issues that suggest ways in which a feminist critic might use the book as a starting point for productive feminist dialogue.

At this point in my book, I decided to depart from the practice of concentrating in each chapter on a particular author or work, and instead to focus on a specific issue using the works of many different authors. I did this partially for the express purpose of transgressing against the organization of my own book, which seemed to me in danger of becoming overlogical. But I also did it because my argument concerning the use of castration images in literature depends upon multiplicity, upon the fact that castration has been used as a literary device many times and in many ways by many different authors. I chose castration as a theme because of its frequent appearance in literature and because it has so often been the focus of the kinds of impoverishing, vulgar Freudian readings that I wanted to call into question. I also chose it because it brings the issue of gender to center stage, and gender is the most important area of transgression to be confronted in the remainder of the book.

I turned from the issue of castration to Virginia Woolf's *Orlando* because of the obvious metaphoric parallel between castration and Orlando's transformation from male to female. *Orlando* is perhaps the classic text of gender transgression in modern literature. But it also raises a number of other important issues, such as history (both literary and in general), and thereby indicates certain relationships between these issues and the issue of gender. *Orlando* also bears some interesting intertextual relationships to its sister text, Woolf's *A Room of One's Own*, one of the Ur-texts of modern feminist criticism.

Monique Wittig seemed an obvious choice for a book of this nature, because her work is so openly transgressive. The Wittig chapter directly follows the Woolf chapter because the two authors have so much in common. Both are engaged in openly feminist projects, and both pursue these projects in highly literary ways, particularly through parody of the male literary tradition. Many critics have seen Wittig's work as adumbrating a new feminine mode of writing, and I felt that reading Wittig through Woolf would help to dispel such readings. In a formal sense, Wittig's work falls directly in line with mainstream modernism, and she shares much in terms of writing technique not only with Woolf, but with male writers such as Joyce and Pynchon as well. But there is something very different about Wittig relative to, say, Joyce, and that difference has to do with the specificity of her social and political position. Wittig's own status as a dedicated Marxist lesbian feminist makes her work ideal for the exploration of the importance of specific positioning in transgression.

Finally, I conclude with a chapter on Djuna Barnes and Angela Carter because a comparison of these two writers so nicely illustrates the dialogue between abjection and the carnivalesque that permeates, however obliquely, all the other texts in this book. Barnes and Carter continue the interrogation of conventional roles that is pursued by Woolf and Wittig. Barnes's *Nightwood* is a text that derives most of its transgressive force from the abject energies so central to it, supplementing those energies with carnivalesque elements that always threaten to break through into the text. Carter's *Nights at the Circus*, on the other hand, derives most of its energy from the carnivalesque, yet gains added power from the suggestion of abject elements just below the surface.

As a final precautionary note, let me also stress that I am not seeking in this study to propose methods for separating "good" (i.e., effectively transgressive) texts from "bad" ones. For one thing, such a method of hierarchical classification is precisely the kind of system that transgressive works deconstruct. For another, all works of literature have some transgressive potential, even when they appear to be fully in complicity with dominant ideologies. Because literature tends to exaggerate the effects and ideas it imports from its cultural and historical context, such works can expose contradictions and "seams" in dominant ideologies that might not otherwise be apparent. Moreover, comparative studies of such works are useful to highlight by contrast the power of works that are effectively transgressive in a more direct sense. The kind of transgressive reading I shall propose is designed specifically to counter the tendency of dominant groups to reject and exclude marginal groups and associated negative images. To oppose this tendency the transgressive critic should operate in a mode not of rejection, but of appropriation, garnering any and all texts that she can use to further the message of transgression. Given the difficulty of initiating any genuine social change, politically committed critics can use all the help they can get.

POSTMODERNISM IN MEDIEVAL ENGLAND:
CHAUCER, PYNCHON, JOYCE,
AND THE POETICS OF FISSION

CHAPTER

1 ───────────────────────────

There is a character in Barry Hannah's short story "Love Too Long" who shares with us reminiscences of his days as a student at Bakersfield Junior College:

I'll tell you what I liked that we studied at Bakersfield. It was old James Joyce and his book *The Canterbury Tales*. You wouldn't have thought anybody would write "A fart that well nigh blinded Absalom" in ancient days. All those people hopping and humping at night, framming around, just like last year at Ollie's party that she and I left when they got into threesomes and Polaroids. (11)

Hannah is having his own particular brand of Southern-fried postmodernist fun here, of course, and the passage serves as an effective deflation of the pretensions of high culture. But it also suggests certain basic similarities between the time of Chaucer and our own unsettled times. Perhaps these similarities render the confusion of Hannah's character understandable; after all, Helen Cooper has recently demonstrated that there are in fact a number of parallels between the work of Joyce and that of Chaucer. But similarities between medieval poetry and the work of Joyce should surprise no one. As Shaun complains of his brother Shem the Penman, Joyce's principal representative in

Finnegans Wake: "He's weird, I tell you, and middayevil down to his vegetable soul" (423.27–28).[1]

On the other hand, if Joyce's work harks back to the Middle Ages, it also just as clearly points forward to postmodernism. Richard Pearce has argued that modernism and postmodernism differ not in the texts themselves but in the expectations that readers bring to those texts. Joyce is just as postmodernist as, say, Pynchon: "It is only that revolutionary writers like Joyce had to be read in a conservative way" (Pearce, "What Joyce" 43). Pearce then suggests that reading Joyce in the light of Pynchon helps to unleash the truly radical potential of Joyce's texts.

Elsewhere, Pearce continues this same argument, suggesting that reading Joyce through Pynchon is especially illuminating for an understanding of the lack of closure in the ending of *Ulysses*. Viewing Molly's final speech as an epilogue, Pearce then compares this ending to the epilogue at the conclusion of Pynchon's *V*. He suggests that this use of an epilogue structure leads to the expectation of closure, which is then subverted: the epilogues may in fact be parodies of epilogues ("Pynchon's Endings").

Among other things, Pearce's argument calls into question the definition (or even existence) of "postmodernism"—and the term should be used with care. Moreover, if Pearce can argue that *Ulysses* is postmodernist because it ends with an epilogue that does not neatly wrap up the rest of the text but instead calls it into question, what are we to make of something like the ending of Chaucer's *Troilus and Criseyde*, or even of the retraction at the end of *The Canterbury Tales*? After all, it seems reasonable to conclude that if Joyce has much in common with Chaucer, and Pynchon has much in common with Joyce, then Pynchon might have something in common with Chaucer. In short, just how far does Pearce's point extend? If reading modernism through postmodernism sheds new light on modernist texts, what about the texts that precede modernism? Can reading Chaucer through the optic of postmodernism illuminate his texts as well?

It should be particularly interesting to compare the dynamics of transgression in postmodernist and medieval texts. According to Bakhtin, the purest spirit of the carnival arises in medieval folk culture, reaching its highest transgressive potential in the works of late medieval authors such as Rabelais. Meanwhile, many have seen postmodernism to embody a resurgence of the carnivalesque spirit. William Spanos, for example, essentially equates postmodernism with the carnivalesque of Bakhtin (193).

That medieval and postmodernist texts do have much in common has been persuasively suggested by Robert Jordan, who notes that "Chaucerian narrative, in highlighting its textuality, its composed quality or 'literariness,' invites primary emphasis on the verbal medium" (16). Jordan then parallels the reflexive concerns with language and with poetic technique shown in works such as the *House of Fame* to similar concerns in postmodernist metafictional writers:

The fiction that is usually designated postmodern or experimental or avant-garde—beginning with Joyce and including Nabokov, Borges, Beckett, Barth, Pynchon, and many others—is largely preoccupied with its own nature as fiction. It is largely preoccupied, that is to say, with the theoretical questions we have come to associate with the *House of Fame*. (25)

In his emphasis on Chaucer's self-conscious concerns with language and poetic technique, Jordan has no doubt identified what, for the modern reader at least, must be the most exciting aspect of Chaucer's project.[2] However, he also suggests (without exploring the implications in detail) that this metafictional concern is not purely formal, but relates to Chaucer's general historical and cultural moment as well. Thus, to Jordan, Chaucer's poetics of uncertainty reflects the general outlook of his time, "a fragmented and problematic outlook, an uncertainty about fundamental truths" (2). Similarly, Gordon Leff writes of the "overall loss of coherence" in the late medieval worldview, which led to a "new openness which complemented the loss of system involved in the redrawing of conceptual boundaries" (11). Thus, one might argue that Chaucer's poetics resembles the poetics of postmodernism because the unsettled character of his times so much resembles that of our own. As Ernest Moody puts it: "our age of analysis has brought us to a point comparable to that of six hundred years ago, when the cosmological and metaphysical framework, within which philosophers had worked for a thousand years, had been dissolved beyond repair" (319).

There are, then, valid historical reasons to expect that interesting results might be achieved by reading the work of Chaucer from the perspective of postmodernist literature. In fact, there are a number of ways in which postmodernist literature can be used to illuminate various aspects of the Chaucerian text. Jordan suggests that the "sympathetic resonance" of Chaucer's poetics with postmodernism derives from its being a "wonderfully flexible and expansive poetics, fundamentally heterodox, open to all modes of discourse, and indifferent to strictures of orthodoxy" (172). In short, both Chaucer and the postmodernists tend to transgress boundaries, destabilize hierarchies, and question authority of all kinds. In this chapter, I shall explore the ways in which Chaucer's texts share with postmodernism a highly critical attitude toward all systems of hierarchy and taxonomy, whether those systems be social, political, literary, or linguistic.

Reading Chaucer through postmodernist authors such as Pynchon and Joyce demonstrates that his language escapes systems of linguistic and literary hierarchy, just as the heteroglossic richness of his texts parallels the postmodernist questioning of social and political hierarchies. These two aspects of the potential subversive force of literary discourse can be roughly associated with the phenomena of polysemy (especially as described by Jacques Derrida) and of polyphony (especially as described by Bakhtin). Thus, the links between Chaucer and postmodernism also involve parallels between Chaucer's attitude toward literature and many of the central developments in modern literary theory.[3] Chaucer's work proves that polyphony and polysemy are not identical and interchangeable. At the same time, as the notion of "transgression" put forth by Stallybrass and White would indicate, polyphony and polysemy, as two separate forms of subversion, are not independent but are in fact intimately related. Thus, among other things, a postmodernist reading of Chaucer suggests certain parallels between the project of Derrida and that of Bakhtin.

THE POETICS OF FISSION: POLYSEMIC LANGUAGE AND THE RADIOACTIVE PUN

One of the difficulties with reading Chaucer through postmodernism is that postmodernism itself is a rather problematically defined entity. Perhaps here I am in danger of repeating the *ignotum per ignocius* of Plato in "The Canon's Yeoman's Tale." However, I believe that the texts of Chaucer and of postmodernism can illuminate each other so that one might gain a clearer view of postmodernism itself. Many attempts have been made to describe the salient features of postmodernism, and I do not have room to review those attempts here.[4] One of the more useful characterizations, I think, has been the suggestion by Jean-Francois Lyotard that the modern can be defined as "any science that legitimates itself with reference to a metadiscourse . . . making explicit appeal to some grand narrative, such as the dialectics of Spirit, the hermeneutics of meaning, the emancipation of the rational or working subject, or the creation of wealth" (xxiii). In contrast, Lyotard defines the postmodern in terms of "incredulity toward metanarratives. This incredulity is undoubtedly a product of progress in the sciences: but that progress in turn presupposes it" (xxiv). For the purposes of this chapter, I will use this "incredulity toward metanarratives" as a starting point for my view of postmodernism. I will, in fact, extend this definition to suggest that it is the essence of postmodernism to call into question systems, hierarchies, and taxonomies of all kinds.

A tremendous amount of subversive energy can be generated through this sort of radically skeptical project. All human systems of hierarchy and categorization are artificial and conventional. As a result, the forcing of people (and ideas) into such systems requires a tremendous amount of social and political "energy." To use a Pynchonian scientific metaphor, it might be compared to the huge amounts of energy required to bind together the various components of the atomic nucleus. But, as we in the twentieth century are all too painfully aware, the awesome force of these nuclear binding energies can be released by splitting the nucleus apart through nuclear fission. Similarly, the "binding energies" required to hold together artificial systems of taxonomy and hierarchy can also be released through the fission of such systems.

On a linguistic and philosophical level, this sort of radical questioning has its modern roots in the program of transvaluation of values undertaken by Nietzsche and its most prominent current avatar in the deconstructive project of Derrida. Clearly, language itself is our most powerful and immanent system of classification and taxonomy, so this nuclear metaphor would be expected to pertain particularly to language. In this respect, one can see that literary language is specially situated to unleash the binding energies of all language.

The energetic effect of poetic language can be visualized by reference to Jakobson's model of language as existing along two different axes, which might variously be figured as paradigmatic and syntagmatic, selection and combination, or metaphor and metonymy. Granted, Jakobson's structuralist model of metaphor and metonymy existing as two separate and opposed poles of language is precisely the sort of circumscribing system that the poststructuralist linguistic theory of Derrida is designed to undermine. However, Jakobson's model is a useful schematic starting point for understanding the energies inherent in polysemic language. According to Jakobson, it is the essence of poetic language that the paradigmatic, or selection, axis is forced onto the axis of combination. This forcible projection not only endows poetic language with additional binding energy, but also renders it unstable, like the nucleus of a radioactive element. Poetic language takes on an aura of strangeness that calls attention to itself and leads to a release of energies through proliferation of meaning.

This model of poetic language is clearly metaphoric, and should not be taken too literally. However, the model is useful and can be taken one step further. What, for example, would occur if an additional projection were performed? What would happen if the axis of combination, now charged with the additional energies of the axis of selection, were itself to be projected back onto its own origin? In this case, both axes would be collapsed onto a single point, and the linguistic energy levels thus obtained would be maximized.

But is such a situation possible? And if so, what would such a situation represent? In the most general case, it would simply represent the word. After all, a single word always exists at the intersection of these two axes, with the potential for metaphoric and metonymic connections already built in. All words contain the "binding energies" of polysemic language, just as all atomic nuclei are held together by their own binding energies. However, most nuclei are quite stable, and their energy is never spontaneously released. Similarly, most words do not in themselves appear to present an especially immediate danger of polysemic decay. They must be destabilized in some way in order for their energies to be released. Literary language (and certainly all tropistic language) represents a step toward such releases of energy. However, at the level of the single word, it would appear that the strongest potential for a release of such energies occurs in that time-honored device, the pun.

The pun openly announces that it contains both metaphoric and metonymic energies. The pun highlights the ambiguity of the selection process of language by refusing to let that selection come to rest; it is a single word that is in fact more than one word. Similarly, the multiple meanings of the pun word cast different meanings upon the other words in the immediate context, confusing the combination process as well. The resultant instability of meaning along both of Jakobson's axes is then analogous to the instability of the nucleus of a radioactive isotope, and the pun is thus among the most efficient means of releasing the stored metaphoric and metonymic energies of language.

Once these mutual energies are released through the action of the pun, explosions of meaning spiral outward from the origin much like the chain reactions that can be initiated from the decay of a radioactive nucleus. As Umberto Eco puts it, "the quarrel between metaphor and metonymy can generate a flight to infinity, in which one moment establishes the other, and vice versa" (73). It is here, in this paradoxical "Strange Loop" relationship between metaphor and metonymy, that Jakobson's view of metaphor and metonymy as separate poles begins to collapse.[5] Clearly, there is more involved in this situation than a simple conflation of the two poles in a "metaphorization" of metonymy or "metonymization" of metaphor. In fact, metaphor and metonymy become a striking example of the sorts of deconstructed oppositions that have figured so prominently in post-Derridean critical discourse, illustrating the way in which deconstruction neither reverses nor simply collapses hierarchies but in fact dynamically destabilizes them in such a way as to demonstrate the ultimate instability (radioactivity?) of all such hierarchies.[6]

From this discussion, it then comes as no surprise that puns are prominent features of postmodernist discourse, Derrida's own work being a notable example. Samuel Beckett's declaration that "in the beginning was the pun" (*Murphy* 65) and Pynchon's suggestion that there is "high magic to low puns" (*Lot 49* 129) stand as central examples of the importance of the pun to postmodernism. But Chaucer, too, is an inveterate punster. Some of his puns, in fact, are quite famous, perhaps most notably the mention of "ars-metrike" in "The Summoner's Tale" (line 2222). Besides being terribly apt (and funny) this particular pun nicely demonstrates the boundary-crossing potential of the pun, combining a reference to high culture (arts) with a reference to what Bakhtin calls the "bodily lower stratum" (arse). One might compare here how Pynchon often constructs puns and metaphors, mixing meanings from highly divergent disciplines or social strata. Thus, in one of the most often cited passages from *The Crying of Lot 49*, Oedipa Maas meditates on the old sailor whom she befriends:

She knew, because she had held him, that he suffered DT's. Behind the initials was a metaphor, a delirium tremens, a trembling unfurrowing of the mind's plowshare. . . . Trembling, unfurrowed, she slipped sidewise, screeching back across grooves of years, to hear again the earnest, high voice of her second or third collegiate love Ray Glozing bitching among "uhs" and the syncopated tonguing of a cavity, about his freshman calculus; "dt," God help this old tattooed man, meant also a time differential, a vanishingly small instant in which change had to be confronted at last for what it was, where it could no longer disguise itself as something innocuous like an average rate; where velocity dwelled in the projectile though the projectile be frozen in midflight, where death dwelled in the cell though the cell looked in on it at its most quick. (128–29)

As Porush points out, Pynchon's technique here (which is a sort of strange combination of pun and metaphor) is extremely complex:

[W]e find ourselves tangled in a metaphor having one word (dt) standing for two vehicles, which in turn may act metaphorically with respect to each other and which both imply several tenors. . . . Finally, the passage is highly self-commenting or reflexive, leading us to grapple with a metaphor that is partly about metaphor itself. (126)

In particular, the conflation of the DT's of the alcoholic and the differential, *dt*, of calculus creates a dialogue that calls into question the privileged position that scientific discourse tends to occupy in Western post-Enlightenment society. Similarly, Chaucer's "ars-metrike" pun calls into question the privileged status of the arts of measurement. This pun also directly illustrates the affinity of Chaucer with postmodernism, because Flann O'Brien deploys precisely the same pun in his *At Swim-Two-Birds*, in which we find Dermot Trellis heading up a stairway directly behind a young servant girl, the stays in whose skirt obscure the "aesthetic" potential of the view: "Ars est celare artem, muttered Trellis, doubtful as to whether he had made a pun" (314).

Trellis (or at least O'Brien) has made a pun indeed, and a double one at that: not only does he reproduce the pun from Chaucer, but the original Latin phrase already contains an embedded pun, since "celare" (to hide) resonates with "caelare" (to engrave, i.e., to make obvious).[7] Thus art simultaneously involves both a hiding and a declaration of art, as O'Brien demonstrates by employing a subtle pun, then explicitly calling attention to it.[8]

Despite their generally comic effect, it would seem that puns are serious things. Indeed, despite the low regard in which puns are sometimes held, they do represent an explicit baring of mechanisms that operate at the heart of all language. The poet James Merrill has described the effect well, noting that the pun

is suffered, by and large, with groans of aversion, as though one had done an unseemly thing in adult society, like slipping a hand up the hostess's dress. Indeed, the punster has touched, and knows it if only for being so promptly shamed, upon a secret, fecund place in language herself. The pun's *objet trouvé* aspect cheapens it further—why? A Freudian slip is taken seriously: it betrays its maker's hidden wish. The pun (or the rhyme, for that matter) "merely" betrays the hidden wish of words. (quoted in Moffett 118)

Of course, one could argue that the above puns on "ars" are relatively stable and well controlled, and do not lead to an extensive proliferation of meaning. After all, it is theoretically possible to control even a nuclear chain reaction within a properly designed device. On the other hand, just as the O'Brien pun is at least double, so too does the "art" in Chaucer's pun evoke both the art of measurement and that other metrical art, namely poetry. Even these relatively tame examples of puns that seem well within the realm of authorial control show the beginning of a proliferation in meaning. This proliferation calls into question the ostensibly well-ordered system of rules and conventions that defines our use of language. We obtain here a fleeting look into the abyss, resulting in Pynchon's "trembling unfurrowing of the mind's plowshare."[9] Attridge describes the potential power of this destabilization of the "grids" of language by the pun, noting that

to obtain a glimpse of the infinite possibility of meaning kept at bay by those grids, to gain a sense that the boundaries upon which our use of language depends are set up under specific historical conditions, is to be made aware of a universe more open to reinterpretation and change than the one we are usually conscious of inhabiting. (*Peculiar Language* 208)

Attridge points out the way in which Joyce's language in *Finnegans Wake* is particularly powerful in this respect, contrasting it with the relatively tame puns employed, say, by Pope. In fact, Attridge suggests that Joyce's Wakean neologisms be classified not as puns, but as portmanteaux. Portmanteaux they are, but my "radioactive" model of the pun would suggest that Joyce's words are in fact decaying puns, linguistic isotopes so unstable that they have already begun to come apart, thus calling particular attention to their instability. As a simple example, consider the way in which Joyce conflates "purpose" with the French "pourquoi" to produce "pourquose" (meaning "why") (18.31). On the surface, this wordplay would seem gratuitous as the two words have roughly the same meaning. However, if we think in the opposite direction, viewing "pourquose" as coming apart rather than being put together, we can see that its multilingual decomposition calls into question the normal boundaries between languages. It thus demonstrates the arbitrary and artificial nature of all linguistic conventions.

Finnegans Wake may be an extreme example of the power of the pun, but R. A. Shoaf has recently noted that Chaucer and other medieval poets also recognized and utilized the violent linguistic energies inherent in the pun. "Puns," says Shoaf, "are about power—puns are power—and they unsettle those who want to be in control, to be on top of things" ("Play of Puns" 44).

He then discusses specific examples of puns from Chaucer's poetry to demonstrate the effects achieved thereby. Shoaf's concern is with polysemy, not polyphony, and his discourse deals with literary, not political matters. However, his appreciation of the potential transgressive violence of the pun goes a long way toward demonstrating its potential political force. He argues that, for Chaucer, "the pun is a device for delaying, interrupting, or otherwise frustrating closure. Often when a character insists on closure and its unisemy, a restriction of meaning, a pun emerges to suggest polysemy and a ludic re-opening of the text" ("Play of Puns" 45).

Clearly, Shoaf is pursuing an insight quite similar to that which Attridge pursues in relation to Joyce. In fact, this destabilizing effect is precisely what puns are all about. Shoaf discusses this punning tendency as an aspect of what he refers to as "juxtology," through which medieval poets link up all sorts of diverse concepts. He notes that these links are made largely through the offices of language itself:

Medieval poets . . . knew full well that language is "in charge."
Juxtologists, as I like to think of them, they recognized that words
yoke themselves together, and together with things, in the most
unpredictable ways. . . . they understood that language exceeds
man's grasp and that that's what heaven is for. ("Play of Puns" 45)

This sort of process by which language "takes charge" is precisely what I have attempted to describe by my image of nuclear decay. Once that first radioactive pun is set free, it can then initiate an ongoing chain reaction of semantic effects beyond human control or intervention. One of Shoaf's favorite examples concerns the reaction of Dorigen in "The Franklin's Tale" when she learns from Aurelius that the rocks have apparently disappeared from the coast of Britanny:

He taketh his leve, and she astoned stood;
In al hir face nas a drope of blood.
She wende nevere han come in swich a trappe.
"Allas," quod she, "that evere this sholde happe!
For wende I nevere by possibilitee
That swich a monstre or merveille myghte be!
(lines 1339–44)

Shoaf demonstrates that "astoned" in line 1339 is a pun meaning both "astonished" and "turned to stone," the latter (especially with the reference to a "monstre" in line 1344) calling forth the episode of the Medusa in canto IX of Dante's *Inferno*. Of course, once this connection is made, the general Dantean motif of using turning to stone as a metaphor for literal and all-encompassing interpretation is evoked as well, adding a special richness to "The Franklin's Tale." The dissemination of meaning thus runs rampant through the Dantean text, connecting to other instances of stony interpretation as well, such as that of Count Ugolino in *Inferno* XXXIII.[10]

The reference to Dante in Chaucer's pun may well have been intentional. But the chain reaction of meaning ultimately acts to escape all questions of authorial intention. Thus, for example, this same pun also evokes Wallace Stevens's "The Man on the Dump," where Stevens, too, attacks the notion of a totalized meaning that shuts off renewal and therefore ends up in the trash. He thus questions the idea that poetry can ever reach a final truth, engraved in stone:

Is it to hear the blatter of grackles and say
Invisible priest; is it to eject, to pull
The day to pieces and cry stanza my stone?
                    (*Collected Poems* 203)

The answer, of course, is no, because with Stevens "it must change." Once the poet's stanza becomes stone, it hardens into a fixed meaning that comes to mistake itself for truth.

Obviously, such connections can be made virtually endlessly once authorial intention is escaped in this way. Here again Chaucer's text parallels *Finnegans Wake*, which, as David Hayman points out, "belongs to a class (not a genre) of works which invite the reader to perpetuate creation" ("Some Writers" 177).[11] But perhaps most important in the proliferation of meaning from this radioactive pun is that the potential connections of the pun "astoned" radiate internally through the rest of Chaucer's text itself. For example, a connection is also made to the philosopher's stone of "The Canon's Yeoman's Tale." The magical chicanery perpetrated upon Dorigen thus resonates with the alchemical shenanigans of that tale, and the general theme of professional trickery in "The Canon's Yeoman's Tale" highlights the betrayals and double-dealing that occur in "The Franklin's Tale." Moreover, given the sexually charged context of Dorigen's astonishment, the semantic explosion that emanates from "astoned" inevitably extends to the stalwart "stoons" of the Nun's Priest that Harry Bailly blesses in the epilogue to "The Nun's Priest's Tale."[12] In this case, being "astoned" thus implies that Dorigen is, as we might say in postmodern vulgar parlance, fucked—and potentially in more ways than one.

Overt puns such as those on "ars-metrike" and "astoned" provide especially obvious examples of the semantic impertinence with which Chaucer's language challenges accepted systems of linguistic orthodoxy. But just as radioactive elements tend to contaminate the more stable elements around them, so too does this "radioactive" language tend to extend (in a very Joycean way) into more apparently stable Chaucerian language as well. For example, it is a commonplace of Chaucer criticism to note the irony that adheres in Chaucer's often using the same terms to describe different pilgrims to very different effect. A good example occurs in his use of the word "worthy" to describe the noble Knight, the corrupt Friar, and the lusty Wife. Thus, early in the "General Prologue," we have the description of the Knight (who comes first in the catalogue of descriptions here, just as he will later be the first tale-teller):

A Knyght ther was, and that a worthy man,
That fro the tyme that he first bigan
To riden out, he loved chivalrie,
Trouthe and honour, fredom and curteisie.
(lines 43–46)

This description, coming so early in the prologue, is as yet unaffected by the descriptions of the other pilgrims. However, the terms in which the Knight is described, perhaps most especially the term "worthy" are already "double-voiced," already colored by a sideward glance at the discourse of the romance/epic tradition. The fact that such terms are obvious clichés of this tradition calls their sincerity into question. Knights are "worthy" by convention, so calling a knight worthy is simply redundant and can convey little descriptive force—unless, of course, it is sarcastic. Thus, Chaucer's entirely conventional language here already hovers on the brink of mockery.

The semantic instability of the Knight's "worthiness" is further increased when, after a long description of the Friar's corruption, we are promptly informed that "This worthy lymytour was cleped Huberd" (line 269). And the Wife of Bath is characterized by worthiness as well:

She was a worthy womman al hir lyve:
Housbondes at chirche dore she hadde fyve,
Withouten oother compaignye in youthe—
                              (lines 459–61)

Here, then, we have the Wife's worthiness juxtaposed with a hint at her promiscuity, which renders the description ironical and echoes the suggested "wantownesse" of the worthy Friar. In particular, the worthiness of the Friar and of the Wife (who represents precisely the sort of aleatory principle that the Knight so abhors), calls into question the worthiness of the Knight. Moreover, the use of the same word in such different contexts calls specific attention to the way in which the same word can have multiple meanings. The word "worthy" is clearly "double-voiced" in the Bakhtinian sense, though its doubleness is of an unusually obvious kind that converts it into a sort of pun.[13]

This "hybrid" pun illustrates how polysemy in Chaucer is not a purely linguistic effect, but often has social and political implications as well. In fact, the radical and subversive energies of all language are unleashed in the pun in such a way as to demonstrate that the true transgressive force of polysemic language (per Derrida) can be quite similar to the force of polyphonic discourse (per Bakhtin). Stallybrass and White note that the pun is a form of "what Bakhtin calls a *grammatica jocosa* whereby grammatical order is transgressed to reveal erotic and obscene or merely materially satisfying counter-meaning" (10–11). Thus Arthur's evaluation of the Bakhtinian carnival gives a special place to the pun, which

violates and so unveils the structure of prevailing (pre-vailing) convention; and so it provokes laughter. Samuel Beckett's punning pronouncement "In the beginning was the Pun" sets pun against official Word and at the same time, as puns often do, sets free a chain of other puns. So, too, carnival sets itself up in a punning relationship with official culture and enables a plural, unfixed, comic view of the world. (1, cited in Stallybrass and White 11)

This suggestion of a relationship between formal linguistic transgressions and political and social transgressions highlights the fact that Bakhtinian politics are inescapably linguistic, just as deconstructive language (because of its attacks on systems and hierarchies of all kinds) is inescapably political.[14] Moreover, medieval authors seem to have recognized this relationship between polysemy and polyphony, long before the advent of Bakhtin and Derrida. After all, Dante has Adam point out that the fundamental sin of man was the "transgression of the sign," suggesting that linguistic impertinences can be used as a figure of rule breaking in general.[15] This relationship highlights the way in which the linguistic emphasis of Bakhtin's project provides a critical perspective for the reading of Chaucer (and of postmodernism) that goes far beyond the carnival per se.[16] Still, it is in the polyphony of the openly carnivalesque nature of much of Chaucer's (and Pynchon's) work that the social and political force of his texts can be seen most clearly. Indeed, it is the textual environment created by the openly social nature of the polyphonic juxtapositions of different voices in this work that lends an inescapably social and political dimension to the polysemic nature of the language in these texts as well, preventing it from collapsing into mere formal play.

POLYPHONIC DISCOURSE: CHAUCER, PYNCHON, AND THE POLITICS OF FISSION

It is central to the Bakhtinian carnival (and to the more general concept of transgression) to have representatives from different social and political strata thrust together in the same physical and social space in such a way that normal hierarchies and class distinctions are rendered ineffective, or at least unstable. This juxtaposition of various voices allows for a polyphonic dialogue that highlights the differences among social groups and generally calls into question the assumptions that would hold certain groups to be ascendant over others. Given this situation, I would suggest that one of the clearest examples of such carnivalistic juxtapositions in all of literature occurs in the gathering of various pilgrims in the "General Prologue" of *The Canterbury Tales*. Here we have twenty-nine (or so) representatives of diverse social categories, ranging from noblemen to "cherls," from cooks to clerics, and from lawyers to wives. Indeed, all major social groups in Chaucer's England are represented, and the opportunities for dialogue would appear to be tremendous.[17]

The gathering of Chaucer's pilgrims provides an excellent illustration of the source from which the fission of boundaries gains its energies. Chaucer's heteroglossic gathering of pilgrims, by allowing a dialogic interaction among different social groups, provides an opportunity for such fission to occur through the clashing of different systems, just as the particles in the atomic nucleus are split apart by bombarding them with other particles. Furthermore, Chaucer's egalitarian plan of allowing the pilgrims to tell their own tales provides an effective framework within which the various discourses can be highlighted in turn, assuring that these sorts of interactions do indeed occur.[18]

The clashes of discourses that thus occur in *The Canterbury Tales* are highly reminiscent of the dialogic effects that form one of the most striking features of the fiction of Pynchon. In works such as *Gravity's Rainbow* one finds the languages of science, technology, psychoanalysis, government, and religion engaged in a complex dialogic struggle with the languages of movies, jazz, locker rooms, bars, and comic books. This interaction generates a polyphonic force that powerfully calls into question all systems of authority and totality through a vivid demonstration of the alternatives that those systems necessarily exclude.

Similar examples of social and political dialogue occur in *The Canterbury Tales*. Indeed, the total amount of dialogic interaction in the *Tales* is virtually unlimited; the overall design of the work is such that any tale can potentially interact with any and all of the others, depending upon connections to be made by the reader. Thus Cooper compares the *Tales* to Joyce's *Ulysses* in terms of the various patterns of cross-references and allusions that permeate the entire work (152). However, Chaucer does take steps to assure that especially promising dialogic interactions are highlighted, the clearest example of this technique being in the juxtaposition of the tales of the Knight and the Miller in the beginning of Fragment A. The Knight–Miller dialogue is then essential to a demonstration of the relevance of using Pynchon and postmodernism to illuminate the dialogic energy of *The Canterbury Tales.*

Reading Chaucer through Pynchon gives "The Knight's Tale" a crucial position. As the first tale, it is set up as an embodiment of the kind of authoritarian, monologic discourse that all of the other tales, if only by their sheer diversity, would seem to call into question. (Of course, all the tales also call one another into question, as I have noted above.) It is entirely appropriate that the Knight, who enjoys the highest social status of all of the pilgrims, should be the first to speak. And the nature of his tale is clearly designed to reinforce that status. "The Knight's Tale," derived from the tradition of the romance/epic, is itself a thoroughly conventional tale delivered in a highly authoritarian mode of discourse. Control is at the heart of the Knight's text, and disorder, disruption, and alien voices of all kinds are scrupulously circumscribed. They are excluded to such an extent, in fact, that the tale self-consciously calls attention to its own authoritarian status. Once this is done, the tale is already teetering on the brink of undercutting itself; a too-zealous exclusion of alien voices emphasizes that such voices do in fact exist.

There is a nagging sense of doubt attached to the authenticity of the Knight's ascendancy from the very beginning of his tale. After all, he is ostensibly chosen to speak first not because of his social status, but through a drawing of lots. His initiatory role thus derives either from sheer chance or from a bogus move on the part of Harry Bailly in determining the outcome of the drawing. In either case, the legitimacy of the Knight's social primacy is immediately called into question. Once the Miller thrusts himself into the order of telling directly after the Knight, disrupting a succession (exploding a hierarchy) that might logically be expected to proceed next to the Monk, then there is little hope that authority of the Knight's position can remain stable. The robust, carnivalistic discourse of the Miller serves to highlight the sterility and inauthenticity of the discourse of the Knight and provides a striking and immediate example of precisely the sorts of voices that the Knight is excluding from his text. Once that example is offered, the Knight's discourse is unavoidably contaminated by that of the Miller; it inevitably turns into a parody of itself. Then, the heteroglossic piling up of tale upon tale, style upon style, and point-of-view upon point-of-view as the work proceeds can do nothing but further undercut the stability of the Knight's position.[19]

The motif of the drawing of lots powerfully calls attention to what is perhaps the strongest tension between the Knight and the Miller: the question of chance. The Knight, seeking to reinforce political hierarchies and strengthen social boundaries, is clearly threatened by the notion of chance occurrences of any kind. The Miller, on the other hand, joyfully accepts the aleatory as one of the richest and most productive parts of life. The aleatory nature of "The Miller's Tale" is emphasized by the freedom that Chaucer's text specifically gives the reader in approaching it. We are granted, in fact, permission to skip over "cherlish" tales such as that told by the Miller entirely:

And therfore, whoso list it nat yheere,
Turne over the leef and chese another tale;
For he shal fynde ynowe, grete and smale,
Of storial thyng that toucheth gentillesse,
And eek moralitee and hoolynesse.
    ("Miller's Prologue," lines 3176–80)

Aside from the fact that this suggestion is fairly likely to assure that the reader will in fact read "The Miller's Tale," this passage clearly endows the entire work with a playful structure that is in fact reminiscent of a number of the works of postmodernism. One thinks here of such examples as the crossword puzzle structure of Milorad Pavić's *Landscape Painted with Tea*, the loose-leaf novel of B. S. Johnson, or Julio Cortázar's *Hopscotch*, which includes suggested alternative orders in which the chapters are to be read at the reader's option. In this light, it is entirely appropriate that the intended order of the various fragments of the *Tales* remains in question. Perhaps the reader should choose his own order.

But this granting of freedom to the reader is more than a formal effect. It introduces an aleatory component that poses a powerfully subversive threat to the stability of systems and taxonomies, and not just in the medieval world. In fact, it is perhaps through the contemporary fiction of Pynchon that we can most clearly understand the stakes that are involved in the opposition between determinism and chance in Chaucer's tales of the Knight and the Miller. Pynchon's fiction mounts nothing less than an all-out assault on the governing ideological systems of our time. In particular, Pynchon is concerned with the ways in which certain dehumanizing and deterministic modes of thought act to limit human freedom. To Pynchon, the determined is always equated with the authoritarian and the monologic, an equation that Chaucer's Knight clearly illustrates. Complexity and diversity, on the other hand, are associated by Pynchon with the aleatory, and the aleatory is in turn associated with freedom.[20]

Pynchon approaches this problem in any number of ways. One of the most striking occurs in *Gravity's Rainbow*, with the opposition that he sets up between the two colleagues, Ned Pointsman and Roger Mexico. Both men are engaged in psychological research at the "White Visitation," but here the similarities end. Pointsman is a devoted disciple of the discourse of determinism, a Pavlovian behaviorist who believes that response must always follow stimulus in a strictly determined and predictable way. Mexico, on the other hand, is a statistician, a believer in probabilities, willing to grant that occurrences in the world contain a stochastic component that makes strict prediction of events impossible. Pynchon's text does not explicitly and unequivocally condemn Pointsman or privilege Mexico. Rather, it allows the two of them to interact in a dialogic confrontation that produces its own energy:

If ever the Antipointsman existed, Roger Mexico is the man. . . . in the domain of zero to one, not-something to something, Pointsman can only possess the zero and the one. He cannot, like Mexico, survive anyplace in between. Like his master I. P. Pavlov before him, he imagines the cortex of the brain as a mosaic of tiny on/off elements. . . . One or zero. . . . But to Mexico belongs the domain between zero and one—the middle Pointsman has excluded from his persuasion—the probabilities.

(*Gravity's Rainbow* 55)

But, of course, once this dialogue is set up, Mexico wins by definition, because he can live with opposition, can accept the contrasting voice of Pointsman. Pointsman, on the other hand, seeks to suppress all alien discourse, so the very presence of that discourse represents his defeat. Pynchon's treatment of this confrontation is highly informed by the World War II setting of the book, and deals extensively in the terminology of twentieth-century life. However, I would suggest that the Pointsman–Mexico confrontation bears some striking resemblances to the similar dialogue that develops in *The Canterbury Tales* between the Knight and the Miller.

Chaucer's Knight, like Pynchon's Pointsman, cannot live in the excluded middle. He is obsessed with the desire to render all of life explicable. He is, in fact, in many ways the prototype of the modern scientific mentality that Pynchon so thoroughly calls into question.[21] Just as Pointsman holds up his hero Pavlov as the embodiment of scientific order, the Knight holds up his own hero, the Duke Theseus, as a similar embodiment of worldly order. In fact, it is in his admiring description of Theseus that the Knight provides us with the clearest statement of his system of values:

> The destinee, minstre general,
> That executeth in the world over al
> The purveiaunce that God hath seyn biforn,
> So strong it is that, though the world had sworn
> The contrarie of a thyng by ye or nay,
> Yet somtyme it shal fallen on a day
> That falleth eft withinne a thousand yeer.
> For certeinly, oure appetites heer,
> Be it of werre, or pees, or hate, or love,
> Al is this reuled by the sighte above.
> This mene I now by myghty Theseus.
>
> (lines 1663–73)

The Miller's exuberant deflation of social decorum is highly similar to Mexico's opposition to the Pavlovian behaviorism of Pointsman. Mexico's appeal to statistical rather than deterministic science seems to lack the carnivalistic exuberance of "The Miller's Tale"; in point of fact nothing could be further from the truth. Pynchon is nothing if not outrageously explicit in his deflation of the pretensions of high culture. Late in the book, for example, Mexico bursts into a high-level board meeting, attended by "Phi Beta Kappa keys, Legions of Honour, Orders of Lenin, Iron Crosses, V.C.s, retirement watchchains, Dewey-for-President lapel pins, half-exposed service revolvers, and even a sawed-off shotgun under the shoulder there" (636). In short, the assembly includes all the accoutrements of establishment power (including the last, which shows how sinister that power can be)[22] whose classical equivalents one might expect to find on any given evening in the banquet hall of the castle of Theseus. Mexico then shows his contempt for all these symbols of social status in a manner that the Miller might appreciate: the "poker-faced men" around the table discovering much to their dismay that he has "unbuttoned his fly, taken his cock out, and is now busy pissing on the shiny table" (636).

Later, Mexico and the inimitable Pig Bodine arrive at a formal banquet only to discover that they themselves are intended to be the "surprise roast" that will serve as the main course. They then save themselves through the power of subversive and aleatory discourse—and of abjection. In particular, they strike back with their vivid descriptions of possible side-dishes such as "snot soup," "menstrual maramalade," and "clot casserole" (715). Like all carnivalistic discourse, this discourse turns out to be contagious, and various members of the audience chime in with contributions such as "puke pancakes," "hemorrhoid hash," and "ringworm relish" (716). These evocations prove sufficiently unappetizing to rout the entire gathering, and Mexico and Bodine escape unscathed.

The distinguished gentlemen who sit around the meeting table in the first example above are the modern literary descendents of the twelve monks who gather around the spokes of a cartwheel at the end of "The Summoner's Tale" in order to sniff their fair shares of the cherl's fart. Similarly, the battle of disgusting discourses in the second example strongly echoes the carnivalesque technique through which Chaucer suggests a clear parallel between the formal chivalric weapons of Arcite and Palamon and hende Nicholas's "fart that well-nigh blinded Absolom." All of these cases, of course, very clearly illustrate the emphasis on the "bodily lower stratum" that Bakhtin sees as being so central to the carnivalesque spirit of Rabelais.

From a modern perspective, the subversive effects of "low" culture when placed in contact with "high" culture are probably more obvious in Pynchon than in Chaucer, if only because Pynchon's contemporaneity renders the various languages more readily recognizable. Reading Chaucer through Pynchon thus sheds new light on certain debates in traditional Chaucer criticism. For example, Derek Brewer presents a strong argument for

Chaucer as a subversive opponent of official culture, reveling in Bakhtinian polyphony amid a culture characterized by plurality and breakdown in official norms and standards, a breakdown that Chaucer clearly encourages. Larry Scanlon, on the other hand, argues that Chaucer's social attitude was one of intense (though critical) Christian conservatism. Reading Chaucer through Pynchon, I would suggest, tells us nothing whatsoever about Chaucer's attitude in this matter. It does, however, tell us a great deal about the effective nature of Chaucer's text, and that nature is clearly of the sort described by Brewer rather than that described by Scanlon.

Scanlon, in fact, anticipates me here. He suggests that our failure to recognize Chaucer's conservatism comes from the "modern humanist tradition to equate critical self-consciousness with its own ideological predispositions" (64). In other words, he suggests that Chaucer is only subversive if read on modern terms. Scanlon clearly believes such reading to be an error, but reading Chaucer on modern terms is precisely what I am trying to do. In fact, that may be the only kind of reading to which we, as modern readers, ultimately have access, try as we might.[23] Moreover, the example of Pynchon demonstrates very clearly the way in which mixing discourses from different social strata is inherently subversive of the "higher" discourse in a way that ultimately escapes all questions of authorial intent. Scanlon suggests that, in "The Nun's Priest's Tale," Chaucer's use of the discourse of the fabular narrative is employed as a sly means of reinforcing the discourse of Christian doctrine. Reading Chaucer through Pynchon (and through Bakhtin) suggests that no such reinforcement is possible. The secular, carnivalesque language of the fable inherently acts to undercut and destabilize the authoritarian discourse of the Church, whether Chaucer intended to do so or not.

Consider that key moment at the end of "The Nun's Priest's Tale" when we are encouraged to see the relevance of the tale to our own lives by an appeal to Christian authority:

For Seint Paule seith that al that writen is,
To oure doctrine it is ywrite, ywis;
Taketh the fruyt, and lat the chaf be stille.

(lines 3441–43)

Donaldson recognizes the ironic twist here, suggesting that the real moral of the tale is precisely the chaff that these lines would seem to have us ignore (88). Still, Scanlon tells us that "Sincere or ironic, this much is clear: these lines portray an attempt to appropriate Christian authority" (49). I do not believe this much is clear at all, and I would suggest that the lines in fact parody the claims of a Christian authority that, in Chaucer's day, was already becoming corrupt and decadent. Scanlon, meanwhile, admits that we are here authorized by Christian tradition to appropriate any and all texts. I would suggest that the monologic authoritarianism evidenced by such blind and single-minded appropriation is called into question by the heteroglossia of *The Canterbury Tales* as a whole, and that Chaucer's text here parodies the tradition of such appropriations. Consider the actual passage from Paul to which these lines refer:

For whatever was written in former days was written for our instruction, that by steadfastness and by the encouragement of the scriptures we might have hope. (Romans 15.4)

Scanlon presents an intelligent discussion of the appropriative tradition in Christianity (which followed the lead of Paul) and suggests that Chaucer is taking his place in this tradition. However, it is clear that Chaucer's statement is far more sweeping than is that of Paul. In fact, it can be read as a parodic reductio ad absurdum of Paul's statement. Chaucer's text appropriates Paul's, turning it against itself, and demonstrating the folly of any system that would seek to silence (even by absorption) all opposing voices. Once Christianity starts to appropriate every text in sight, we will soon find our religious authority based not on the Word of God, but on tales of cocks and foxes—or of a cock and bull.

The above "quotation" from Paul is given special significance in *The Canterbury Tales* by being repeated in Chaucer's ending retraction. It is here that the real force of this appropriation of Paul becomes fully evident. Obviously, if it is true that "Al that writen is" is written "to oure doctrine," then there can be no chance of tales that "sownen into synne." Thus, the very existence of the retraction radically undermines the suggested universality of Christian appropriation. Furthermore, the conspicuous inclusion of the statement of such appropriation within the retraction itself very clearly calls attention to this fact and in turn undercuts the retraction. The retraction, like all palinodes, does not erase the tales that "sownen into synne," though it may place them under erasure. In a sense, the retraction merely reactivates the carnivalistic energies of such tales and underscores the existence in the *Tales* of voices that oppose the hegemony of Christian doctrine, while doing so within the discourse of that doctrine itself. But this sort of destabilizing ending brings me back to where I began, with Pearce's comparison of Pynchon and Joyce. The special effectiveness of such contradictory endings highlights the way in which subversion of closure can have a special force in terms of transgression of hierarchies. Indeed, the avoidance of closure is closely related to the effects of polysemy and polyphony that I have been discussing.

ON CONCLUSIONS IN WHICH NOTHING IS CONCLUDED

The palinodic technique embodied in Chaucer's retraction was a common one in medieval literature. Jeremy Tambling, for example, discusses the frequent use of palinodes in Dante, noting precisely the effect I have described here in relation to Chaucer: "These palinodes suggest re-writing, rather than development, discontinuity rather than consistency, and qualify unitary truths with the sense of lability, doubleness, and difference" (132). Furthermore, Tambling argues that the use of palinodes in Chaucer is merely an aspect of the general oscillation of tones and voices within his work, so that "the palinode is with him a literary type, a mode of writing which need have nothing of sincerity about it" (133).

Interestingly, a similar type of "unstable" palinode turns out to be a very common feature of postmodernist literature as well. The unstable palinodic endings of Chaucerian works such as the *Tales* and *Troilus and Criseyde* bear clear similarities to the nonclosure of endings such as those employed by Pynchon, the "anti-epilogue" noted by Pearce at the end of *V.* being a clear example. Pynchon makes especially good use of the reader's expectation of an ending in *The Crying of Lot 49.* Ostensibly modeled on the genre of the detective story, all of *Lot 49* seems oriented toward an epistemological solution of the mysteries at hand, but no solution is ever given. Actually, at least one mystery is solved in the end, that being the meaning of the enigmatic title. This revelation acts to heighten our expectations concerning the importance of the stamp auction, but we go with Oedipa Maas to the final auction in search of critical clues to the central Tristero mystery only to find that the book ends as the auction begins, leaving us stranded.

Chaucer, in *The Canterbury Tales*, has a special opportunity for dealing with questions of endings, because each individual tale has an ending of its own. Some of these endings are truncated by interruption, achieving an effect of incompleteness quite similar to that achieved by Pynchon in *The Crying of Lot 49*. However, it is in the tales that apparently do close that Chaucer displays his most subtle (and powerful) subversions of closure. "The Knight's Tale," with its neat ending, is again a principal target. Generically, this tale has much in common with those later told by the Wife of Bath, the Squire, and the Franklin. But the Wife's tale, with its hidden internal polemic against the sexual exploitation of women,[24] reaches closure only by an exaggerately arbitrary means.[25] "The Squire's Tale," with its hyperbolic use of romance devices, demonstrates the inauthenticity of the romance tradition, and reaches no closure because it is interrupted by the Franklin. The Franklin then proceeds to tell a tale whose underlying theme of corruption and betrayal shows the rotten core that lies at the heart of the world of chivalry embodied by the Knight. It, too, closes in a clearly artificial manner. The effect of the dialogue among these generically related tales is to expose the falseness of the Knight's position and to reveal that the closure of his tale is in fact an arbitrary and impoverishing imposition of political power.

The lack of closure in such "conclusions" is especially striking because of the significance that attaches to endings in general. However, in its more general aspect, closure involves far more than simply the sense of an ending. It also involves the establishment of stable interpretations all through the reading process. For example, *Gravity's Rainbow* contains palinodic oscillations throughout, constantly teetering on the brink of ontological chaos. Situations are presented, then retracted, then presented again, to the point where it is nearly impossible to tell what is "really" happening from what occurs in dreams, paranoid fantasies, drug-induced hallucinations, and so on. We see Thanatz's memory of Blicero becoming unstable: "Of course it happened. Of course it didn't happen" (667). Or, in the midst of a discussion of drug-induced dreams, Tyrone Slothrop tells us, "A-and who sez it's a dream, huh? M-maybe it exists" (699). In fact, Brian McHale argues that the technique of putting characters, places, events, and so on "under erasure" is a central feature of postmodernist fiction. He then calls Slothrop the "most spectacular" example of a character who is himself placed under erasure (105).[26]

Perhaps the best-known postmodernist example of this technique occurs in the fiction of Samuel Beckett, where statements are constantly being made, then immediately withdrawn or contradicted. This effect can be particularly striking when (like the retraction to *The Canterbury Tales*) it occurs at the end of a work: it leaves the reader suspended in uncertainty. Thus Beckett ends Molloy with "It is midnight. The rain is beating on the windows. It was not midnight. It was not raining" (176). And we have the famous ending of *The Unnameable:* "I can't go on, I'll go on" (414). Wolfgang Iser discusses this aspect of Beckett's work, and suggests that it "results in a total devaluation of language by accentuating the arbitrariness with which it is applied to the objects it seeks to grasp" (165). The end result is that all arbitrary systems are called into question, releasing an energy whose effect is "to set the self free to pursue a course of endless self-discovery" (178). In other words, it releases creative energy as it destabilizes systems of taxonomy by demonstrating their artificial and conventional natures.[27]

In Chaucer, this kind of ongoing and continual lack of closure is clearly related to the instability of meaning that results from the polysemy and polyphony of his texts, as Shoaf notes in his discussion of Chaucer's puns. In *The Canterbury Tales*, this effect can be particularly related to the clashes among genres that occur in this work. As Barbara Herrnstein Smith points out in her general discussion of poetic closure, an effect of closure in a poem is intimately related to a perception of structure on the part of the reader. This perception is closely related to the generic expectations that the reader brings to the poem from his previous experience with other poems of the same genre (29–30). In *The Canterbury Tales*, however, the genre constantly changes, and the reader is never allowed to develop a coherent set of expectations with which to perceive a stable view of the poem. The most obvious modern analogue to this effect would be *Ulysses,* where Joyce's constant changes of style and genre from one chapter to the next subvert any attempts at univocal interpretation. But authors such as Pynchon derive a tremendous amount of mileage from the subversion of genre expectations as well, as I shall discuss in more detail in Chapter 7.

This sort of subversion of closure through denial of the reader's generic expectations is more obviously a literary effect than a political one, and it is certainly true that many of the clashes that occur in *The Canterbury Tales* are literary rather than social, at least on the surface. I would suggest, however, that these literary clashes are not innocent; indeed, they parallel and mirror the social ones. Just as the work entails a juxtaposition of a heterogenous group of pilgrims from various social strata, so too does it include a wide range of literary styles and genres. David Benson has recently presented an extensive discussion of this aspect of the *Tales:* "After opening with the startling contrast between *The Knight's Tale* and *The Miller's Tale,* Chaucer goes on to offer the reader an astonishing mixture of themes, genres, and narrative styles. The holy occurs next to the shameless and slapstick farce next to learned sermons" (20).

Thus, one of the systems of hierarchy and taxonomy that Chaucer calls into question is that involving literary genres. Benson appears headed here for a rather Bakhtinian approach, but he never takes that step, limiting his discussion to stylistic features and opting not to explore the social and political implications of those features. But a Bakhtinian analysis (especially with the notion of carnival replaced by the more general notion of transgression or fission) reveals that such implications can be strong indeed. As Stallybrass and White note, "the ranking of literary genres or authors in a hierarchy analogous to social classes is a particularly clear example of a much broader and more complex cultural process" (2).

This mutual implication of social and literary hierarchies is especially clear in Chaucer. Cook, in discussing the carnivalistic aspects of the "General Prologue," notes:

Each pilgrim represents a form of life; each gravitates towards one domain or another of medieval culture: the courtly, the pious, the carnivalesque, or some admixture of these. These are so many styles, but not in an exclusively literary sense: we need to extend a sense of style to include allegiance to particular beliefs and an implicit conception of social relations. (178)

But of course this conflation of literary and social dialogue in Chaucer is not surprising from a Bakhtinian perspective. Generic clashes are at the heart of Bakhtin's notion of Menippean satire, the genre (or antigenre) that best exemplifies the carnivalesque in literature. One might compare here Derrida's classification of his own *Glas* as a work of Menippean satire:

I think that a text like *Glas* is neither philosophic nor poetic. It circulates between these two genres, trying meanwhile to produce another text which would be of another genre or without genre. On the other hand, if one insists on defining genres at all costs, one could refer historically to Menippean satire, to 'anatomy' (as in *The Anatomy of Melancholy*), or to something like philosophic parody where all genres—poetry, philosophy, theater, et cetera—are summoned up at once. (In McDonald 140–41)

The multiplicity of genres included within the Menippean satire, then, acts to call into question the status and authority of all genres, and (by implication) of all systems of hierarchy. This inclusion of multiple genres (of which *The Canterbury Tales* is an excellent example) is one of the ways in which the Menippean satire maintains a subversive polyphonic force, never allowing itself to settle into a single univocal interpretation. Thus, the multigeneric character of the *Tales* can be seen as another of Chaucer's techniques for the avoidance of closure. Sklute sees Chaucer's entire career as building toward this form, which well suited his distaste for closure: "the entire form of *The Canterbury Tales* suggests, finally, that for Chaucer conclusive meaning in literature is neither possible nor desirable" (137). Sklute indicates that the structure of the poem, which is potentially infinitely expandable through addition of more tales, allows it to be endlessly open. I would argue, however, that the poem is already endlessly open, even without the potential for more tales. "Conclusive meaning" is always already undermined merely by the complex and dynamic dialogue that occurs among the existing tales.

The polysemic and polyphonic nature of *The Canterbury*

Tales and of works of postmodernists such as Pynchon powerfully contests the imposition of impoverishing univocal meanings in the process of reading literature. However, I have suggested throughout this chapter that the destabilizing process of reading these texts has implications that go far beyond the literary, extending to the ways in which we make meaning in all aspects of life. In the next chapter, I shall explore the work of Salman Rushdie, a contemporary author whose work is centrally informed by the transgression of boundaries and deconstruction of hierarchies in a way that particularly emphasizes the political implications of these literary techniques.

BEAUTY AND THE BEAST:
DUALISM AS DESPOTISM IN
THE FICTION OF SALMAN RUSHDIE

CHAPTER
2 ─────────────────────────

One of the most telling and significant passages in all of the complex fiction of Salman Rushdie occurs in his discussion of the game of "Snakes and Ladders" in *Midnight's Children*. This passage illustrates Rushdie's ability to evoke memories of childhood with a tenderness and nostalgia that rival Proust or Nabokov. It also shows the way in which Rushdie so effectively employs images from popular culture in the construction of his highly literary fictions, as "Snakes and Ladders" itself is of central thematic importance to the structure of *Midnight's Children*. In this simple children's game, alternatives are clear and unproblematic. Ladders lead up and are good; snakes send one sliding downward and are bad. But Rushdie's narrator, the harried Saleem Sinai, notes the way in which this apparently innocent game figures a much less innocent tendency toward dualistic thinking in general:

implicit in the game is the unchanging twoness of things, the duality of up against down, good against evil . . . metaphorically, all conceivable oppositions, Alpha against Omega, father against mother. (*Midnight's Children* 167)

In Rushdie's world, however, things are never quite so simple, and Sinai finds that such neat polar oppositions inevitably fall apart:

but I found, very early in my life, that the game lacked one crucial dimension, that of ambiguity . . . it is also possible to slither down a ladder and climb to triumph on the venom of a snake. (167)

This crucial element of ambiguity and multiple possibilities, emphasized as it is by the self-contradictory Shandean narrative excesses of Sinai himself, becomes in fact central to the entire book. But, like Tristram Shandy, Sinai is actually quite charming in his contradictoriness, and, as Maria Couto points out, his inconsistency "enhances one of the novel's most engaging qualities—its pervasive tone of uncertainty" (62). In the case of *Midnight's Children* this theme is linked in an obvious way to the use of *Tristram Shandy* as a narrative model, but in fact all of Rushdie's narrators operate much in the same way.[1] For example, the narrator of *Shame* explains his ability to be unbothered by apparent contradiction: "The inconsistency doesn't matter; I myself manage to hold large numbers of wholly irreconcilable views simultaneously, without the least difficulty. I do not think others are less versatile" (267).

Certainly it would be egregiously naive to take statements made by any of Rushdie's rhetorically complex narrators for the opinions of Rushdie himself, although recent events indicate that one might have a difficult time explaining that fact to certain Islamic fundamentalist elements.[2] Still, this Nietzschean–Whitmanesque mode of acceptance of contradiction might serve not only as a central theme of *Shame*, but of all Rushdie's fiction. His fiction consistently embraces contradiction, privileging the plural over the singular, the polyphonic over the monologic. One of the clearest ways in which it does so is by carefully constructing dual oppositions—like the snakes and ladders of Sinai's children's game—only to deconstruct those oppositions by demonstrating that the apparent polar opposites are in fact interchangeable and mutually interdependent. This deconstruction of oppositions functions as a transgression of the boundaries societies (especially authoritarian ones) maintain to define themselves. These boundaries exclude others; thus, transgressing them has highly political implications.

Rushdie's major novels are all highly political. In *Midnight's Children* he traces the history of a group of children born at or near midnight on India's day of independence from British rule, paralleling their stories very directly with that of the Indian Republic and including some very topical attacks on Indira Gandhi and other Indian political leaders. He also evokes the richly heteroglossic world of Indian culture in vivid fashion, and builds his plot around real events such as the partition of India and the resulting conflicts over that partition. In *Shame* he continues this motif, setting the novel in Pakistan and telling the story of Pakistan's oppressive political structure via a highly self-conscious metafictional narrative written in the tone of a fairy tale, a tone that eerily contrasts with the subject matter. And in *The Satanic Verses*—which in a sense combines the intense cultural vividness of *Midnight's Children* with the ostentatious artifice of *Shame*—he addresses very directly the cultural legacy of British imperialism as it affects the plight of modern-day immigrants, as well as exploring the complicity between authoritarian political thinking and the ideology of religion. In all of these books, Rushdie's incessant assault on totalitarianism involves attacks on dualistic thinking.

The most obvious way in which Rushdie launches his attack on dualistic thinking is through the use of paired characters. The most important characters tend to be shadowed by doubles in Rushdie's texts. A good example of such pairings involves Saleem Sinai and his alter ego, Shiva. Sinai is ostensibly the hero of the book, even if he is a hero in a decidedly ironic way. The sinister Shiva, on the other hand, is presented as the very embodiment of evil. These two opposing characters were both ominously born at the stroke of midnight on India's day of independence from British rule, one to the well-to-do Sinai family, one to a family of paupers. But the two infants were in fact switched at birth by Mary Pereira, the Sinai family ayah who sought to impress her Marxist boyfriend with this bit of prince-and-the-pauper subversion of social hierarchies. In a sense, then, Sinai is "really" Shiva, and Shiva is "really" Sinai, so that the polar opposition is rendered severely problematic.

Rushdie continues this motif of paired characters in *Shame*, though more complexly, because in *Shame* there is no single major character on whom to focus. As a result there are a number of important pairings in this later novel, including Iskander

Harappa and Raza Hyder, Harappa and Maulana Dawood, and Rani Harappa and Bilquìs Hyder. In *The Satanic Verses*, however, the text again centers on a single pairing, in the persons of Gibreel Farishta and Saladin Chamcha, though Rushdie builds on that pairing in an extremely sophisticated way: "For are they not conjoined opposites, these two, each man the other's shadow?" (426). The use of such character pairings is quite common in modern literature, of course, and one immediately thinks of the doppelgänger of Nabokov, or of pairings such as Stephen–Bloom or Shem–Shaun in Joyce. However, Rushdie (like Joyce) goes much deeper in his deconstruction of oppositions than the questioning of apparent differences between separate characters; he delves into the interior of the individual psyche itself.[3]

In John Fowles's *The French Lieutenant's Woman* the narrator suggests that a tendency toward dualistic thinking was the central characteristic of Victorian England, which makes "the best guidebook to the age very possibly *Dr. Jekyll and Mr. Hyde*" (289). Indeed, Stevenson's classic tale of the duality of human nature stands as a strong literary paradigm of dualisms in general. It is appropriate, then, that Rushdie's *Shame* (a text that deals so extensively with the theme of duality) should adopt *Dr. Jekyll and Mr. Hyde* (along with its fairy-tale counterpart, *Beauty and the Beast*) as a central intertextual model. Musing on the possibility that a Beast may in fact lurk inside the Beauty who is Naveed "Good News" Hyder, Rushdie's narrator imagines a nameless "Great Poet" explaining the impossibility of such a conjunction:

As Mr. Stevenson has shown in his *Dr. Jekyll and Mr. Hyde*, such saint-and-monster conjunctions are conceivable in the case of men; alas! such is our nature. But the whole essence of Woman denies such a possibility. (*Shame* 173)

This statement, of course, is made with typical Rushdie irony. A central plot line of *Shame* involves the literal transformation of Naveed's beautiful sister Sufiya Zinobia Hyder into a beast who hypnotizes and seduces young men, then rips off their heads with superhuman strength.[4] Rushdie carefully indicates the parallel between Sufiya Zinobia and Stevenson's hero, referring to her marriage to Omar Khayyam Shakil as "[h]er transformation from Miss Hyder into Mrs. Shakil" (188). Names are usually significant in Rushdie, even if ironically so: Omar Khayyam, for example, never writes a line of poetry. Here, the phonetic parallel between Jekyll–Hyde and Shakil–Hyder is quite obvious, though the pairing is (not insignificantly) reversed: Sufiya Zinobia is a beauty as Hyder, a beast as Shakil.[5]

The kinds of human-beast transformations undergone by Sufiya Zinobia Hyder enact a fundamental transgression of the boundary between human and animal. Such transgressions represent a favorite Rushdie motif. In *Midnight's Children*, Saleem Sinai is at one point used as a "man-dog," employed by the Pakistani "Canine Unit for Tracking and Intelligence" to sniff out enemies with his redoubtable nose.[6] *The Satanic Verses* actually features a number of such human-beast transgressions, the most striking of which is the mysterious metamorphosis of Chamcha into a devilish goatlike beast. And when the transformed Chamcha participates in a mass escape from the hospital where he is confined, he enters a nightmare vision inhabited by all sorts of similarly metamorphosed creatures:

Chamcha glimpsed beings he could never have imagined, men and women who were also partially plants, or giant insects, or even, on occasion, built partly of brick or stone; there were men with rhinoceros horns instead of noses and women with necks as long as any giraffe. (*Satanic Verses* 171)

Bizarre as they may seem, these kinds of transformations are quite central to the Menippean tradition to which Rushdie is such a clear heir. As Mikhail Bakhtin notes, "[t]he folktale image of man—throughout the extraordinary variety of folkloric narratives—always orders itself around the motifs of transformation and identity" (*Dialogic Imagination* 112). The classic work of Menippean human-animal metamorphosis is Apuleius's *The Golden Ass*, and the transformation of Chamcha into a goatlike beast parallels the transformation of Apuleius's Lucius into an ass in a number of important ways. Like Chamcha, Lucius undergoes considerable hardship and severe mistreatment while in this animal state, but later regains his humanity. Indeed, Rushdie acknowledges his debt to his great Menippean predecessor for this motif by having Muhammad Sufyan quote from Apuleius upon seeing the transformed Chamcha for the first time (*Satanic Verses* 243).

Bakhtin notes that such transformations allow representation in shorthand form of the development and change of the individual as he goes through life: "Metamorphosis serves as the basis for a method of portraying the whole of an individual's life in its more important moments of crisis: for showing how an individual becomes other than what he was" (*Dialogic Imagination* 115). Thus, such metamorphoses powerfully question the view of the self as a stable, self-contained entity by showing the drastic changes that the self can undergo in the course of life.[7] Moreover, the resultant confusion between human and animal brings about a transgressive reminder of certain abject, animalistic aspects of human nature that society generally attempts to repress.[8] The ability of the self to be transformed into something that formerly seemed totally alien to itself interrogates the boundary between self and other, challenging the validity of even that fundamental duality.[9]

In Rushdie, the boundary between self and other is always problematic. His characters tend to be complex, multiple, and highly variable, and he emphasizes the manifoldness of identity in numerous ways. Thus Saleem Sinai explains the difficulty of relating his life in any simple way by the fact that he, like Whitman, contains multitudes: "Consumed multitudes are jostling and shoving inside me" (*Midnight's Children* 4).

In *The Satanic Verses* Rushdie again employs this image of jostling multiple selves, this time enhanced by one of his many allusions to popular culture:

O, the conflicting selves jostling and joggling within these bags of skin. No wonder we are unable to remain focused on anything for very long; no wonder we invent remote-control channel-hopping devices. If we turned these instruments upon ourselves we'd discover more channels than a cable or satellite mogul ever dreamed of. (519)[10]

Finally, he even states this multiplicity clearly in terms of a deconstruction of the opposition between self and other:

Because a human being, inside himself, is anything but a whole, anything but homogeneous; all kinds of everywhichthing are jumbled up inside him and he is one person one minute and another the next. (*Midnight's Children* 283)

This instability of identity, we are told, occurs because people tend to blend together "like flavours when you cook" (*Midnight's Children* 38). Such a mixing of identities is particularly explicit in *Shame* during the gestation of Omar Khayyam Shakil. One of three sisters is bearing him (we never learn the identity of the father), but the other sisters are so close that they share the experience with her, helping her to bear the stigma of unwed pregnancy: "twin phantom pregnancies accompanied the real one; while the simultaneity of their behaviour suggests the operation of some form of communal mind" (13). The communal nature of the identity of these three sisters is so strong, in fact, that no one can tell the real pregnancy from the phantom ones, and neither the reader nor Omar Khayyam ever learns which of the three sisters is his true biological mother. And years later, when the sisters begin to argue over Omar Khayyam's fateful birthday wish to be allowed to leave their barricaded home and enter the outside world for the first time, they discover that such arguments are made difficult because even they have reached the point where they cannot tell themselves apart:

they had been indistinguishable too long to retain any exact sense of their former selves . . . and of course this confused separation of personalities carried with it the implication that they were still not genuinely discrete. (*Shame* 36)

Finally, in *The Satanic Verses*, all identities are radically unstable, with most of the characters being shown to bear artificially created identities that they themselves have largely made up: "Fictions were walking around wherever he went, Gibreel reflected, fictions masquerading as real human beings" (*Satanic Verses* 192). This artificiality of identity is particularly strong in the case of Chamcha, who has made up his name, changed his voice, even changed his face in order to try to fit in better in Britain.[11] As a result, his identity is hopelessly multiple, as emphasized by his professional role as the "Man of a Thousand Voices and a Voice": "Once, in a radio play for thirty-seven voices, he interpreted every single part under a variety of pseudonyms and nobody ever worked it out" (*Satanic Verses* 60). Of course, as a result of such artificiality, his identity is also highly changeable:

When he was young . . . each phase of his life, each self he tried on, had seemed reassuringly temporary. Its imperfections didn't matter, because he could easily replace one moment by the next, one Saladin by another. (*Satanic Verses* 63)

Later, the narrator suggests that the fundamental difference between Chamcha and Gibreel may in fact be that Chamcha undergoes his various changes in identity willingly, but that Gibreel seeks (unsuccessfully) to maintain his "true" self. But of course in Rushdie there is no "true" self, and this dual opposition is fated to break down:

this sounds, does it not, dangerously like an intentionalist fallacy?—Such distinctions, resting as they must on an idea of the self as being (ideally) homogeneous, non-hybrid, "pure",—an utterly fantastic notion!—cannot, must not, suffice. (*Satanic Verses* 427)

One of the most vivid representations of this theme of unstable identity involves Saleem Sinai in *Midnight's Children*, who is physically (or at least so he believes) cracking and fragmenting into pieces. Saleem also serves as a particularly apt figure of the instability of identity because he is literally not himself. Secretly switched at birth with the infant who grows up to become the sinister Major Shiva, he is brought up by parents who are not his own. Moreover, his parentage is doubly contestable: his real biological father is the Englishman William Methwold, not the husband of his biological mother. Clearly, to Rushdie (as to Joyce's Stephen Dedalus) paternity is a legal fiction, but Rushdie even expands this principle to make maternity a legal fiction as well.[12]

Questionable parentage is one way in which Rushdie calls the illusion of identity into question. In *Shame* we know the identity of neither of Omar Khayyam's parents. Meanwhile, both Iskander Harappa and Naveed Hyder are revealed to be of illegitimate parentage, and this theme is most strikingly emphasized in the scene in the women's dormitory where the husbands enact conjugal visits en masse under a cover of darkness so absolute that proper pairing is highly doubtful. As Rani tells Bilquìs:

who would know if her real husband had come to her? And who could complain? I tell you, Billoo, these married men and ladies are having a pretty good time in this joint family set-up. I swear, maybe uncles with nieces, brothers with their brothers' wives, we'll never know who the children's daddies really are! (*Shame* 75)

But if the very idea of a stable, unified self is revealed by Rushdie to be a fiction, then the Romantic notion of the self as a basis of authority or source of truth must be a fiction as well. This attack on the authority of the individual in Rushdie is particularly evidenced by his narrators, who are extremely unreliable, being not only inconsistent and contradictory, but oftentimes downright mendacious. Saleem Sinai closely ties his narrative to events in actual Indian history, yet gets dates wrong, confuses causes with effects, and fabricates information when he has no facts. He even invents entire episodes, such as the death of Shiva, though he later confesses to his invention:

To tell the truth, I lied about Shiva's death. My first out-and-out lie—although my presentation of the Emergency in the guise of a six-hundred-and-thirty-five-day-long midnight was perhaps excessively romantic, and certainly contradicted by the available meteorological data. (*Midnight's Children* 529)

In this passage, Saleem admits a lie, claims it was his only one, then immediately admits (though more obliquely) a second lie. The net result is an evocation of the liar paradox: the reader finds it impossible to reach any satisfactory conclusion as to what in the text is true and what is false. Moreover, by tying his text so closely to history, Rushdie suggests that the authority of all of our representations of the past may be somewhat questionable. Sinai explains his lie about Shiva in a way that has ominous implications concerning the construction of history in general:

I fell victim to the temptation of every autobiographer, to the illusion that since the past exists only in one's memories and the words which strive vainly to encapsulate them, it is possible to create past events simply by saying they occurred. (*Midnight's Children* 529)

The authority of Sinai's narrative is further undermined by the way in which he himself calls attention to flaws in his own narrative. Admitting that he has given the wrong date for the assassination of Gandhi, Sinai then muses on the implications of this error for the rest of his narrative, again with a reference to the authority of history:

Does one error invalidate the entire fabric? Am I so far gone, in my desperate need for meaning, that I'm prepared to distort everything—to re-write the whole history of my times purely in order to place myself in a central role? (*Midnight's Children* 198)

Rushdie continues his questioning of the authority of both narrative and history in his later novels as well. In *Shame* the intrusive narrator repeatedly reminds us of the fictionality of his story, emphasizing that fictionality with a variety of fantastic elements, yet tying it closely to the actual history of Pakistan as well. For example, as Raza Hyder plots the overthrow of Iskander Harappa, the narrator steps in:

Well, well, I mustn't forget I'm only telling a fairy-story. My dictator will be toppled by goblinish, faery means. "Makes it pretty easy for you," is the obvious criticism; and I agree, I agree. But add, even if it does sound a little peevish: "You try and get rid of a dictator some time." (*Shame* 284)[13]

In addition, the self-conscious fictionality of the narrative is directly linked to the artificiality of our constructions of history. This connection is particularly reinforced by the Pakistani setting, as Pakistan itself is an artificially created country that came into existence only with the partition that occurred with India's independence from Britain. As a result, Pakistan is a country whose history must be fabricated from scratch:

To build Pakistan it was necessary to cover up Indian history, to deny that Indian centuries lay just beneath the surface of Pakistani Standard Time. The past was rewritten; there was nothing else to be done. (*Shame* 91)

This phenomenon of rewriting is one that occurs again and again in Rushdie's fiction: we are given an account of events, then that account is retracted and we are given an alternative, contradictory account. The reader thus finds herself very much in the position of *Shame*'s Raza Hyder, who, having assumed the presidency of Rushdie's mythical version of Pakistan, is haunted by opposing voices. In his right ear, he hears the voice of the dead Muslim religious fanatic Maulana Dawood; in his left, the voice of Harappa, Hyder's deposed predecessor: "God on his right shoulder, the Devil on his left" (*Shame* 263). This motif evokes the well-known cartoon image in which the central character is torn between the contradictory advice of a winged angel on the one hand and pitchfork-bearing devil on the other. In Rushdie, however, such an evocation is not surprising; he is probably rivalled only by Thomas Pynchon as a contemporary poet of cartoons, comic books, and commercials. There is clearly a carnivalesque aspect to this juxtaposition of cartoon imagery with serious political and religious issues, a suggestion that the way we typically deal with those serious issues may not be so far removed from the silliness of cartoons as we would like to believe. Moreover, the Harappa–Dawood dichotomy shows that even the distinction between God and the Devil is not a pure-and-simple one. In *Shame* we find that Harappa commits a number of atrocities, but definitely has a good side as well. Meanwhile, the holy man Dawood is a cruel and sinister (if also patently ridiculous) figure.

Of all the dual oppositions that are called into question by Rushdie's fiction, this one between God and the Devil may be the most powerful, as the recent violent reaction of Islamic fundamentalists to *The Satanic Verses* strikingly demonstrates. The dualistic opposition between Gibreel Farishta and Saladin Chamcha moves to a decidedly theological plane as Gibreel spends much of the book in the throes of a transformation (maybe) into his namesake the archangel, while Chamcha is being transformed (maybe) into a goatish devil. Amid the general postmodern ontological confusion of the book, however, it is impossible to develop any satisfactorily stable understanding of the exact meaning and status of these problematic transformations. Moreover, the "devil" Saladin is generally treated more sympathetically and humanly than is the "angel" Gibreel, though it is perhaps Saladin (whose intentional subversion of the relationship between Gibreel and Alleluia Cone leads to the deaths of both lovers) who commits the most devilish act in the book. In short, it is ultimately impossible to decide who is the "good guy" and who is the "bad guy." Such oppositions simply do not apply in Rushdie's world.

The action of *The Satanic Verses* occurs on a number of different ontological levels, and the angel-devil dichotomy represented by Gibreel and Saladin is reproduced in a number of ways throughout the book. Even the prophet Muhammad (here, Mahound) seems unable to tell angels from devils. He ascends Mount Cone and receives, presumably from the archangel Gibreel, "permission" to accept the female deities of the city of Jahilia as secondary gods in order to facilitate the conversion of the people of the city to Islam. He recites this revelation in verse to the people of Jahilia, but then later receives a second revelation from Gibreel telling him that the first had been a trick on the part of Satan. Therefore, he is forced to issue a palinode retracting those first Satanic verses.[14] But this retraction, like all palinodes, cannot fully erase the earlier verses, though it may place them "under erasure." In a sense, the retraction merely reactivates the carnivalesque energies of those earlier verses, much like Chaucer's retraction at the end of *The Canterbury Tales*.

Of course, the very use of the name "Mahound" participates in this confusion. Again, names in Rushdie's fiction are charged with significance. The name "Mahound," like so much in Rushdie, was apparently derived from the Western literary tradition. "Mahound" appears in various guises both in medieval mystery plays and in Spenser, but always as a sort of diabolic figure. To make matters more complicated, the narrator suggests that the prophet himself has chosen to use this diabolic name as a means of disarming his opponents:

Here he is neither Mahomet nor Moehammered; has adopted, instead, the demon-tag the farangis hung around his neck. To turn insults into strengths, whigs, tories, Blacks all chose to wear with pride the names they were given in scorn; likewise, our mountain-climbing, prophet-motivated solitary is to be the medieval baby-frightener, the Devil's synonym: Mahound. (*Satanic Verses* 93)

Thus, the use of this name for the prophet Muhammad emphasizes the indistinguishability of the divine and the diabolic in Rushdie's latest book.[15]

All of this is complicated in that the reader shares Mahound's confusion: we, too, cannot tell God from Devil, Gibreel from Satan (who, after all, is a former archangel himself). In fact, even as Mahound issues his palinode, that palinode is itself subverted by the text:

Gibreel, hovering-watching from his highest camera angle, knows one small detail, just one tiny thing that's a bit of a problem here, namely that it was me both times, baba, me first and second also me. From my mouth, both the statement and the repudiation, verses and converses, universes and reverses, the whole thing, and we all know how my mouth got worked. (*Satanic Verses* 123)

This statement not only illustrates Rushdie's frequent and effective use of film imagery and terminology (again à la Pynchon), but also effects a deconstruction and mutual implication of oppositions that would do Derrida proud. Angel and devil here are not opposites at all, but one and the same. Moreover, Gibreel's speech shows how the Satanic verses recited by Mahound serve as an internal duplication of Rushdie's text as a whole. That text works constantly in a mode of statement and retraction. In the very beginning of the book, we are presented with the spectacle of Chamcha and Farishta conversing and singing as they fall from an aircraft that has exploded at high altitude:

Let's face it: it was impossible for them to have heard one another, much less conversed and also competed thus in song. Accelerating towards the planet, atmosphere roaring around them, how could they? But let's face this, too: they did. (*Satanic Verses* 6)

Or, as we are repeatedly reminded throughout the book, "it was and it was not so, as the old stories used to say, it happened and it never did" (*Satanic Verses* 35).[16]

This palinodic mode of narration serves to heighten the confusion of the reader. Faced with the choice between so and not so, real and not real, the reader is thwarted in his efforts to reach a comfortable solution. Such either-or, yes-no choices are constantly subverted within Rushdie's overall assault on polar logic. This manipulative mode of narration is another Rushdie trademark. His work tends to feature unreliable, intrusive narrators who openly break the frame of the fiction to reveal the processes of composition, disturbing any attempts at a naturalistic recuperation of those fictions, even though the bulk of the narration may proceed in a largely naturalistic mode. Thus, in *The Satanic Verses*, we do indeed know how Gibreel's "mouth got worked." Like everything in Rushdie's fiction, it got worked by the narrator. In *Satanic Verses* the narrator is less overtly manipulative and intrusive than in *Midnight's Children* (where the narrator is also the main character) or *Shame* (where the narrator continually reminds us that we are reading a fiction that he made up). However, he is still an important figure, always pulling the strings; the identity of the narrator is one of the puzzles the reader encounters in negotiating the book.

Very early on (on the second page of the book), the narrator challenges us to guess his identity: "Who am I?" he asks. "Who else is there?" he responds (*Satanic Verses* 4). Soon afterward, he repeats this same question, after presenting the song of Farishta falling through the sky: "Of what type—angelic, satanic—was Farishta's song? Who am I?" (10). But in *The Satanic Verses* it is never possible to reach a comfortable distinction between angelic and satanic, and the narrator here implicates his own identity in this same unanswerable question. Like Mahound, the reader of Rushdie's book cannot tell if the words she receives are of divine or of diabolic origin.

There are many indications in the book that the narrator is, in fact, Satan. For one thing, the title itself points in that direction. We also have specific hints: "I know; devil talk. Shaitan interrupting Gibreel. Me?" (*Satanic Verses* 93). Later, the narrator compares his own fall to that of Chamcha and Farishta: "You think they fell a long way? In the matter of tumbles, I yield pride of place to no personage, whether mortal or im——" (133). From such passages, the narrator's Satanic identity seems quite clear. Yet, later in the book Gibreel sees a vision of God himself, though it is a vision of a rather unimpressive, bearded, balding God with the appearance of a "myopic scrivener," who curiously seems to look a lot like Rushdie. We find, however, that this vision is the narrator. In *The Satanic Verses* God and Satan are indistinguishable, irrevocably intertwined, and the narrator himself does nothing to clear up the confusion: "I'm saying nothing. Don't ask me to clear things up one way or the other; the time of revelations is long gone" (*Satanic Verses* 408).

Clearly, Rushdie's attacks on the authority of texts and his attacks on the authority of religion are closely related, as well they might be: religions commonly base their authorities on central texts. It is not surprising, then, that one of Rushdie's central assaults on textual authority has as its target the Koran, the authoritative text of Islam. The Koran was supposedly dictated to Muhammad by Gibreel, but we already know that Mahound has difficulty distinguishing Gibreel from Satan. If he mistakenly accepted Satanic verses once, how do we know that he won't do so again? Moreover, Mahound in turn dictates the revelation of scripture to his scribe, called (appropriately enough) Salman. But Salman, concerned over Mahound's patriarchal insistence on the submissiveness of women, begins to wonder if the prophet has his own less-than-pure motives for this insistence. So he decides to put Mahound to the test, altering the dictation slightly, only to discover that Mahound can't tell the difference:

Here's the point: Mahound did not notice the alterations. So there I was, actually writing the Book, or rewriting, anyway, polluting the word of God with my own profane language. But, good heavens, if my poor words could not be distinguished from the Revelation by God's own Messenger, then what did that mean? (*Satanic Verses* 367)

Or, as Salman later states, "It's his Word against mine" (*Satanic Verses* 368). By challenging the authority of that ultimate monologic word, the Word of God, Rushdie (like Bakhtin) emphasizes the inherent dialogic power of words. No word can have unquestionable authority, because all words inherently contain the potential echoes of responses from opposing voices. This is not, however, to say that language cannot be used in the service of despotism; it can. In *Shame* Rushdie's narrator specifically links Islamic fundamentalism in Pakistan to political oppression, and especially to the oppressive potential of official language:

So-called Islamic "fundamentalism" does not spring, in Pakistan, from the people. It is imposed on them from above. Autocratic regimes find it useful to espouse the rhetoric of faith, because people respect that language, are reluctant to oppose it. This is how religions shore up dictators; by encircling them with words of power. (*Shame* 278)

But if language can be used in the interest of oppression, it can also be used to oppose that oppression. Against the oppressive authoritarian language of the dictators, Rushdie opposes his own language of freedom and multiplicity. Thus, in an article printed in the *New York Review of Books*, Rushdie notes that the uproar over *The Satanic Verses* is "a clash of languages" ("The Book Burning" 26).

Because of the inherent dialogic potential of language itself, the seemingly clear linguistic opposition between the sacred and the profane is in Rushdie not so simple after all. Moreover, by questioning the authority of such seemingly truth-based texts as history and the Koran, Rushdie even confounds so simple an opposition as that between the true and the false, the real and the not-real. The difficulty of this distinction is highlighted by the way in which Rushdie's self-consciously literary fiction engages in a direct and intense dialogue with the social and political issues of the real world. Whether it be political oppression in Pakistan or religious fanaticism in Iran, the targets of Rushdie's anti-authoritarian satire are not only modes of philosophical speculation, but also living, breathing autocrats. *Shame*, for example, unashamedly depicts the tumultuous history of Pakistan, from its formation in 1947 up to the time of the writing of the book, while at the same time continually proclaiming its own fictionality. The narrator explains:

The country in this story is not Pakistan, or not quite. There are two countries, real and fictional, occupying the same space, or almost the same space. My story, my fictional country exist, like myself, at a slight angle to reality. (*Shame* 23–24)

This theme of two contradictory realities occupying the same space is a favorite one in Rushdie's fiction. Much of the premise of Grimus, for example, involves a science-fiction–like speculation on the existence of alternate dimensions within the same space. In *Shame* he uses this same idea to describe the duality of Sufiya Zinobia Hyder, noting that "the edges of Sufiya Zinobia were beginning to become uncertain, as if there were two beings occupying the same air-space, competing for it, two entities of identical shape but of tragically opposed nature" (*Shame* 259). But if two "tragically opposed" entities, two incompatible and contradictory alternative realities, can occupy the same space, then the very notions of "identity" and "reality" are called into question. The narrator of *Shame*, realizing the volatility of the material with which he is dealing, expresses his gratitude that he is not writing a realistic novel. As a result, he will not have to mention certain controversial real-world issues, which he then promptly lists. Then he notes what a good thing it is that he does not have to include this material (which he has just included) in his book:

> By now, if I had been writing a book of this nature, it would have done me no good to protest that I was writing universally, not only about Pakistan. The book would have been banned, dumped in the rubbish bin, burned. All that effort for nothing! Realism can break a writer's heart.
>
> Fortunately, however, I am only telling a sort of modern fairy-tale, so that's all right; nobody need get upset, or take anything I say too seriously. No drastic action need be taken, either. (*Shame* 72)

The ironic humor of this passage is obvious in the context of the book, but in light of the recent "drastic action" taken by Iran's Ayatollah Khomeini in response to *The Satanic Verses*, this passage takes on a rather chilling quality.[17] This action, in addition to providing a dramatic instantiation of Rushdie's questioning of the boundaries between fact and fiction, also spectacularly illustrates why Islam so often surfaces in Rushdie's fiction as a symbol of monological thought. Time and again, Rushdie emphasizes the fact that Islam is the religion of one God, a monotheism that forms a particularly striking symbol in the context of heteroglossic, polytheistic India. As recent reactions to Rushdie's work so vividly demonstrate, it is characteristic of certain fanatical devotees of this particularly single-minded religion to be totally intolerant of all alternative modes of thought. This intolerance of otherness amounts to an opposition between self and other of the type that Rushdie relentlessly challenges in his fiction. For example, the narrator of *The Satanic Verses* indicates that such oppositions are related to the tendency to see God and the Devil as two separate and opposing forces rather than as related parts of the same force. He then presents textual evidence to argue that such a separation has no basis in older religious texts: "This notion of separation of functions, light versus dark, evil versus good, may be straightforward enough in Islam . . . but go back a bit and you see that it's a pretty recent fabrication" (*Satanic Verses* 323).

Still, it is important to recognize that Rushdie's enemy is not Islam itself, but dogmatism in general (read "oppression"), just as Nietzsche opposed the dogmatism of Christianity more than any particular tenets of the Christian religion. Indeed, Rushdie's thought seems to resemble that of Nietzsche in many key ways.[18] But Rushdie's deconstruction of polar oppositions as a means of challenging monological authority has a number of parallels in modern critical discourse. From Nietzsche's transvaluation of values to the deconstructive project of Jacques Derrida, a number of modern thinkers have argued that the dualistic thinking so central to the history of Western civilization has tended inevitably toward the establishment of hierarchies: one term in a pair is privileged over the other so that what is "good" becomes defined by its difference from what is "bad." Dualistic thinking thus allows complex issues to be reduced to questions of black-and-white, good-and-bad. It allows the identification of the opposition as the Other, as evil, and provides a justification for the violent oppression of that opposition.[19]

In *Shame* Rushdie demonstrates that this tendency toward hierarchical dualisms is in fact not restricted to the West. One of the most striking and important effects of his fiction in general is the way in which it obfuscates the popular adjective "Western" that has come to be associated (generally in a pejorative sense) with so many political, philosophical, and historical concepts in recent years. But that is as it should be. In Rushdie, simple dual oppositions such as East versus West are never to be trusted. One of the ways in which he breaks down this distinction in *Shame* is through his use of the French Revolution as an intertext for the various coups and other incidences of political violence in modern-day Pakistan. Rushdie evokes Georg Büchner's play *Danton's Death*, which depicts the apparently polar opposition between the French revolutionary figures Danton and Robespierre, linking that opposition to an epicureanism-puritanism dialectic model of history. But then, in exploring the sympathies of the play's audience with these two figures, he discovers that the opposition is not a simple one at all: "The people are not only like Robespierre. They, we, are Danton, too. We are Robeston and Danpierre" (Shame 267).[20] Further, he uses this insight to confound a similar political opposition in Shame itself: "Iskander Harappa was not just Danton; Raza Hyder wasn't Robespierre pure-and-simple" (Shame 267).

But of course nothing is ever "pure-and-simple" in Rushdie's fiction, and the manifoldness of his vision links his work not only with the line of modern philosophy that runs from Nietzsche to Derrida, but also to the carnivalesque Menippean literary tradition within which he writes.[21] Within this tradition, Rushdie's clear predecessors are authors such as Rabelais, Swift, and Sterne, while his modern-day company includes such members as Joyce, Pynchon, and Günter Grass.[22] Central to the work of all of these writers (and to Menippean satire in general) is a questioning of traditional authority, and particularly of traditional forms of logic, forms that depend greatly on dualistic oppositions (especially the Aristotelian principle of noncontradiction) for their structure.

Julia Kristeva outlines this philosophical aspect of Menippean satire (and its modern-day heir, the "polyphonic novel"), noting that "Menippean discourse develops in times of opposition against Aristotelianism, and writers of polyphonic novels seem to disapprove of the very structures of official thought founded on formal logic" ("Word" 85). This rejection of Aristotelianism leads, according to Kristeva, to the rejection of a whole panoply of related concepts; the notions of "identity, substance, causality and definition are transgressed so that others may be adopted: analogy, relation, opposition, and therefore dialogism and Menippean ambivalence" (86). But to Kristeva there is more at stake than abstract ideas in the philosophical subversion inherent in the polyphonic novel. It is characteristic of Menippean satire to be invested with political force, to be a satire of something, and literary works in the Menippean tradition tend to be intensely involved with the sociohistorical moment in which they are produced. "Disputing laws of language based on the 0–1 interval, the carnival challenges God, authority and social law; in so far as it is dialogical, it is rebellious" (79).

The challenge to God that Kristeva mentions here particularly emphasizes her contention that the subversive force of the modern polyphonic novel differs from that of its Menippean forerunners in one important way:

In the Middle Ages, Menippean tendencies were held in check by the authority of the religious text; in the bourgeois era, they were contained by the absolutism of individuals and things. Only modernity—when freed of "God"—releases the Menippean force of the novel. (85)

To Kristeva, then, it is precisely the loss of monologic authority associated with the Nietzschean death of God that energizes the modern polyphonic text. In this sense, Rushdie's work is paradigmatic of the genre as Kristeva defines it. Not only is his work intensely involved with its real-world context, but that involvement quite often explores alternatives to the concept of theological authority.

Rushdie, however, is not an antireligious writer.[23] Like Nietzsche before him, he rejects religious dogmatism while at the same time recognizing that human beings have a fundamental need for beliefs and values. There is a character (Aadam Aziz) in *Midnight's Children* who, having lost his religious faith, experiences the sensation of a hole at the heart of his very self. Rushdie himself admits that he, too, has suffered such an experience of loss: "Unable to accept the unarguable absolutes of religion, I have tried to fill up the hole with literature" ("The Book Burning" 26). Rushdie's fiction, then, can be seen as his contribution to the development of alternative myths for the modern age. Similarly, the narrator of *Shame* acknowledges that an alternative to the myth of fundamentalist religion is the development of new myths. He unabashedly recommends three such myths derived directly from the Western Enlightenment: "liberty; equality; fraternity" (*Shame* 278).

Rushdie's contention is not that we should not have faith, but that each of us should have the freedom and opportunity to explore and enact his own faith in his own way. Rushdie is an apostle of freedom, proclaiming the creed that none of us can be truly free as long as any of us remain oppressed. In this regard, it is significant that he has become more and more concerned with the oppression of women in Islamic society. After all, the male-female distinction is among the most important of the dual oppositions that Rushdie consistently attacks, and as long as women are oppressed, men cannot have true freedom either:

Repression is a seamless garment; a society which is authoritarian in its social and sexual codes, which crushes its women beneath the intolerable burdens of honour and propriety, breeds repressions of other kinds as well. Contrariwise: dictators are always—or at least in public, on other people's behalf—puritanical. So it turns out that my "male" and "female" plots are the same story, after all. (Shame 189)[24]

Rushdie clearly recognizes that the ideals of liberty, equality, and fraternity are myths instituted for pragmatic purposes and does not attempt to render them universal truths. Still, despite his questioning of the stable, unified subject and despite a some- what modern (though not radical, by feminist standards) sen- sitivity to gender issues, his basic political vision seems in- formed by a remarkably traditional liberal humanism, garnered straight from the slogans of the French Revolution. All of this seems pretty unobjectionable, even clichéd, by Western stan- dards, yet at the date of this writing Rushdie remains a marked man, sentenced to death by Khomeini for the transgressions committed against Islam in *The Satanic Verses* (even though Khomeini himself has since died).

Khomeini's seemingly bizarre reaction to *The Satanic Verses* emphasizes the profoundly contextual nature of Rushdie's fic- tion, and of transgressive literature in general. In order to be transgressive, literature must have something specific to trans- gress against. Rushdie's fiction, viewed narrowly within the Western tradition, is inventive and provocative, but does not appear to be especially radical or subversive. Viewed from the Islamic perspective of Iran or Pakistan, however, the deconstruc- tion of dualities and concommitant questioning of authority inherent in Rushdie's fiction are so powerfully subversive that Khomeini has declared that Rushdie must die.

Preposterous as it seems from our Western perspective, Kho- meini's death sentence would apparently be in perfect accor- dance with Muslim law, except that the simple-minded Ayatol- lah hermeneutics used to reach this verdict (clearly based upon techniques of reading the Koran as the univocal Word of God) are incapable of dealing with the rhetorical complexities of a text such as *The Satanic Verses*. Apparently Khomeini has not heeded Rushdie's narrator's warnings against the "intentionalist fallacy," but then it is also a pretty safe bet that Khomeini hasn't read Wimsatt and Beardsley, or (for that matter) *The Satanic Verses* itself. In any case, this attempt to literalize Barthes's death of the author in the case of Rushdie indicates that there is a quite tangible real-world relevance for both literature and literary studies.[25] This relevance, in fact, is one of the prime points made by Rushdie's fiction, even without the Ayatollah's "help." In fact, Rushdie sees the very notion that literature might be divorced from real-world political issues as an illusion arising from the comforts of advanced Western societies:

In the rich, powerful societies of the West, it is possible to exclude politics from fiction; to treat public affairs as peripheral and faintly disreputable. From outside the West, this looks like the sort of position one can only take up inside a cocoon of privilege. ("The Empire" 8).

Rushdie's encounter with Khomeini highlights graphically (and frighteningly) the interrelatedness of literature and politics outside that Western cocoon of privilege. Rushdie has declined to seek the safety of that cocoon, and one can only hope that his courageous literary attacks on the real-world despotism of regimes such as Khomeini's have not placed him in the position in which George Miranda of *The Satanic Verses* sees Gibreel's last controversial religious movie as having placed Gibreel: "Looks like he's trying deliberately to set up a final confrontation with religious sectarians, knowing he can't win, that he'll be broken into bits" (*Satanic Verses* 539).

The specificity of Rushdie's targets, whether they be Muslim fundamentalism in general, or specific authoritarian regimes in Pakistan or Iran, provides an important insight into the mechanism of literary transgression. Rushdie's deconstruction of oppositions and transgression of normal boundaries is genuinely subversive largely because of the specificity of these targets. Of course, a transgressive reader might be able to marshal the lessons of Rushdie's fiction against other targets as well, but in general transgressive reading is greatly facilitated when the text itself already posits a target. In the next chapter I shall look at

Gilbert Sorrentino's *Mulligan Stew*. This recent text, although possessing an extreme diversity of styles, generic multiplicity, and avant-garde technique, does not fully succeed as a transgressive work—largely because it seems to lack specific social and political targets.

THE DYNAMICS OF LITERARY TRANSGRESSION IN SORRENTINO'S **MULLIGAN STEW**

CHAPTER

3 _____

One reviewer of Gilbert Sorrentino's *Mulligan Stew* called the book a "suicide-kit of modernism," though perhaps it might have been equally descriptive to refer to it as a tool-kit of post-modernism. Sorrentino's book displays a broad and impressive array of fictional devices and techniques that have come to be identified either with postmodernism, or metafiction, or both. Clearly the book is technically impressive, but one is tempted to ask if it is not *too* impressive, placing it in severe danger of collapsing into an empty formalism that is all style and no sub-stance. On the other hand, one could argue that style is the substance of this book, and so on, until the arguments become more and more circular and confused, collapsing back onto themselves in a midden heap. It is precisely because of such difficulties that *Mulligan Stew* would seem to be an ideal text within which to explore the fundamental question of the ef-ficacy of postmodernist metafiction as a transgressive form.

Sorrentino's book appears a prime candidate for transgressive reading, if only because it openly violates so many conventions of fiction. Though the book has a plot (actually several plots, on different ontological levels), that plot is of relatively little impor-tance. The book roughly concerns the efforts of struggling writer Antony Lamont to pursue his craft, especially in the writing of a ridiculous detective novel in which Martin Halpin attempts to decipher the clues concerning the death of Ned Beaumont. But *Mulligan Stew* is really the story of the construction of *Mulligan Stew* from bits and pieces of the literary tradition. It consists of a bricolage of different styles and genres, constructed by patching together a variety of heterogenous documents, including letters, a scientific treatise, a play, pornographic poetry, notebook and journal entries, a detective novel, magazine articles, and so on. Even the characters are taken from other books. By leaving the seams between these patches so openly exposed, Sorrentino challenges the paradigms of realistic fiction and the ideology upon which they are based. The question, however, is whether Sorrentino's quest for obviousness goes so far that it undercuts his own project.

Charles Altieri sees modernism as perhaps the apex of the humanist tradition, as a movement that "seeks to bring individuals and the culture to more complete, more fully humane uses of human energy." Postmodernism, on the other hand, grows out of the failure of this vision, out of an environment in which "it has become almost impossible to believe that culture as we know it can be a creative force awakening humanity to its own possibilities" (*Enlarging the Temple* 38). Elsewhere, Altieri notes the way in which modernist poets (particularly Stevens) sought to give us a means of envisioning our own nobility, while in the postmodern era, "few of us, I suspect, escape dramas of self-reflection where we try to distinguish those assertions about ourselves in which we can take pride from those that end in self-parody" ("Why Stevens Must Be Abstract" 89).

Altieri's assessment of the postmodern condition can lend considerable insight into the trials and tribulations of postmodern literature. Caught up in this atmosphere of skepticism, the postmodern author faces a difficult quandary: how to make a useful contribution to society in a time when a spiraling sense of irony ultimately threatens to turn any statement she might make into a mere parody of itself. This tendency toward self-parody would seem to be particularly acute in overtly metafictional works, given that (at least on the most obvious level) such works are principally concerned with themselves.

Presumably, metafiction reveals in an obvious way the inner workings of a mechanism that is in fact constantly ticking away inside of all fiction. As such, it can tell us a great deal about the assumptions and conventions that we bring to the reading of fictional texts in general. Thus John O'Brien (echoing Viktor Shklovsky's famous discussion of *Tristram Shandy*) argues that *Mulligan Stew*

> is a typical novel in that it acts more or less as a paradigm of what fiction is and does. The codes, conventions, and languages of fiction, displayed in all their artificial splendor, form the novel's very substance. *Mulligan Stew* is a primer for the reading of novels. (63)

O'Brien goes on to argue for a strict separation of art and life in reading Sorrentino's novel, and his invocation of the Russian Formalist Shklovsky raises the question of the transgressive power of Sorrentino's text. There seems little doubt that *Mulligan Stew* can tell us a great deal about fiction, but can it tell us anything about anything else? The Russian Formalist model of literary history gives a central role to transgression: literature evolves as new rule-breaking works come along to redefine the literary. But, as Bakhtin (among others) has pointed out, this Formalist notion of literary evolution tends to divorce itself from events in the the world outside of literature, being concerned only with the "intrinsic, immanent laws of the development of forms within a closed, purely literary system" (Bakhtin and Medvedev 159).[1] Bakhtin's point is that no strict separation between literature and the society around it is possible. It is obvious that *Mulligan Stew* does not mirror nature in a referential way; nonetheless those "codes, conventions, and languages of fiction" have a great deal to do with the codes, conventions, and languages that operate in the world outside of fiction as well. If nothing else, we as readers approach the text with our own preexisting tool-kits of interpretive techniques, techniques that derive not only from our previous encounters with fiction, but also from our interactions with the world at large. Yet O'Brien's formalist approach to the metafictional text would seem to seal such texts off from the real-world experience of the reader and to deny them any valid social or political force. At one point, for example, he states that in art the "sole purpose is to be beautiful" (71). Such an attitude is not unfamiliar in twentieth-century criticism, of course, as the obvious example of the New Critics immediately shows. But it is an attitude that much of postmodernism has come to challenge. William Spanos explains:

> The objective interpretive methodology of modernism, in other words, is grounded in an ideology sealed off from dialogic encounter. A postmodern hermeneutics, on the other hand, recognizes, with Heidegger, that there can be no presuppositionless understanding of literary texts. (224)

Spanos here seems in danger of confusing modernism with the New Criticism (and he is certainly not alone); nevertheless his point concerning the situatedness of all readings and of all texts is important. We *do* approach texts with presuppositions, and one of the most powerful functions of metafictional texts is to challenge those presuppositions, making us examine and question the validity of culturally inscribed assumptions that we might otherwise mistake for universal truths. But is it possible, through form alone, for a text to mount a genuinely transgressive force?

Spanos's emphasis here on dialogic encounter shows the influence of Bakhtin on his vision of postmodernism; at one point he essentially equates the postmodern with Bakhtin's concept of the carnivalesque (193). Indeed, Bakhtin's work provides a number of insights into the potential political force of metafictional texts such as *Mulligan Stew*. In particular, Bakhtin teaches us that a text's concern with its own status as a linguistic artifact can have profound implications for the world outside of the text. He notes, for example, that the "auto-criticism of discourse is one of the primary distinguishing features of the novel as a genre" (*Dialogic Imagination* 412). Further, he goes on to discuss different forms that this auto-criticism might take, including a type that "introduces an author who is in the process of writing the novel" (413). Bakhtin correctly identifies this kind of auto-criticism with the Formalist concept of the "baring of the device," and it is clear that this phenomenon corresponds quite closely to what is going on in modern metafictional texts. Moreover, Bakhtin's suggestion that such self-examination is central to the novel as a genre (particularly what he terms the "Second Line" novel) places such metafictional texts at the very heart of the process through which novels interrogate the various languages and discourse structures that constitute the contemporary social and historical moment in which they are produced.

To Bakhtin, language is always interested, always invested with ideological force. Any work that seeks to explore the workings of language investigates the ideological climate of its world: "In the novel formal markers of languages, manners and styles are symbols for sets of social beliefs" (*Dialogic Imagination* 357). As a result, self-referential fiction is not only relevant to the real world, but perhaps considerably more so than so-called realistic fiction, which on the surface appears to engage that world more directly. In contrast to his rival Georg Lukács, Bakhtin implies that "realistic" fiction (roughly associated with the "First Line" novel) merely operates in complicity with existing authoritarian value structures, and thereby can have only a conservative political force. Meanwhile, works that interrogate their own modes of discourse call existing value structures into question at a fundamental level, and thus have the potential for instigating significant changes of attitude and viable social reform.

The relevance of Bakhtin's arguments to *Mulligan Stew* is obvious even on a cursory reading. Though the book is impossible to summarize simply, its principal structural device is the depiction of a writer writing a novel, in this case Antony Lamont in the process of writing his unfortunate *Guinea Red* (later retitled *Crocodile Tears*). Moreover, *Mulligan Stew* reminds us time and again that the main issue in the book is language itself. A Bakhtinian reading of Sorrentino's book, then, would seem to offer great promise for an exploration of the potential political force of the work. At first glance, the book seems indeed to be an almost ideal Bakhtinian novel of linguistic subversion. On the other hand, the extremity of its metafictional technique recalls Altieri's comments about postmodernist self-parody and makes one wonder whether *Mulligan Stew* really subverts anything other than itself. Spanos, for example, banishes Sorrentino from his republic of postmodernist authors, claiming that his emphasis on form itself "tends to reappropriate the logocentric spatial form of early modernism in an even purer way" (259). Sorrentino, apparently (like certain political figures who might be accused of being so left-wing that they are right-wing, or vice versa), is so postmodernist that he circles the globe of literary history and winds up back in the camp of the modernists.

PSEUDOSTYLIC SHAMIANA: FICTION AS APPROPRIATION

The novelist-narrator of Flann O'Brien's *At Swim-Two-Birds* makes it clear that he has little use for the Great Tradition of realistic fiction, noting that "the novel should be a self-evident sham to which the reader could regulate at will the degree of his credulity" (33). Further, he offers the following advice to other would-be authors of modern literary works:

The entire corpus of existing literature should be regarded as a limbo from which discerning authors could draw their characters as required, creating only when they failed to find a suitable existing puppet. The modern novel should be largely a work of reference. Most authors spend their time saying what has been said before— usually said much better. A wealth of references to existing works would acquaint the reader instantaneously with the nature of each character, would obviate tiresome explanations and would effectively preclude mountebanks, upstarts, thimbleriggers and persons of inferior education from an understanding of contemporary literature. (33)

While it is true that the narrator's friend Brinsley (playing Lynch to the narrator's Stephen) immediately muddles this statement with his response of "That is all my bum," it is also true that this passage stands as a striking summation of the kind of allusiveness that has characterized many modern literary works. Most obvious among these is O'Brien's text itself, but this method of composition by appropriation brings to mind the works of a number of other authors, among whom James Joyce and Thomas Pynchon immediately leap to mind. But the work that has perhaps taken this advice most to heart is *Mulligan Stew*, a text that (significantly) makes extensive use of both O'Brien and Joyce as intertextual fodder. Antony Lamont, for example, is lifted directly form the pages of *At Swim-Two-Birds*, as are his sister Sheila and his archenemy Dermot Trellis.

Sorrentino's book spectacularly instantiates O'Brien's narrator's program for the modern novel, not only blatantly lifting its characters, settings, and motifs from other novels, but even appropriating its very language from other sources, resulting in a dazzling montage of parody, pastiche, and outright mimicry of everything from "high" literature to cheap detective fiction to newspaper reports to pornography. Indeed, an (appropriately) unidentified voice in a section of *Mulligan Stew* labeled "An Anonymous Sketch" launches a vitriolic attack on an unnamed novelist (presumably Lamont, but obviously Sorrentino as well), accusing that novelist of a variety of offenses, including plagiarism:

Borrowing? Aye! From the base, the sublime, from the low to the high this thief took his ore. Reading a read of a novel he'd pull out a phrase or a line; he ransacked the news; squeezed out the juice from advertisements; was pleased when a song had a word he could use; in the blues he perversely found humor; from Natchez to Mobile he ranged, from the shining mind of heaven to the primordial ooze. A persistent and underground rumor ran thus: that with unparalleled insolence he stole his very characters—all of whom (but of course) were invented by better than he. (261)

This passage describes the method of construction of Sorrentino's novel quite well, as its very title might indicate. After all, a mulligan stew is distinguished precisely by its being prepared from whatever ingredients happen to be on hand. This self-conscious statement of his own appropriative technique places Sorrentino firmly in the tradition of Joyce and O'Brien. David Hayman even invokes a similar culinary metaphor to describe Joyce's method of composition, noting that: "Like a thrifty housewife, Joyce used the stock and ingredients from yesterday's soup to flavor today's casserole" ("*Ulysses*" 15). Indeed, the above attack on plagiarism from *Mulligan Stew* may itself be borrowed from Joyce. It sounds suspiciously similar to some of Shaun's libelous descriptions of his brother Shem (and of Joyce) in *Finnegans Wake*:

One cannot even begin to post figure out a statuesquo ante as to how slow in reality the excommunicated Drumcondriac, nate Hamis, really was. Who can say how many pseudostylic shamiana, how few or how many of the most venerated public impostures, how very many piously forged palimpsests slipped in the first place by this morbid process from his pelagiarist pen? (181.34–182.3)

Among other things, the method of composition employed by Shem (and by Joyce and Sorrentino) powerfully calls into question the traditional view of the author as creator and source of meaning in a text. As Gerald Bruns notes, "*Mulligan Stew* is a celebration of doubtful authorship; that is, it takes plagiary as its theme, and plagiarisms of various sorts are among its most telling ingredients" (96). Most important, *Mulligan Stew* suggests that perhaps all authorship is necessarily a plagiarism of sorts, even in texts that purport to be original.

The work of Bakhtin contributes to an understanding of this view of authorship as inheritance rather than creation. In his important late essay "The Problem of Speech Genres" Bakhtin outlines his theory of the utterance as the basic unit of actual speech practice. However, unlike the parole of Saussure to which it is often compared, every utterance belongs to a specific speech genre, with certain generic conventions constraining the form that the utterance might take. Furthermore, these generic conventions imply specific worldviews and ideological investments. Thus, the utterance is inevitably implicated in the contemporary social and political moment in which it is produced. All utterances are thus profoundly historicized, and historical changes in language are closely linked to historical changes in the world at large. As Bakhtin puts it: "Utterances and their types, that is, speech genres, are the drive belts from the history of society to the history of language" (*Speech Genres* 65).

Bakhtin's dynamic historical view of the utterance implies that all utterances within a specific genre are produced in a dialogue with previous utterances in that genre. Any speaker (or writer) is thus inevitably not only expressing his own ideas, but repeating and responding to the ideas of others as well:

He is not, after all, the first speaker, the one who disturbs the eternal silence of the universe. And he presupposes not only the existence of the language system he is using, but also the existence of preceding utterances—his own and others'—with which his given utterance enters into one kind of relation or another (builds on them, polemicizes them, or simply presumes that they are already known to the listener). Any utterance is a link in a very complexly organized chain of other utterances. (*Speech Genre* 69)

This understanding of the profound historicity of all language use supports the view of historical embeddedness and situatedness of all discourse that Spanos and others have described in relation to postmodernism. No text is produced in a vacuum; each exists as part of an entire social, historical, and cultural moment. This being the case, it is clear that the Romantic notion of the artist-creator does not provide an accurate description of the actual mechanics by which texts come to be. By openly foregrounding the inherited nature of the cultural and linguistic materials with which he constructs *Mulligan Stew*, Sorrentino calls attention to the fact that authorship is a social, rather than individual phenomenon. Of course, the view of author-as-creator is profoundly ideological and linked to the entire Western tradition of the stable, unified subject. Any work that attacks this conventional theological model of authorship would then appear to have considerable subversive potential.

MULLIGAN STEW AND THE ASSAULT ON CHARACTER

Unfortunately, it turns out that subverting the traditional image of the author is not nearly so easy to effect as it might at first appear. In *Mulligan Stew*, for example, one can see a number of devices that call attention to the discourse of the book's coming from a variety of sources. Antony Lamont, for example, stands in the text as a dramatized figure of the author who loses control of his text. Indeed, the "Like Blowing Flower Stilled" chapter of *Guinea Red / Crocodile Tears*—in which a bizarre Elizabethan ghost (with an occasional hint of Irish brogue) confronts and terrifies Martin Halpin—seems to have arisen literally out of the pool of intertextuality without authorial intervention. Lamont, now totally paranoid, finds the completed chapter on his desk, and concludes that it must be part of the plot against him:

I did not write this chapter.

Typed on my machine. My paper. No notes, no rough drafts, no corrections. A perfect, finished copy.

They of course have done it. (400)

Lamont's disclaimer of authorship can be attributed to his growing insanity, of course, but it is interesting (though not ultimately interpretable) that Halpin himself agrees:

Lamont could not have done this. But then if he didn't, who did? And if nobody did it? What then? (401)

Curiously, though, Lamont's difficulties are almost too literal. He seems to be a vision of the traditional author twice removed, functioning not so much as a parody of the conventional author-creator as a parody of a parody of such an author. The dialogue here circles back on itself, and the net result may be that the traditional view of the author is actually supported by Sorrentino's depiction of Lamont. Similarly, despite all the technical devices that call attention to the "borrowed" nature of *Mulligan Stew*, it is Sorrentino himself who would seem to be in charge of marshaling these devices; the sheer technical brilliance of the book has a way of turning back on itself, emphasizing the central importance of an author who is capable of such artistry. We laugh as Lamont loses control of his text, but somehow we feel that Sorrentino is firmly in command of his.

Of course, the author is in a double bind here. One is reminded of the myth of the invisible modernist author, made so by a work whose technical virtuosity theoretically effaced all "brush-strokes," all evidence of the maker's hand. But of course this very virtuosity itself calls attention to the artist's work. In many ways *Mulligan Stew* represents a sort of extension of this phenomenon ad absurdum, so that the real target of Sorrentino's "plagiary" is not the myth of the author-as-creator, but the myth of the autonomous text that stands apart from any authorial presence. As such, it would again seem to emphasize, rather than efface, the presence of the author in the text. The book makes some interesting points about authorship, but these points are not ultimately subversive ones.

In an era after Barthes and after Foucault, the decentered model of authorship posited by Sorrentino is common currency. Even his especially direct depiction of Lamont's authorial travails is no longer unusual. Books about the writing of books have become extremely common in this century. Alastair Fowler suggests that "the most outstanding fictional genre of recent decades has surely been the poioumenon, or work-in-progress-novel—the narrative of the making of a work of art" ("Future of Genre Theory" 294). Fowler notes that this "new" genre has roots that go back at least to Sterne, but that "as a prominent genre it is distinctively modern." In short, by the late 1970s, Sorrentino's "radical" treatment of authorship seems to be highly conventional.

If *Mulligan Stew* does mount an attack on conventional notions of the unified subject, that attack consists not so much in its questioning of the role of the author as in its treatment of character. After all, the characters in a fictional text are the most obvious representations of that text's attitude toward subjectivity and therefore provide the most direct means of communication with the reader's own attitudes. As Hélène Cixous puts it, "through 'character' is established the identification circuit with the reader: the more 'character' fulfills the norms, the better the reader recognizes it and recognizes himself" ("Character" 385).

But the identification between reader as unified subject and character as representation of the same is clearly an ideological one, related to the entire tradition of realism. Cixous goes on to note that

[t]he ideology underlying this fetishization of "character" is that of an "I" who is a whole subject (that of the "character" as well as that of the author), conscious, knowable; and the enunciatory "I" expresses himself in the text, just as the world is represented complementarily in the text in a form equivalent to pictorial representation, as a simulacrum. (385)

Presumably, any text that challenges traditional notions of characterization will challenge traditional notions of the subject as well; Cixous mentions Virginia Woolf's *The Waves* and Joyce's *Ulysses* as specific examples of such challenges (389). *Mulligan Stew* clearly opposes the notion of characters as whole, autonomous subjects as well. Donald Greiner notes Sorrentino's contempt for the conventional notion of "rounded" characters, arguing, for example, that "Sorrentino, the real novelist, makes the point that Martin Halpin is not a round character about to walk off the page or even a flat character about to be forgotten, but merely language" (107). Indeed, at one point late in the text "Martin Halpin" is forced to play both his role and that of "Ned Beaumont," who has already fled the text due to his frustration at Lamont's authorial incompetence. Curiously, though, Greiner finds the figure of Lamont nonetheless convincing:

While laughing at Lamont, we do visualize him, care for him. He may not walk off the page, but he is there in the page, a fictional character who struggles with his own characters much as we struggle with Sorrentino's. We care about Lamont because we hear his voice and read his language even as we are always aware that he is no more than a construct of words which the real author consciously manipulates. (106)

I do not agree with Greiner's assessment of the reality of Lamont; it seems to me that by borrowing both characters from other texts (Halpin is taken from *Finnegans Wake* just as Lamont is taken from *At Swim-Two-Birds*), Sorrentino grants both characters an equal (and equally artificial) ontological status. As a result, Sorrentino's characterization loses much of its power to trouble the reader and to make her question her conception of her own identity. A comparison with *At Swim-Two-Birds* is helpful here. In O'Brien's book, the ontological levels are clearly layered, or nested. The unnamed narrator provides a level of "reality" that within the world of the text corresponds to the reader's own reality. Trellis is one level "down," being created by the narrator, while Lamont and friends are still farther removed, being created by Trellis.

But of course we realize that Trellis is no more real than Lamont. By extension, the narrator is no more real than Trellis. Here is where O'Brien's text achieves its troubling power: the reader has identified the narrator's reality with her own. The result is an ontological transgression that leads to the infinite and vertiginous situation known in recent critical discourse as the *mise en abîme*. The relationship between the *mise en abîme* and meditations on ontology was recognized early on by Borges, who uses the play-within-a-play in *Hamlet* as an illustration of the effect in his essay "Partial Magic in the *Quixote*" (193–96). Borges does not use the term *mise en abîme*, which had not then come into general use in the discussion of literature,[2] but he notes that the same effect was produced by Josiah Royce in 1899 in discussing the case in which a map is traced in the soil of

England—a map so detailed that it includes itself, and so on to infinity. Borges then relates this situation to the unsettling effects of certain works of literature:

Why does it disturb us that the map be included in the map and the thousand and one nights in the book of the *Thousand and One Nights*? Why does it disturb us that Don Quixote be a reader of the *Quixote* and Hamlet a spectator of *Hamlet*? I believe I have found the reason: these inversions suggest that if the characters of a fictional work can be readers or spectators, we, its readers and spectators, can be fictitious. (196)

O'Brien's text achieves precisely this effect of making us question our own reality. Sorrentino's text, however, does not. Even though Halpin is a character in Lamont's book, it is blatantly clear to the reader that both are equally fictitious. Both characters are merely linguistic constructs, both lifted from other works of literature. This coequal status is emphasized late in the text when Halpin, trying to be both "himself" and Beaumont, becomes indistinguishable from either Beaumont or Lamont. All three are hopelessly intermixed in the linguistic texture of the book.

Sorrentino's "experimental" writing also again loses force from having too many predecessors: O'Brien, Pirandello's *Six Characters in Search of an Author*, and Queneau's *The Flight of Icarus*. A fictional character's leaping out of the text and into reality has already become a stock device. Still, Greiner's comment on the "reality" of Lamont here is a monument to the power of the convention of reader identification with the characters in a text. Fully cognizant of Sorrentino's attack on the notion of realistic characters, Greiner still finds Lamont oddly believable. In fact, he goes on to suggest that Sorrentino's fragmented characters reflect the fragmentation of the modern world, so that the apparently nontraditional characterization in *Mulligan Stew* in fact has a mimetic function (106–7). Obviously, the phenomenon of reader identification with fictional characters will vary from reader to reader and from character to character, though a recognition of the linguistic nature of character helps to show why such identifications do seem to follow certain broad trends rather then being totally subjective.

This notion of the linguistic construction of character is

prominent in contemporary critical discourse, and bears directly on the conceptions of subjectivity argued by such theorists as Bakhtin and Lacan. Such conceptions provide powerful challenges to conventional models of the subject, and works such as those of Joyce and Woolf provide ample evidence that literary works can provide similar challenges. But to be truly effective, such representations of character-as-language must attack conventional characterization at the root level of language itself. Discussing Joyce's strategy of characterization in *Finnegans Wake*, Derek Attridge suggests:

> If Joyce is truly to undermine character as personage, then, he must also undermine character as sign. This is most obvious in the case of the proper name: if the word under which character traits are assembled retains its transcendent discreteness, coherence, and uniqueness, the essential identity of character will survive all vicissitudes of behavior. ("Joyce" 155)

But it is precisely this kind of fundamental Joycean subversion of the word as a bounded, knowable entity that *Mulligan Stew* lacks; as a result its characterization is not ultimately subversive. Joyce presents us with characters that teeter on the brink of roundedness, characters in whom we want to believe, but in whom we cannot finally believe because the language itself denies all our attempts to get a grip on them. We are lured—certainly in *Ulysses*, but also in *Finnegans Wake*—into an attempted recuperation of Joyce's characters on realistic terms, but then frustrated in those attempts. Greiner's comments on Lamont aside, most readers would not be tempted to read the characters in *Mulligan Stew* as realistic. It is simply too easy to recuperate Sorrentino's characters as amusing artifacts of textual play; his characterization is not troubling, and therefore not ultimately subversive. In fact, Greiner himself notes as much, arguing that, confronted with Sorrentino's obviously artificial characters, "any intelligent reader does not complain but laughs" (107).[3]

LOST PIECES TO DIFFERENT JIGSAW PUZZLES: SUBVERSION AND BRICOLAGE

If Sorrentino's attacks on the integrity of the author and of character are not finally effective, it is still possible that his mulligan-stew method of text construction can itself be political. After all, such a piecemeal and fragmentary mode of construction has the potential to comment powerfully on traditional authoritarian concepts such as wholeness and fullness of presence. Critics have noted this method of construction in many modern texts, sometimes linking it to Lévi-Strauss's concept of bricolage. The bricoleur is a sort of junk man who randomly collects odd items without any particular plan, and then uses those diverse materials as the need arises. Lévi-Strauss sees this technique as analogous to the way in which myths are often constructed: "Now, the characteristic feature of mythical thought, as of 'bricolage' on the practical plane, is that it builds up structured sets, not directly with other structured sets but by using the remains and debris of events . . . odds and ends in English" (21).

It is fundamental to the evolution of a myth that the bricolage character of its original construction becomes lost, so that its final form appears natural and inevitable. A text such as *Mulligan Stew*, however, refuses to let this sort of naturalization occur. By specifically calling attention to the arbitrariness of its method of construction, it asks us to consider whether the other texts we encounter (literary or otherwise) are not in fact constructed in a similarly arbitrary fashion, regardless of how natural and well made they might seek to appear.

Because of this ability to challenge assumptions about the natural or "logical" way in which texts are supposed to be composed, the concept of bricolage has gained considerable prominence in recent critical discourse. Jacques Derrida has related his own methods of composition to those of the bricoleur, and even suggests that, due to the "necessity of borrowing one's concepts from the text of a heritage which is more or less coherent or ruined, it must be said that every discourse is bricoleur" ("Structure" 255). In this vein, Derrida speaks of the way in which his texts are quite literally "assembled":

I insist on the word "assemblage" here. . . . The word "assemblage" seems more apt for suggesting that the kind of bringing-together proposed here has the structure of an interlacing, a weaving, or a web, which would allow different threads and different lines of sense or force to bring others together. (*Speech and Phenomena* 132)

Derrida's suggestion that his writing be considered assemblage brings to mind a statement made by a certain "James Joyce," who appears as a character in Flann O'Brien's *The Dalkey Archive*, and who notes that, in his own case: "Writing is not quite the word. Assembly, perhaps, is better—or accretion" (145). This "James Joyce" is a fictional character, not *the* James Joyce, but then the parallel is close, and Joyce stands as perhaps the most formidable bricoleur in modern literature. Joyce himself once declared (in a letter to George Antheil, January 3, 1931) that he was "quite content to go down to posterity as a scissors and paste man for that seems to me a harsh but not unjust description" (*Letters* 297).

Derrida emphasizes the subversive potential of the bricolage technique by employing it strictly within the framework and tradition of philosophy, a context within which it gains effect largely by its sheer difference from the norm. By employing this seemingly random method of composition in a field where one especially expects coherence and logic, Derrida calls into question the assumptions that underlie those expectations. Similarly, Joyce's bricolage constructions are powerful largely because of the way in which they oppose efforts to force them to make sense conventionally. In *Ulysses*, he employs the technique within a novel that has so many naturalistic elements, especially early on, that one is tempted to read the entire book as a work of naturalism, only to be defeated by the many lists and random textual intrusions that gradually break down the traditional coherence of the book. *Finnegans Wake*, on the other hand, would never be mistaken for a naturalistic text. Rather, it subverts reader expectations on a more fundamental level, that of the words themselves. After all, any reader is likely to approach a text assuming at least that it will be constructed of words, but in the *Wake* words themselves are bricolage constructions, composed of bits and pieces of found phonemes. In this way, Joyce's last novel challenges our most cherished assumptions about the nature of language as a medium of rational discourse.

As the examples of Derrida and Joyce show, there is a strong subversive potential in the bricolage technique. This does not mean that any text constructed according to this principle will inherently be subversive. Subversion requires a target; transgression of boundaries requires that those boundaries initially be in place. In the case of Derrida and Joyce, bricolage becomes an effective technique largely because their texts are constructed in such a way and within such contexts that one would naturally read them as other than bricolage. Their texts' subsequent resistance to these attempts at recuperation is a powerful challenge of the assumptions upon which those attempts are based.

In short, in order to be effectively subversive, the bricolage technique (like unconventional treatments of character) must be troubling. It is here, I think, that *Mulligan Stew* again falls short. Certainly, in some ways the bricolage nature of Sorrentino's text is even more obvious than that of Joyce's, with the entire book being quite literally a collection of found scraps, orts, and fragments, pieced together with virtually no semblance of order or plan. We find pieces of Lamont's work-in-progress, snatches of his previous work, passages from the work of his archenemy Dermot Trellis, a learned treatise on mathematics, various journal entries, letters, songs, poems, jottings, advertisements, and so on. As with Joyce, any attempt to read Sorrentino's novel according to traditional conventions of narrative structure can lead only to frustration. However, I would suggest that the reader of *Mulligan Stew* is never really tempted to employ such conventions. The *Stew* is linguistically complex, but its language is not troubling and challenging in the way that the language of *Finnegans Wake* is. Moreover, the book is so obviously metafictional that one is never tempted (as one is with *Ulysses*) to recuperate it as a conventional unified narrative with theme, plot, character, and so on.

Of course, a metafictional text need not tempt the reader to recuperate the entire work in terms of a single narrative structure in order to be effectively subversive. The bricolage technique can also achieve a subversive effect in relation to traditional narrative expectations through the use of bits and pieces of apparently unrelated narrative, each individual segment of which is itself narratively coherent. The various digressions in *Tristram Shandy* are an important forerunner of this technique, but it is also employed effectively in a number of modern texts. Italo Calvino's *If on a winter's night a traveler* relates the adventures of a reader ("The Reader") who attempts to read a number of different narratives, only to have each of them broken off just as "The Reader" begins to be caught up in them. The reader of Calvino's book experiences similar difficulties, because the individual narrative fragments can be quite engrossing. Kathryn Hume notes: "The richness of plot, outlook, subject, and style raises a a sufficiently strong desire to read further that some critics have resented Calvino's refusal to complete the novels" (75).

Calvino's fragments are to some extent tied together by the story of "The Reader," but Georges Perec's *Life: A User's Manual* has no main narrative whatsoever; it is composed strictly as a series of digressions. Each one of those individual digressions, however, is itself constructed as a convincing and conventional narrative. As a result, the text calls into question the traditional view that digressions must somehow be subordinate to some central thread from which they digress. Attridge notes that *Finnegans Wake* performs precisely this same deconstruction of the traditional hierarchy of central narrative versus marginal digression, with powerful effect: "The result is that the reader is weaned from dependence on the illusion that novels are reports on the real world and is encouraged to enjoy the writing as writing, in all its uncertainty, prolixity, contradictoriness, and materiality" (*Peculiar Language* 228).

Perec's *Life* calls attention to its bricolage structure through its explicit use of the jigsaw puzzle as a structural device. Indeed, it offers a self-referential description of the interaction between author and reader through its description of the relationship between the maker and solver of a jigsaw, noting

the ultimate truth of jigsaw puzzles: despite appearances, puzzling is not a solitary game: every move the puzzler makes, the puzzle-maker has made before; every piece the puzzler picks up, and picks up again, and studies and strokes, every combination he tries, and tries a second time, every blunder and every insight, each hope and each discouragement have all been designed, calculated, and decided by the other. (191)

This metaphor is extremely apt, and the reader of Perec's text finds himself precisely imitating the actions of the puzzler, vainly attempting to put the various pieces of the text together in terms of some coherent whole. The book explicitly invites this sort of detective work on the part of the reader, including devices such as a detailed index and an appended chronology of events to aid in the effort. Approximately midway through the book we are treated to a tantalizing description of the painter Valène reflexively painting himself painting a picture which in turn contains essentially all the key motifs in Perec's book itself. We are even given a detailed, numbered listing of 179 items appearing in the painting, presented in near-letter-quality dot matrix that sets it off from the remainder of the text and gives it a computerized quality that adds to the impression that *here* is the key information needed to decipher the text. I have not attempted to match all of the items in this list to the text, but I did check a significant number of them, and all of these did indeed appear somewhere in the book. But one suspects that no matter how much effort one puts into solving the puzzle of Perec's text, one will ultimately fail, much like Percival Bartlebooth, the afficionado of jigsaw puzzles whose efforts to solve a series of puzzles are a central motif of the book. The book ends, in fact, with Bartlebooth's death, an unsolved puzzle sitting before him:

On the tablecloth, somewhere in the crepuscular sky of the four hundred and thirty-ninth puzzle, the black hole of the sole piece not yet filled in has the almost perfect shape of an X. But the ironical thing, which could have been foreseen long ago, is that the piece the dead man holds between his fingers in shaped like a W. (497)

But even this blatant clue that the puzzle of the text cannot be solved has a tendency to inspire further attempts. It points, for example, to Perec's previous novel, which was called *W*. *W* involves a complex counterpoint between two seemingly unrelated plot lines, much like William Faulkner's *Go Down, Moses* or Pynchon's similarly titled *V.* In fact, Stencil's search for "V." in Pynchon's book involves precisely the same sort of incomplete quest as Bartlebooth's puzzle solving, and Perec's translator begins *W* with a reminder that in French the letter "W" carries the resonance of a double "V." Perec's use of the puzzle metaphor (ideal for the description of the bricolage text) also echoes the work of Pynchon. For example, early in *Gravity's Rainbow* Pynchon presents a list of the diverse items to be found atop Tyrone Slothrop's desk, and it is clear that the list serves as a self-referential description of the bricolage nature of

Gravity's Rainbow as a whole. Significantly, among the items in the list are "lost pieces to different jigsaw puzzles" (18). Pynchon then constructs a narrative that refuses to obey traditional rules of logic, even though it consistently hovers so close to those rules that the reader constantly attempts a conventional recuperation. Pynchon's narrator even taunts the reader about these attempts, stating at one point: "You will want cause and effect. All right" (663). He then follows with a preposterously deterministic bit of narrative that mocks the whole idea of such conventionally metonymic narrative structures.

Mulligan Stew uses the jigsaw puzzle device as well. In the first chapter of Lamont's novel, we find Martin Halpin ruminating on this metaphor:

Perhaps as I talk the pieces will fall into place like the pieces of a gigantic jigsaw puzzle, and the truth will be seen plain. Perhaps God, or Fate, plays with us as we play with the pieces of a jigsaw puzzle, toying with us, trying to make us fit where we don't belong, dropping us to the floor. (3)

Again, this passage is obviously self-referential, and on the very next page Lamont explains in a letter to Professor Roche that "I have always thought of the experimental novel . . . as a kind of elaborate jigsaw puzzle." However, in Perec and Pynchon one has hints of conventional narrative and is therefore tempted to try to put the puzzle together, though ultimately thwarted in the attempt. In *Mulligan Stew* one never even tries to put the pieces of the text together; its fragmentation is amusing, but not ultimately troubling or challenging.

Mulligan Stew does posit a traditional narrative structure that might be transgressed against, in the form of the detective novel being composed by Antony Lamont. This use of the detective story as a structural device is quite common in postmodernist fiction. As Michael Holquist puts it, "What myth was to experimental fiction before World War II, detective fiction is to avant-garde prose after World War II" (148). However, Holquist further notes that the postmodernist author typically subverts the usual expectations of the detective story, delivering not orderliness and neat epistemological closure, but chaos. Thus, "by exploiting the conventions of the detective story such men as Borges and Robbe-Grillet have fought against the Modernist attempt to fill the void of the world with rediscovered mythical symbols. Rather, they dramatize the void" (155).

Texts such as Robbe-Grillet's *The Erasers* and Pynchon's *The Crying of Lot 49* are paradigmatic of this technique: both employ the detective-story motif in such a way that the reader becomes implicated in the traditional expectations of epistemological closure associated with the genre, genuinely seeking a solution to the mysteries that are posed. When the trap springs shut and we realize that no solution is to be found, we are disappointed and uncomfortable, but at the same time we have learned a valuable lesson about the follies of such expectations of closure. In *Mulligan Stew*, however, the embedded detective story is so obviously artificial that the reader neither expects nor really cares about the solution to the central mystery. After all, that mystery concerns the manner of Ned Beaumont's death, yet throughout the text he is not "really" dead. Thus, as with his treatment of character, Sorrentino's subversion of the detective story goes too far, becoming a parody of a parody. *Guinea Red / Crocodile Tears* reads not so much like a parody of, say, Dashiell Hammett (from whose *The Glass Key* Ned Beaumont has been lifted) as a parody of other parodists of the detective story, such as Pynchon and Robbe-Grillet.

It would seem, then, that the narrative structure (or lack thereof) in *Mulligan Stew* does not itself effectively subvert traditional reader expectations. Readers who read conventionally for plot are apt to reject the book out of hand; more sophisticated readers—those who are "in on the joke"—are apt to be amused, but little else. Still, there is one final way in which the bricolage construction of Sorrentino's text might lead to subversive effects. After all, the bricolage method of construction involves more than the formal device of paratactic structure. Remember that the bits and pieces of a bricolage construction come from somewhere. The power of bricolage construction derives largely from the way in which traces of these sources remain, initiating a dialogue between the appropriating text and the source being appropriated. In the case of *Mulligan Stew*, the appropriated fragments come primarily from a variety of other written texts, ranging (as Sorrentino's above anonymous voice notes) "from the low to the high." This sort of mixture of languages immediately recalls the work of Bakhtin on the carnivalesque in literature. To Bakhtin, the celebration of misrule and subversion of hierarchies associated with the medieval carnival is a metaphor for transgression in literary texts. Languages from "high" and "low" culture interact in the carnivalesque text much in the same way that persons from different social strata intermix during the carnival itself. This intermixing (and the associated breaking of rules in general) then subversively calls into question the validity of hierarchies that reign during normal periods.

BREAKING THE RULES: SUBVERSION AND TRANSGRESSION

Unfortunately, not only is Bakhtin's carnival metaphor somewhat problematic, but Bakhtin himself primarily invokes the energies of the *medieval* carnival, admitting that the modern carnival is a degraded form that has lost most of its subversive force. By extension, the same might be said for carnivalesque texts. In a survey of the carnivalesque impulse toward transgression in modern literature, Allon White has noted the troublesome link between rule-breaking art and political subversion, concluding that "[t]here are profoundly complex links between transgressive aesthetics and radical politics, but they are neither essential nor univocal" ("Pigs and Pierrots" 53). Again, the key element here is subjective: a carnivalesque mixing of languages and breaking of traditional rules in literature can be subversive only if it has a troubling effect on the reader that results in his reexamining the hierarchies normally accepted by his society. On the other hand, if an intermixing of languages is not troubling, it can indeed act to reinforce traditional distinctions between low and high. In a given text, the subversive force of a carnivalesque mixing of languages will generally lie somewhere between these extremes, with the exact position on the continuum varying from reader to reader according to individual reactions. In the case of *Mulligan Stew*, the fragmentation of the text is such that high and low elements are never truly intermixed, but merely exist simultaneously in separate fragments, so that Sorrentino's text probably lies somewhere midway on this continuum.[4]

But this emphasis on the individual reader also highlights another complication of the subversive potential of transgressive literature. To be truly effective in a political sense, transgression must have a strong communal element. As I noted in the Introduction, bourgeois society is remarkably resistant to any kind of transgression that is formulated in terms of individual rebellion. Thus, the "troubling" effect I refer to must involve not only private emotional reactions, but public responses as well. The reader must interrogate the broad social conventions that underlie political practice, thereby calling into question the hierarchies and institutions that promulgate these conventions and that are in turn made possible by them. It is, however, this emphasis on the social and the public that is lacking in much of modern (post-Romantic) transgressive literature, which has come more and more to rely upon the terror and abjection of subjective experience (especially sexuality) to achieve its transgressive effect. Thus, White notes that "[i]t is precisely because transgression becomes subjectivized in romanticism that modern theory has the utmost difficulty in reconstituting its public domain. . . . The traditional carnival attack on social oppression gives way to a subjectivized attack on individual repression" ("Pigs and Pierrots" 69).

But Bakhtin and others have argued that subjectivity is in fact communal and that the self is constituted through intersubjective relations in language. In this case, the potential for political force in *Mulligan Stew* would appear especially strong, as it is precisely this emphasis on language itself that is the most striking feature of Sorrentino's book. If the book has a representational function at all, it is in the representation of language itself as an object, a representation in which Bakhtin sees exciting potential for transgression and subversion. This kind of subversion occurs, for Bakhtin, primarily through the medium of parody, so it seems promising that Sorrentino utilizes parody so extensively in *Mulligan Stew*.

When Sorrentino re-creates Joyce's "Circe" in his "Flawless Play Restored," when he mimics Nabokov in "A Bag of Blues," and when he parodies erotic poetry with Lorna Flambeaux's "The Sweat of Love," it is clear that the object of representation lies not in the referents of the language, but in the language itself. Indeed, virtually all of the language in the book has a borrowed quality that calls attention to the language itself as language. The use of parody allows Sorrentino to enter into a dialogic exchange with the various languages that he draws into his texts, an exchange that can subvert the assumptions upon which those languages are based. Such dialogue requires that parody be employed not in the sense of a mocking of a previous text, but rather in the Bakhtinian sense of "an intentional dialogized hybrid. Within it, languages and styles actively and mutually illuminate one another" (*Dialogic Imagination* 76). In short, effective parody must be transformative; it must change the way we look at the texts being parodied. It must, again, be troubling.[5] Among the more striking examples of such troubling parodies in modern literature are Joyce's parodies of religious language and ritual in *Ulysses* and (especially) in *Finnegans Wake*, as well as Pynchon's parodies of the language of science in *Gravity's Rainbow* and elsewhere. These parodies, of course, are able to achieve their troubling effects partially because they attack discourses that maintain such powerful authority in the societies in which Joyce and Pynchon write—much like the unsettling effect that the work of Rushdie has had in the Muslim world. About the closest Sorrentino comes to this kind of effect in *Mulligan Stew* is in his presentation of a mock mathematical treatise in the section entitled "Recent Studies in Contravariant Behavior Processes in Complex Resolutions." This highly amusing section makes a mockery of the claims to truth and objectivity that the language of such treatises normally makes for itself, and in that sense it does have an effective force. However, it may be too much of a mockery. Unlike Pynchon, who employs scientific terminology in authentic ways that are undermined only by context, Sorrentino undercuts the language itself and never gives it a voice in the text. One need only review the published critical discourse on Pynchon to realize the extent to which his readers are duped into taking his use of scientific terminology seriously, thus attempting to develop interpretations of his works based on various scientific principles. This apparent scientific authenticity, which subsequently turns out to be an illusion, comments powerfully upon the illusory nature of much of our traditional confidence in science. That one cannot decide whether Pynchon's use of scientific terminology is serious or parodic adds greatly to its troubling effect. But one is not even tempted to take Sorrentino's use of mathematical language seriously; it is pure farce and loses much of its subversive energy accordingly.

In short, Sorrentino uses the language of the mathematical treatise in "Recent Studies," but he does not transform that language. He does not make us forever after see that language in a different way. Again, the section reads more like a parody of Pynchon than of science, and Sorrentino's text remains thoroughly inscribed in the world of literature. Bakhtin describes this sort of phenomenon as "canonization," in which different languages brought into a literary text

> already have lost their flavor of 'belonging to another language'; they may already have been canonized by literary language, and are consequently sensed by the author as no longer within the system of provincial patois or professional jargon but as belonging rather to the system of literary language. (*Dialogic Imagination* 418)

In many ways the referent of Sorrentino's "Recent Studies" does not seem to be mathematical language at all, but the language of the "Nightlessons" section of *Finnegans Wake*; Sorrentino's preposterous and largely irrelevant footnotes are particularly reminiscent of Joyce's chapter. Indeed, Sorrentino's parodies are almost exclusively literary, and if there is any effective parodic dialogue in *Mulligan Stew* one would expect it to occur with the literary tradition. This fact does not preclude his parodies from having political force, however, as literature is implicated in many of the same systems and assumptions that support structures of political authority.

Joyce is the master of literary parody, so it comes as no surprise that he enjoys such a prominent presence in Sorrentino's text. In fact, the works of Joyce are among the most important sources of material for Sorrentino's own parodies. However, Sorrentino's relationship to Joyce is not truly parodic, at least not in the dialogic sense meant by Bakhtin. Quotations from Joyce (especially from *Finnegans Wake*) have a tendency to pop up in Sorrentino's text at odd times, but the sense of these quotations seldom has any parodic force and seems to be more an acknowledgement of an important predecessor than of a dialogic encounter. Even more extended Joycean motifs, such as the retelling of "Circe" in "Flawless Play," have little parodic force. After all, "Circe" itself is already more outrageous and parodic than is Sorrentino's parody of it.

It may be that Joyce is an impossible target for parody in general. As Terry Caesar points out in regard to the *Wake*, "Joyce has written a book that cannot be parodied, and it cannot be parodied because he has already parodied it himself" (234). The language of the *Wake* seems to be constantly in motion, constantly reappropriating and transforming itself from within, so that there is no target upon which an external parody can establish a fixed purchase. As Clive Hart puts it, this effect results in "a kind of endless regress of self-parody" (41–42). Thus, if *Finnegans Wake* is already a parody of itself, then the best one can hope for in an external parody is an authentic reproduction of what the *Wake* already is, which obviously can have no transformative function. Joyce's work has a quality of absorbing all attempts at parody without itself being altered in the process, just as it also has a way of absorbing any and all attempts at critical commentary. As Derrida notes,

nothing can be invented on the subject of Joyce. Everything we can say about *Ulysses*, for example, has already been anticipated . . . to say nothing of *Finnegans Wake*, by a hypermnesis machine capable of storing in an immense epic work, with the Western memory and virtually all languages in the world including traces of the future. ("Ulysses Gramophone" 48)

In fact, not only is it impossible to parody Joyce, but Joyce's work has a tendency to reflect any attempts at parody back on the source, so that the parodying text in effect becomes a parody not of Joyce but of itself. This phenomenon comes through very clearly in Sorrentino's attempt to parody the soliloquy of Molly Bloom in *Mulligan Stew*:

He bought me an orange dress once that he called my Florida dress it was soft buttersoft and fit my body to a t marvelous it was actually it was called my Florida frock he had the most extraordinary habit of painting a moustache on his face whenever he felt blue do you like the way I'm talking on and on without any pauses or punctuation it's my consciousness just simply streaming. (230)

This passage clearly comments more on what Sorrentino is doing in *Mulligan Stew* than on what Joyce is doing in *Ulysses*. In the encounter between Joyce and Sorrentino, Joyce's text overwhelms that of Sorrentino to the extent that Joyce transforms

Sorrentino, rather than vice versa. Joyce effectively parodies Sorrentino, but Sorrentino does not effectively parody Joyce.

Joyce is a special case, but the Sorrentino–Joyce encounter is typical of the generally self-referential character of the parody in *Mulligan Stew*. Sorrentino's parody of the detective story never establishes a dialogic relation with the traditions of that genre, and essentially becomes a parody of such parodies. The parody of erotic poetry in "The Sweat of Love" comes closer to true parody: there the poetry, bad as it may be, does come close enough to authenticity that a true dialogue might be possible. However, as John O'Brien points out, "there is no way of successfully parodying erotic poetry except to reproduce it; its very stylization and formulas require it to parody itself, so that the parody and the original would be almost indistinguishable" (67). Moreover, it is difficult to see any subversive potential in the parody of a genre that is already itself marginal. O'Brien goes on to argue that "The Sweat of Love" is not a parody at all, but merely a comic device within the context of the rest of the book. In short, its dialogue is not with the tradition of erotic poetry but with the context of the rest of *Mulligan Stew*.

If, then, there is true subversive potential within *Mulligan Stew*, that potential arises from its dialogue with itself. By parodying and undercutting itself at every turn, the book is consistently different from itself, avoiding monologism and questioning traditional notions of self-identity and fullness of presence. As *Finnegans Wake* amply demonstrates, a text that parodies itself always has the potential of initiating an infinite regress of meaning that defeats all attempts at interpretive recuperation. In order to be powerful such texts must undermine all attempts at interpretation, including the interpretation that they undermine all attempts at interpretation. In short, they must defeat attempts to recuperate the text comfortably by hypostatization of indeterminacy itself as the meaning of the text. But *Mulligan Stew* does not successfully evade attempts at such recuperation. Because of its lack of elements that tempt the reader to seek certainty, it allows the reader to reach closure quite comfortably simply by determining that it is not possible to reach closure. As Hugh Kenner noted in an early review of *Mulligan Stew*, "When the band plays fortissimo for seventeen hours people do not notice haphazard key shiftings" (89).

Mulligan Stew employs a number of devices that would appear to carry potential for subversive political force. In all cases, however, the book goes too far with its self-reflexive techniques, failing to engage the reader in a reexamination of the presuppositions with which she initially approached the text. It ends up an amusing formal exercise that in the final analysis is about nothing but itself. It becomes a parody of itself. On the other hand, by the very fact of doing so, the book has a curious way of moving beyond itself and commenting upon the difficult situation in which postmodernist and metafictional works generally find themselves. Such works are always in danger of collapsing into the same kind of solipsism that I see in *Mulligan Stew*. They are always in danger of going too far; inherently transgressive, they run a danger of being too successful in the crossing of boundaries and deconstruction of hierarchies, leaving themselves nothing to transgress against except themselves.

While I have generally suggested that *Mulligan Stew* does, in large measure, fall prey to these dangers, I also suggest that whether a given work is effectively subversive in any real social sense depends upon much more than any property inherent in the text, be it of form or of content. The impact of a work depends upon the context in which it is read, the other texts to which it is compared, and the position occupied by the reader who encounters it. Moreover, the case of *Mulligan Stew* raises several issues that will be crucial in my considerations of transgressive literature in the coming chapters. Three of these are especially important to keep in mind. First, there is the question of historical context. Much of what makes Sorrentino's novel seem relatively devoid of transgressive energy derives from its various experiments' having already been performed by a number of other works. Each literary work arises not only in a specific social and historical context, but also against a background of previous literary works. Joyce, writing against a background of nineteenth-century realism, achieved powerful subversive effects with his experimental writing. But Sorrentino writes against a background that has already been substantially modified by predecessors such as Joyce, in a sense depriving him of a target. As Hal Foster asks of postmodernism in general, "how can we exceed the modern? How can we break with a program that makes a value of crisis . . . or progress beyond the era of

Progress . . . or transgress the ideology of the transgressive?" (ix). Thus, the question of literary history is crucial to any consideration of transgression in literature.

Second, there arises in *Mulligan Stew* a question of definition. Mere rule breaking for the sake of rule breaking may be shocking, annoying, or exhilarating to various readers depending upon their particular points of view. A work that includes radical formal innovation, or even radical content (such as scenes of shocking violence or extreme sexual behavior) is likely to seem "transgressive" to many and to have a powerful impact on some. But the question remains whether such individual subjective effects are truly transgressive in a genuine political sense (i.e., challenging existing dominant ideologies in a way that contributes to the process of social change).

Finally, I am aware that my suggestion that genuinely transgressive fiction must be "troubling," whereas Sorrentino's work is often merely entertaining, echoes the distinction drawn by Roland Barthes between texts of pleasure and texts of *jouissance*. I am also aware that this distinction very easily slides into the traditional one between "high" art (the difficult modernist texts of *jouissance*) and "low" art (the popular forms that merely give pleasure). While many modern theorists such as Theodor Adorno have had no problem with this distinction, finding it quite comfortable to argue that high art can be genuinely subversive whereas popular art is just another opiate of the masses, I am not so comfortable. One might just as easily argue that it is in fact the privileging of high art that is in complicity with reigning values of bourgeois society—a view supported by the ease with which modernist art was institutionalized in the West. Moreover, feminist theorists have recently made clear the historical tendency to associate high art with masculine values and popular art with feminine ones, so that the privileging of high art at the expense of popular art becomes at least in part a strategy for perpetuating a myth of the artistic and intellectual inferiority of women.[6]

All of these questions need to be kept in mind, though one should also remember that transgression itself operates more in a mode of raising questions than of answering them. In the next chapter I shall look at some of the mechanisms of transgression in John Fowles's *The French Lieutenant's Woman*, a text that especially addresses all of these issues. Fowles's book deals with issues of jouissance and feminine sexuality that resonate interestingly with the work of Barthes, whom it directly cites. It also employs the question of historical perspective as a central object of inquiry. Finally, the rejection of Fowles's work in general as mere popular literature not worthy of serious study places it squarely in the midst of the high art–low art debate.

TRANSGRESSION WITHOUT GOD: SEXUALITY, TEXTUALITY, AND INFINITY IN *THE FRENCH LIEUTENANT'S WOMAN*

CHAPTER

4 ───────────────────────────────────

"They order," says Laurence Sterne's Parson Yorick in the beginning of *A Sentimental Journey*, "this matter better in France." Yorick never fully clarifies the nature of "this matter," but Richard Howard suggests that it is a question of sexuality and ways of expressing it in language (v). I think he is right. Though Sterne was writing over two hundred years ago, his comment would be even more apt today. In the last few decades, French thinkers such as Barthes, Foucault, Lacan, Kristeva, and Derrida have repeatedly reminded us of the intimate and inextricable links that exist between sexuality and language. It seems highly appropriate, then, to turn to John Fowles's *The French Lieutenant's Woman*. Sexuality, textuality, and the links between the two are pivotal issues in Fowles's novel. In particular, this novel provides striking dramatizations of how both sexuality and textuality lead to irreducible ambiguities of interpretation. Neither concept can be circumscribed within a univocal structure of totalized meaning. Because of the resultant impossibility of final interpretation, both sexuality and textuality lead directly to a confrontation with infinity, hence their vertiginous force.

Infinity is the most staggering concept with which modern man has had to come to grips. Not that infinity has not always been with us; it has. However, throughout most of Western intellectual history the idea of infinity has been circumscribed and contained within the comforting concept of an omnipotent God. Descartes, for example, considered the very fact that we can even conceive of the infinite as proof of God's existence: from where else could such a concept arise? Beginning with the secularization of the sublime that M. H. Abrams notes in relation to the Romantics, though, and especially with the death of God announced by that late Romantic Friedrich Nietzsche, we have lost that easy way out.[1] Infinity is now within the purview of humanity, and now we must face it head-on. Wallace Stevens, in his poem "The American Sublime," has perhaps best and most succinctly expressed this modern predicament. Indeed, without God to fall back on and yet faced with the awesome silence of infinity, what wine does one drink, and what bread does one eat?

Stevens is not alone in having recognized the centrality of this problem. Jorge Luis Borges is another modern writer who has shown an explicit fascination with infinity: "There is a concept which corrupts and upsets all others. I refer not to Evil, whose limited realm is that of ethics; I refer to the infinite" (202). Borges's own fiction explores the notion of infinity in a number of provocative and exciting ways, as do the works of many modern authors. Time after time, we find modern literary characters (and texts) attempting to come to grips with our modern existential predicament, seeking to follow Hemingway's Lady Brett Ashley in reaching some determination of exactly what it is that we have instead of God. Among the more interesting of such texts to appear in the last couple of decades is *The French Lieutenant's Woman*. This text is fascinating from a number of perspectives, but it is especially so in of its treatment of the secularization of infinity in modern literature. Infinity, though, cannot be directly represented, but only figured, and it is precisely the twin concepts of sexuality and textuality that Fowles employs as his figures of infinity. Fowles's treatment of these figures confronts directly those issues such as framing and boundaries that are fundamental to the character of postmodernist art in general.

SEXUALITY, INFINITY, AND TRANSGRESSION

That the sublime (or any concept of infinity) is related to the general question of framing and boundaries is clear: the infinite is by definition that which exceeds all bounds. As a result, the very concept of infinity presents a special point of view from which to view questions of boundaries and frames of all kinds. In particular, the infinite presents us with a paradigm for the transgression of boundaries. Michel Foucault recognizes this very point when he argues the importance of a concept of the sacred to the very notion of transgression. Transgression requires boundaries, and the boundlessness of infinity highlights the artificiality of the various systems of boundaries that society constructs. To Foucault, having lost God we must seek some other arena in which to formulate boundaries and thus transgressive ideas. He suggests (following Bataille) that twentieth-century culture has adopted sexuality as the arena in which this reformulation occurs:

Thus, at the root of sexuality, of the movement that nothing can ever limit (because it is, from its birth and in its totality, constantly involved with the limit), and at the root of this discourse on God which Western culture has maintained for so long . . . a singular experience is shaped: that of transgression. ("Preface to Transgression" 33)

The difficulty noted by Foucault of formulating an effective notion of transgression in a posttheological world parallels the situation of postmodernism that I noted in the last chapter. Coming after modernism has already broken down most traditional barriers, postmodernism faces the challenge of finding a legitimate target for its transgressive energies. Foucault, in his emphasis on sexuality and transgression within the dynamics of power mirrors the movement in which a number of writers have sought to formulate their transgressive programs in the area of the sexual. One thinks, for example, of the sometimes outrageous sexual imagery of a William S. Burroughs, or of the gallery of sexual misfits inhabiting the fiction of Vladimir Nabokov.[2]

Foucault's link between sexuality and infinity also parallels the work of Jacques Lacan. The strange hybrid of ecstasy and terror that constitutes the Lacanian experience of *jouissance*, that unrepresentable moment of a sudden and stunning glimpse into the Real, is very closely linked to the concept of the sublime. The transgressive potential of *jouissance* is brought home by Kristeva's essential equation between *jouissance* and abjection, and it is interesting to note that she relates abjection directly to the sublime as well: "The abject is edged with the sublime. It is not the same moment on the journey, but the same subject and speech bring them into being" (*Powers of Horror* 11). Lacan was an important influence on Kristeva, although Kristeva adds an explicitly political element to her relation between sexuality and transgression that is lacking in Lacan. And Foucault evades the psychoanalytic perspective entirely, denying the primacy of sexuality and arguing that the sex drive is in fact secondary to a broader and more fundamental will to knowledge.

Lacan himself has explicitly linked *jouissance* to both sexuality (especially feminine sexuality) and God:

What was tried at the end of the last century, at the time of Freud, by all kinds of worthy people in the circle of Charcot and the rest, was an attempt to reduce the mystical to questions of fucking. If you look carefully, that is not what it is all about. Might not this *jouissance* which one experiences and knows nothing of, be that which puts us on the path of ex-istence? And why not interpret one face of the Other, the God face, as supported by feminine *jouissance*? (*Feminine Sexuality* 147)

If Lacan is right that feminine sexuality embodies the potential for a special access to *jouissance* (that is, to the sublime), then it would seem clear that the feminine also presents the potential for a special transgressive force. Feminist theory counts on just this force, and here Lacan, whose phallocentric language has rendered questionable his relationship to feminist theory, would certainly seem to be privileging the feminine. On the other hand, Lacan's view does not seem far from an old romantic notion of the mysteries of the feminine, a notion that in our day survives on a more pedestrian level in concepts such as "feminine intuition." Kristeva's link between *jouissance* and the abject also raises the question of whether Lacan's view participates in the historical trend of associating the physicality of women with abject images of filth and decay. It is not clear whether Lacan's notion of this special woman's *jouissance* is a genuinely positive feminine attribute or a projection of male fantasy. But it is precisely this same uncertainty that surrounds the radical and mysterious alterity (and sublimity) of the feminine as embodied in Fowles's Sarah Woodruff.[3] Alien, enigmatic, and touched with a hint of forbidden sexuality, her attraction for Charles Smithson would seem to be very much a matter of her special access to the *jouissance* of the woman. Further, she has the additional advantage (if one wants to seem radically Other) of being apparently mad—providing another link to the interests of Foucault.

The special import of Sarah's sublime Otherness is made clear by the "Victorian" context of her story.[4] If the secularization (and thus unleashing) of the sublime is the hallmark of Romanticism, then it is precisely the attempt to come to grips with this unleashing that is the hallmark of the Victorian era. The Victorian response is simple: to contain, delimit, and circumscribe the sublime in any way possible. From this response arise the Victorian mania for taxonomy and classification and the Victorian obsession with scientific description and explanation. And, if I am correct in relating the sublime to Lacan's concept of *jouissance*, one would expect the Victorians to be particularly concerned with suppressing the dangerous energies of sexuality in general, and especially of feminine sexuality.

That the Victorians were in fact greatly concerned with such suppression goes without saying, and this concern plays a large part in Fowles's novel. The book indicates a definite relationship between the Victorian denial of feminine sexuality and the more general Victorian terror of the transgression of boundaries of all kinds. For example, Fowles's narrator suggests that Charles and Sarah's difficulties in communication arise largely from the Victorian denial of the body, which results from the strict dichotomy that the Victorians maintained between soul and body, a dichotomy in which the soul is privileged and which is itself "perhaps the most dreadful result of their mania for categorization" (288). Sexuality, then, suggests an immediate rupture of the usual soul-body (or thought-feeling) hierarchy that so characterizes the Victorian era. This dualism in fact informs the entire history of Western civilization at least since Aristotle (which makes its transgression all the more significant), but the narrator goes on to suggest that such dichotomies are especially central to the Victorian period, "and this, I think, makes the best guidebook to the age very possibly *Dr. Jekyll and Mr. Hyde*" (289).

The relationship between the unleashing of feminine sexuality and transgression of taxonomies and hierarchies in general is also stressed elsewhere. For example, late in the book, when Charles rediscovers Sarah in the Rossetti house, he compares her mode of dress with that he had observed among the young women of America:

In the United States Charles had found the style, with its sly and paradoxically coquettish hints at emancipation in other ways, very charming; now, and under so many other suspicions, his cheeks took a color not far removed from the dianthus pink of the stripes on her shirt. (347)

Roland Barthes (in *Système de la Mode*) has taught us that conventions in fashion can serve as a paradigm for conventional systems and taxonomies of all kinds. Transgressions of accepted modes of dress, then, can function as powerful reminders of the possibility of other types of transgressions as well, of "emancipation in other ways." America is already itself an image of unruliness for a Victorian (which is why it is the perfect place for Charles's Byronic exile late in the book), so a lack of decorum in style of dress would not be out of place there. But in Victorian England such a lack is frightening indeed, as shown by the strength of Charles's emotional reaction. This reaction is partially due to the fact that Charles is still reeling from the discovery that Sarah has apparently come up in the world since leaving him, when all the dictates of Victorian logic indicate that she was supposed to have come down:

He saw nothing; but only the folly of his own assumption that fallen women must continue falling—for had he not come to arrest the law of gravity? He was as shaken as a man who suddenly finds the world around him standing on its head. (347)

This link to the world of nineteenth-century, Newtonian, deterministic science is important, and what better symbol of that world can there be (as Pynchon, among others, has so thoroughly recognized) than the law of gravity? Moreover, this motif of the "world upside down" (a standard theme of the Bakhtinian carnival) illustrates the way in which the polar hierarchies of the Victorians were so easily susceptible to inversion. The supreme transgression (for a Victorian) rears its head in Fowles's text soon afterwards, as Charles suddenly considers the unthinkable possibility of that ultimate unleashing of the subversive possibilities of feminine sexuality: lesbianism.

What new enormity was threatened now! Another woman, who knew and understood her better than . . . that hatred of man . . . this house inhabited by . . . he dared not say it to himself. (357, Fowles's ellipses)[5]

Still worse, the suspected lesbian lover of Sarah is none other than the notorious Christina Rossetti herself, the poetess whose verse had always contained, for Charles, threatening touches of feminine *jouissance*, with its built-in hints of the infinite and of the transgression of boundaries:

Of course! Had he not always found in her verse, on the rare occasions he had looked at it, a certain incomprehensible mysticism? A passionate obscurity, the sense of a mind too inward and femininely involute; to be frank, rather absurdly muddled over the frontiers of human and divine love? (357)

Charles's fears turn out to be unfounded, but the very fact that they occur to him as they do indicate the power with which they threaten and destabilize his well-ordered Victorian view of the world. Charles, despite being (especially in his own mind) somewhat beyond the average in terms of sophistication and liberality, is an ideal specimen of the Victorian mind. Not only does he fundamentally accept the overall Victorian worldview, but his fascination with paleontology provides a direct representation of the drive toward classification and categorization that so characterized the era. The compulsion to classify, name, define, and circumscribe all aspects of life is perhaps the driving force behind Victorian science in general. By challenging this compulsion through a demonstration of the way in which the infinite mystery of the world (especially as figured by feminine sexuality) ultimately eludes all taxonomies and hierarchies, Fowles powerfully calls into question the fundamental assumptions upon which Victorian science and society were constructed.

For Fowles's purposes, Charles's paleontological endeavors provide an especially apt example of the Victorian fascination with and confidence in the ability of science to circumscribe the strangeness of nature. In particular, Charles's typically Victorian misreading of evolution as a teleological process obeying strictly predictable laws of cause-and-effect provides a direct link to the concomitant Victorian faith in progress in general. Thus, when Charles is attempting to explain evolution to Mr. Freeman, he depicts it as an orderly process of adaptation and improvement, explaining that a species must change "[i]n order to survive. It must adapt itself to changes in the environment" (228). Charles here shows precisely the lack of appreciation for the contingent and aleatory nature of evolution that led to such theories as social Darwinism among his contemporaries. And the response of Mr. Freeman links this misreading of evolution to the broader Victorian view of social and historical progression:

Just so. Now that I can believe. I am twenty years older than you. Moreover, I have spent my life in a situation where if one does not—and very smartly—change oneself to meet the taste of the day, then one does not survive. One goes bankrupt. Times are changing, you know. This is a great age of progress. And progress is like a lively horse. Either one rides it, or it rides one. (228)

These assumptions are not only central to Victorian notions of history, science, sociology, and the like, but also form the fundamental structural principle of the typical Victorian novel, which Fowles's book so effectively parodies. Indeed, through many explicit and striking metafictional devices, Fowles tellingly questions the assumptions upon which narrative is constructed and interpreted.

Charles's ideas concerning paleontology and evolution are basically narrative ones. He tends to view his own actions in highly narrative terms, often self-consciously choosing his own course in life in terms of what would fit the expectations of narrative convention. The most obvious example of such expectations concerns his entire view of his relationship with Sarah. At first, such a relationship is simply out of the question because it violates so many of the rules of Victorian narrative. And then, when his desire (whatever its nature) for Sarah reaches the point that he is willing to pursue her regardless, he is able to do so largely by finding another narrative convention in which that pursuit can take place. She may be a fallen woman, but he begins to see her as a noble one. She needs him; he will come to her rescue. Thus he begins to see himself as a knight in shining armor, riding onto the scene to rescue his damsel in distress.

Fowles makes this picture explicit: "He had come to raise her from penury, from some crabbed post in a crabbed house. In full armor, ready to slay the dragon."

But here, as everywhere in the world of Fowles's text, the pre-fabricated narrative structure is inadequate to cope with the realities of sexuality and textuality. Unfortunately for Charles, the damsel in question has another agenda. Sarah has no desire or need to be saved: "and now the damsel had broken all the rules. No chains, no sobs, no beseeching hands." Once again, this upset to Charles's neatly compartmentalized conception of the world leaves him confused and disoriented. He may be acting as a character from literature, but he has stepped into the wrong script, even the wrong genre: "He was the man who appears at a formal soirée under the impression it was to be a fancy dress ball" (349).

Sarah is also highly influenced by literary convention. We discover that she, as a schoolgirl, had not gotten along well with her fellow students:

Thus it had come about that she had read far more fiction, and far more poetry, those two sanctuaries of the lonely, than most of her kind. They served as a substitute for experience. Without realizing it she judged people as much by the standards of Walter Scott and Jane Austen as by any empirically arrived at; seeing those around her as fictional characters, and making poetic judgments on them. (48)

This picture of Sarah as being constituted by the literature that she reads is a familiar one, and goes back in the tradition of the novel to Cervantes. Here, however, it would seem to evoke a particularly strong connection to Flaubert's Emma Bovary. Thus it comes as no surprise that a novelist as self-conscious as Fowles later makes this connection explicit. Charles condescendingly opts to temper his condemnation of Sarah's apparent sexual transgressions with a realization that his view of Darwinism implies a kind of determinism that suggests that we are not necessarily responsible for our own actions:

Partly then, his scientific hobbies . . . but Charles had also the advantage of having read—very much in private, for the book had been prosecuted for obscenity—a novel that had appeared in France some ten years before; a novel profoundly deterministic in its assumptions, the celebrated *Madame Bovary*. And as he looked down at the face beside him, it was suddenly, out of nowhere, that Emma Bovary's name sprang into his mind. (99–100, Fowles's ellipsis)

The evocation of Flaubert is important for several reasons. For one thing, it creates an interesting double twist, with Charles relating his experience in life to a book about a character who related her experiences in life to other books. It thus furnishes a particularly good example of the way in which Charles develops his expectations of life from the literature that he has read. It is also another link to things foreign and French in the book, links that themselves suggest transgression of neat Victorian (English) categories. Here it is particularly important to note that *Madame Bovary* is a book whose central theme of adultery concerns precisely the sorts of transgressive sexuality that are so important in Fowles's book.[6] In addition, Flaubert's notorious disgust with the bourgeois society of his own country suggests that many of the invidious aspects of Victorian society were not strictly English phenomena. Flaubert's *Bouvard and Pécuchet* powerfully condemns precisely the sorts of systematization and classification that Fowles's novel attacks. It also employs sexuality as a metaphor for the ultimate insufficiency of taxonomy. When that great amateur of systems, Pécuchet, overhears the encounter between Gorju and Mme. Castillon, he is suddenly confronted with the way in which sexuality exceeds all systems of enclosure, resulting in

the discovery of a new world—an entire new world—which contained dazzling radiances, riotous bursts of blossom, oceans, tempests, treasures, and abysses of infinite depth. What matter that it was charged with terror! (207)

Pécuchet has, in fact, come face to face with *jouissance*, or with the sublime. However, his own single attempt at a first-hand investigation of the sublimity of sexuality (in his unfortunate encounter with the servant-girl Mélie) yields results that are disappointing, to say the least. The "innocent" young girl turns out not to be so innocent after all, and Pécuchet receives little for his trouble except a case of syphilis.

Perhaps Pécuchet's disappointment is not surprising; after all, one of Lacan's most famous pronouncements is that "there is no sexual relation." This special *jouissance* of the woman of which Lacan speaks is apparently not so easy to come by; for a man, it may be impossible. Charles Smithson, too, finds that the physical realities of sex do not necessarily measure up to the sublime mysteries of sexuality in the abstract. He has some past sexual experience, but in the first attempt to which we as readers bear witness, he becomes ill and vomits into a prostitute's pillow. In fact, like Pécuchet, he manages only a single specifically represented sexual encounter in Fowles's book, though his experience in some ways turns out to be almost the direct opposite of that undergone by Flaubert's character. When at last Charles "seduces" (thanks to her orchestration) the mysterious Sarah Woodruff, he learns that in this case a fallen women turns out to be innocent, or at least apparently so. However, like Pécuchet's, his experience is a disappointing one, and the results of this encounter are comically deflating (to the reader, if not to Charles) after nearly three hundred pages of suspenseful preparation and textual foreplay.

The blow-by-blow account of the encounter between Charles and Sarah begins by openly linking the pleasure of the experience (at least for Charles; here, as elsewhere, we never quite know what Sarah thinks about it all) to the notion of transgression. In a variation of the forbidden-fruit theme, the narrator suggests that the restrictions imposed by Victorian society on sexual enjoyment actually added to that enjoyment, and that in fact an additional thrill was available through the analogy with transgression in other areas as well. As Charles makes his climactic move, we are told that:

[h]e strained that body into his, straining his mouth upon hers,
with all the hunger of a long frustration—not merely sexual, for a
whole ungovernable torrent of things banned, romance, adventure,
sin, madness, animality, all these coursed wildly through him. (274)

We see here the general link between sexuality and transgression erupting in all its might, so much so that its power is only slightly undercut at this point by all that straining and by the comically hyperbolic nature of the language in this passage. The scene quickly degenerates into farce, however, with Sarah melodramatically faking a swoon (something on the order of a silent-movie heroine) and Charles frantically ripping off his clothes, sending buttons flying. We are then treated to the vivid picture of Charles with "his member erect and thrusting out his shirt," followed by a frantic and clumsy coupling. "Precisely ninety seconds had passed since he had left her to look into the bed-room" preparatory to the act (274–75).

The narration of this scene points out the jarring disjunction between the physical reality and brutality of this coupling and the mystery of sexuality that surrounds it. Thus, as Charles achieves penetration we are told in hyperbolically romantic terms that "her arms flung round him as if she would bind him to her for that eternity he could not dream without her." But this evocation of the sublimity of eternity is already put in question by that crucial "as if," by the fact that Sarah's actions throughout this scene are hardly spontaneous. This passage is further destabilized in that the eternity invoked by Sarah's action comes not from her dreams, but from his. And this elevated notion is undercut even more by the information that "[h]e began to ejaculate at once" (274). In short, the long-awaited orgasm is an anticlimax. Infinity cannot be circumscribed; sexuality cannot be contained within sex. As Lacan inimitably points out, *jouissance* is not merely a matter of fucking.

TEXTUALITY, FRAMING, AND REFLEXIVITY

If Lacan employs the term *jouissance* to describe the ultimate intensity of the sexual experience, then it is certainly interesting to note that Barthes uses the same sexually charged French word to describe the ultimate intensity of the experience of reading texts. Such confluences of terms occur quite frequently in French, a language distinguished by its unusually high degree of polysemy. However, if we have learned anything from the developments in French theory in the last few decades it is that such linguistic "accidents" can in fact be highly significant. Thus, while the *jouissance* that Barthes describes in relation to textuality is generally taken to be an experience of pleasure that lacks the dimension of abysmal terror involved in Lacan's *jouissance* of sexuality, there is in fact a highly unsettling quality to Barthes' textual *jouissance*. Thus Barthes defines the "text of bliss" as "the text that imposes a state of loss, the text that discomforts (perhaps to the point of a certain boredom), unsettles the reader's historical, cultural, psychological assumptions, the consistency of his tastes, values, memories, brings to a crisis his relations with language" (*Pleasure of the Text* 14).[7]

The "state of loss" associated by Barthes with the *jouissance* of textuality arises largely from the emptiness (and liberty) at the heart of things that occurs as a result of the death of God. As Barthes himself puts it, "to refuse to fix meaning is, in the end, to refuse God and his hypostases—reason, science, law" ("Death of the Author" 147). *The French Lieutenant's Woman* is a "text of bliss" that provides a vivid enactment of the confluence of these sexual and textual versions of *jouissance*, utilizing both as figures of nontheological infinity. The book is explicitly concerned with the mystery and transgressive potential of sexuality. At the same time, it is equally concerned with its own textuality, which turns out to be a similarly uncontainable force; we find that the unfathomable mysteries of Sarah Woodruff are closely related to the unfathomable mysteries of the workings of texts and narratives. Just as Charles can never reach a final interpretation of Sarah, so can we as readers never reach a final interpretation of the text in which she appears and to which she gives the title.

I would suggest that the premature ejaculation experienced by Charles in his attempt to gain mastery of Sarah provides a precise analogue for the sort of premature and totalizing interpretation that occurs whenever any reader seeks to master a text and thereby circumscribe and finalize its meaning. In both cases closure is achieved at the expense of most of the action. The complexities of the scene of consummation between Charles and Sarah point to the mutual coimplication of sexuality and textuality throughout *The French Lieutenant's Woman*. The ambiguities of the scene, in fact, are essential to both concepts. As Shoshana Felman points out, sexuality is fundamentally constituted by an undecidable conflict between opposing forces, especially desire and repression:

If, far from implying the simplicity of a self-present literal meaning, sexuality points rather to a multiplicity of conflicting forces, to the complexity of its own divisiveness and contradiction, its meaning can by no means be univocal or unified, but must necessarily be ambiguous. It is thus not rhetoric which disguises and hides sex; sexuality is rhetoric, since it essentially consists of ambiguity: it is the coexistence of dynamically antagonistic meanings. Sexuality is the division of meaning; it is meaning as division, meaning as conflict. (112)

Ambiguity is the primary mode of Fowles's text, and his choosing sexuality to instantiate his vision of ambiguous, non-totalizable meaning is entirely appropriate. Sexuality is the perfect correlative for the functioning of Fowles's text, which specifically demonstrates the parallelism of sexuality and textuality in a number of ways. One of the most striking illustrations occurs as Charles listens to Sarah's story of her affair with Varguennes, projecting his own desire into the narrative:

He was at one and the same time Varguennes enjoying her and the man who sprang forward and struck him down; just as Sarah was to him both an innocent victim and a wild, abandoned woman. Deep in himself he forgave her her unchastity; and glimpsed the dark shadows where he might have enjoyed it himself. (143)

Clearly, Charles functions here in the role of reader to Sarah's role of author, and indeed the (especially male) reader of Fowles's text, despite the many reminders of its fictionality, experiences similar identifications not only here with Varguennes, but later with Charles as he finally does "enjoy it himself."[8] Indeed, the link between the process of reading and that of voyeurism is integral to the entire novel; it is one of Fowles's clearest statements of the parallelism between sexuality and textuality. The explicit presentation of details in Charles's encounter with the prostitute and later in his eventual seduction of Sarah are clearly designed to implicate the desires of the reader. Moreover, as the narrator presents us with the scene at Ma Terpsichore's, it is interesting that he does so primarily by quoting from a text, the bawdy eighteenth-century novel *The History of the Human Heart*.

Sarah, meanwhile, functions both as the embodiment of feminine sexuality and as a figure of the author not only as she tells Charles about Varguennes, but throughout the book. The way in which Sarah spins invented tales and manipulates people and events is clearly parallel to the way in which authors manipulate characters and plots in their own invented tales. When Charles shows up at the Rossetti house to "save" Sarah, she does not respond with the expected gratitude, but instead turns Charles away, aborting their relationship as an author destroys a draft of a work that is not proceeding satisfactorily:

I was told that if an artist is not his own sternest judge, he is not fit to be an artist. I believe that is right. I believe I was right to destroy what had begun between us. There was a falsehood in it. (351)

While much of the action in Fowles's novel can be illuminated by considering Sarah as a figure of the author and Charles as a figure of the reader, it is also important to remember that these positions are not simple polar opposites. If it is clear that Sarah's mysteriousness is largely a projection of male fantasy, it is equally clear that the traditional notion of the creating author is largely a projection of our own individual fantasies of autonomy and power. The same might be said for the traditional notion of God. But as both Barthes and Foucault have argued in their separate ways, this view of the author is a highly theological one: the demystification of the role of the author in modern critical discourse is closely related to Nietzsche's death of God. Barthes's notorious "death of the author" is perhaps the best known statement of this notion:

We know now that a text is not a line of words releasing a single "theological" meaning (the "message" of the Author-God) but a multi-dimensional space in which a variety of writings, none of them original, blend and clash. The text is a tissue of quotations drawn from the innumerable centres of culture. Similar to *Bouvard and Pécuchet*, those eternal copyists, at once sublime and comic whose profound ridiculousness indicates precisely the truth of writing, the writer can only imitate a gesture that is always anterior, never original. His only power is to mix writings, to counter the ones with the others, in such a way as never to rest on any one of them. ("Death of the Author" 146)

Fowles's narrator openly reminds us that he is writing in the age of textuality, noting that "I live in the age of Alain Robbe-Grillet and Roland Barthes" (80). The work of Barthes is one of the many intertexts that plays constantly in the margins of *The French Lieutenant's Woman*. Thus Sarah, though an authorial figure, is herself constituted by the discourses of romantic literature and of conventional male fantasy. She does not create her narratives ex nihilo, but within a preexisting discursive context; she "mixes writings, countering the ones with others." Fowles's self-consciously intertextual book presents itself (like *Bouvard and Pécuchet*) as an explicit demonstration of Barthes's notion that "the text is a tissue of quotations."

But if all texts are constructed of discourse borrowed from other texts, then those other texts are themselves always already constructed from still other texts, and so on ad infinitum. Intertextuality is an infinite concept. As Derrida and others have shown, the web of intertextual connection ultimately extends to the entire linguistic structure in a way far more fundamental and immanent than the mere allusion to specific texts. This effect occurs in all texts, but *The French Lieutenant's Woman* makes it especially obvious with its variety of explicit metafictional devices such as the various epigraphs and the numerous footnotes that compromise the frame around the fictional text. These epigraphs and footnotes blur the distinction between inside and outside, openly proclaiming the infinite extendibility of all texts, the intertextuality of all narratives, and reminding us of the Derridean dictum that "there is nothing outside of the text."

In *The French Lieutenant's Woman*, the infinity of textuality points inward as well as outward. The self-referential nature of Fowles's text and language triggers the infinite regression of mirror reflections that has come to be known in recent critical discourse as the *mise en abîme*. When Fowles's narrator steps forward to announce (with the authority of an author) that the author has no authority, we are clearly confronting a paradox similar to the one that occurs when Sarah transcends the boundaries of Victorian male dominance by assuming a mysteriousness and resistance to interpretation that remain strictly inscribed within the limits of male fantasy. When that narrator proclaims the fictionality of his text, when he warns us that "I am lying," he is repeating the gesture of Epimenides, a gesture that leads to an infinite regression of back-and-forth cancellation and restatement of meaning.

This self-referential "liar paradox" effect is critical to the dynamics of Fowles's text, undermining as it does the attempt to reduce any aspect of the book to a univocal interpretation or even to peacefully coexisting multiple interpretations along the lines of a New Critical appeal to unity in multiplicity via concepts such as irony or ambiguity. The undecidability embodied in *The French Lieutenant's Woman* (either the novel or the character of Sarah) is infinite and can never be brought to rest by appeals to irony and ambiguity as hypostatized categories of textual functioning. Textuality, like sexuality, escapes all attempts at such categorization. Fowles's text turns back on itself, openly declaring itself as a work of fiction and clearly setting itself off from any illusion of reality. At the same time, this clearly intertextual book reaches outward toward an infinite web of connections beyond its own boundaries. Thus Fowles's novel clearly delineates itself as a fictional artifact, while at the same time suggesting that the frame thus established cannot ultimately contain the immense energies that inhere in the book. A single text cannot contain the infinity of textuality, just as the physical act of sex cannot contain the infinity of sexuality.

The fact that Fowles's text simultaneously employs both an "inward" and an "outward" approach to textual infinity suggests that perhaps these two approaches are not entirely separate after all. It suggests that the reflexivity of the *mise en abîme*, often considered to be a purely formal effect that seals a text off from the real world, is in fact a powerful means of engaging and commenting upon that world. Fowles goes to great lengths to frame his book as a work of fiction, to call our attention to its artifice, yet he continually suggests parallels between his fictional world and our "real" one. In the notorious intrusion of chapter 13 of the novel, Fowles's narrator steps outside the frame to present us with a digression on the art of the novel, explaining that novelists are motivated by the desire to "create worlds as real as, but other than the world that is" (81). But if these novelistic worlds are in fact as real as the "world that is," then the implication must be that the "real" world is itself constructed via fictions. Indeed, the narrator goes on to suggest that his control over his characters is quite similar to that which we have over the people with whom we interact in our everyday lives.

But this is preposterous? A character is either "real" or "imaginary"? If you think that, hypocrite lecteur, I can only smile. You do not even think of your own past as quite real; you dress it up, you gild it or blacken it, censor it, tinker with it . . . fictionalize it, in a word, and put it away on a shelf—your book, your romanced autobiography. (82, Fowles's ellipsis)

Fowles quite explicitly points out that it is not just Charles who constructs his own life according to the conventions of narrative. Nor is this mode of behavior limited to the narrative-minded Victorians. It is, in fact, the fundamental way in which we all approach the world. Such fictionalization is, we are told, "a basic definition of Homo sapiens" (82).

Clearly, if all of us approach the world in this way, then the "real" world is itself a fictional text. A book such as *The French Lieutenant's Woman*, with its self-conscious commentary on the means by which fictional narratives are constructed, is thereby commenting on the "real" world as well. This commentary is related to the question of framing and of boundaries of works of art, but it is also closely linked to the more general way in which society imposes conventional frames and boundaries to divide experience into artificially compartmentalized segments. Robert Siegle has discussed in some detail the political implications of reflexive narratives, citing *The French Lieutenant's Woman* as a principal example. He notes that

any code system divides up an expression continuum (from sounds and marks to phonemes and graphemes) by an arbitrary act that parallels the equally arbitrary way culture segments the content continuum (of things and experiences) and elaborates rules for the combination of these units (grammar and syntax for language, clothing and mores for behavior, politics and economics for group behavior, genres and conventions for art, concepts and theoretical systems for philosophy or theology or poetics). (10)

Siegle and others make a strong case for the potential political relevance of metafictional texts as forces for the destabilization of received ideas. *The French Lieutenant's Woman* lends particularly strong support to this argument through its explicit involvement in such issues, drawing parallels between its fictional world and the "real" world such as those that I have noted above. The book makes an especially strong claim for the political relevance of its metafictional devices to the real world by constantly inviting comparison between narrative conventions and conventions of viewing history. After all, as Hayden White and others have shown, the history that we write depends very heavily upon the narrative models that we use in writing that history. Here, Fowles's choice of a Victorian setting for his work is especially important, given the mutual implication of Victorian narrative conventions and the conventional Western post-Hegelian view of history. However, this coimplication indicates that the Victorian novel was perhaps not a subversive force, but in fact a conservative one. The strong intertextual presence of Matthew Arnold becomes highly relevant here. To Arnold, what we have instead of God is culture, and it is the role of culture (including literature) to act as a stabilizing force that helps resist the encroachments of anarchy resulting from the loss of divine guidance. Charles is something of an Arnold devotee, but the narrator is not. Instead, he openly attacks this conservative view of the function of art in society, clearly preferring the subversive view instead. He derides the "stupid and pernicious" sentimentality of certain works of Victorian art and declares:

Each age, each guilty age, builds high walls round its Versailles; and personally I hate those walls most when they are made by literature and art. (129)

At one point, in fact, Charles experiences a flash of insight in which he suddenly appears to understand the fictive nature of the Victorian bourgeois view of history, and its implications for social institutions in general:

he saw that all life was parallel: that evolution was not vertical, ascending to a perfection, but horizontal. Time was the great fallacy; existence was without history, was always now, was always this being caught in the same fiendish machine. All those painted screens erected by man to shut out reality—history, religion, duty, social position, all were illusions, mere opium fantasies. (165)

The specific use of "opium" here to describe the delusive effects of Victorian social institutions evokes the figure of Marx, and it is significant that, among the many sources of epigraphs used to head chapters in the book, it is the text of Marx that heads the book itself. The transgressive voice of Marx sounds ominously in the margins throughout Fowles's evocation of Victorian bourgeois society, suggesting that the smugly confident world of the Victorians was never quite so securely monolithic as they would have liked to believe. Indeed, Fowles's text openly invites a Marxist reading, and class distinctions are among the many hierarchies that the book addresses. On the other hand, this text goes even further, calling historical progression so strongly into question that a classical Marxist reading, too, is undercut, despite the constant presence of Marx as a privileged voice. Marxism itself is seen as merely another opiate of the masses; both the Victorian bourgeois notion of progress and the Marxist notion of dialectical history depend fundamentally upon the same Hegelian narrative of history that Fowles's text confounds.

Fowles's novel sets these two opposing views of history one against the other and then makes it impossible to establish a preference of one over the other. This interrogation of the Hegelian model of teleological history depends upon that model for its effects and thus cannot be read as a denial of or as an attempt at an "escape" from history. It does, however, suggest that our models of history are determined by textual convention and not by any standard of "truth." This observation is no longer particularly novel, but in *The French Lieutenant's Woman* the links between sexuality and textuality are so strong that the text can be seen to question even something as apparently natural as the sex act itself. The copulation between Charles and Sarah is informed by the typical Victorian model of the sex act as consisting of intercourse leading directly to (especially male) orgasm. But this model (which in many ways has not changed so much in the intervening century) turns out not to be based on the "facts of life," but to be discursively constructed, participating in much of the same ideology as the Hegelian model of teleological history. Feminine sexuality thus takes on a special transgressive force because of its failure to comply with this model of sexual intercourse as the ultimate Hegelian synthesis (between male desire and female submission).

In *The French Lieutenant's Woman* the undecidable oppositions between different views of history participate in the characteristic mode in which the entire text operates, and also provide a further link between sexuality and textuality. Sexuality, according to Felman, is fundamentally informed by an ambiguity arising from the unresolved (and unresolvable) conflict between opposing forces, and Fowles's text realizes most of its ambiguity from exactly the same source. The most important example of such oppositions derives from Fowles's complex treatment of Victorian society and particularly from the highly sophisticated parody of the conventions of Victorian fiction, a treatment that sets the Victorian age in direct opposition to our modern one, and then makes it impossible to choose between the two. While it may be true that the traditional readings of most Victorian novels places those novels in complicity with the prevailing bourgeois ideology of the time, it is also possible to read those novels in productive and subversive new ways simply by going against the grain and refusing to grant the validity of that ideology. Fowles here performs in fiction the same sort of rereading and reenergizing of the Victorian novel that readers such as Barthes and J. Hillis Miller have performed in criticism.[9] Fowles does not mock and ridicule Victorian novels; on the contrary he produces (with a few destabilizing exceptions, such as frequent references to twentieth-century authors and ideas) a reasonably authentic replica. The book is a parody, then, not in the sense of one text that mocks or ridicules another, but in the Bakhtinian sense of "an intentional dialogized hybrid. Within it, languages and styles actively and mutually illuminate one another" (*Dialogic Imagination* 76).

The text is walking a fine line here. Parody, while beginning in similarity, generally derives its force from the difference between the parodying text and the text being parodied. That *The French Lieutenant's Woman* can be both an authentic Victorian novel and at the same time an effective parody of a Victorian novel attests both to the dexterity of the construction of the book and to the properties of the Victorian novel itself, a genre so extreme that it constantly teeters on the brink of its own parody. Primarily, however, the force of Fowles's parody is historical: the difference between his text and the texts being parodied derives mostly from their having been written in different centuries ruled, as Foucault might put it, by different epistemes. By writing a nineteenth-century novel in the twentieth century, Fowles produces a "Pierre Menard" effect that allows the two centuries to interact dialogically in a highly unstable dynamic equilibrium, commenting each upon the other. As a result, every word in the book is double-voiced, pointing both to the context of Victorian fiction and to the context of postmodern metafiction, thus contributing even further to the text's radical instability of meaning. As a Victorian novel, the book demands that the reader suspend disbelief and agree to pretend that the words in the text represent real events. As a metafictional novel, the book demands that the reader suspend belief and participate in the rhetorical games involved in producing the text, agreeing not to be taken in by the seductive lure of the narrative.

The complex double-voiced discourse of *The French Lieutenant's Woman* also contributes to the text's conflation of textuality and sexuality. The book provides a powerful critique of the Victorian world, but even more powerful is its subtle suggestion that many of the same criticisms apply to our own world as well. After all, our notion that we have advanced so far beyond the Victorians itself derives merely from an extension of the Victorian notion of history-as-progress that Fowles so strongly calls into question. Fowles's narrator addresses this question openly in the case of sexuality. While we may deplore the Victorian repression of sexuality, he suggests that we ourselves may not be so much better off, that by bringing sexuality out into the open we may have deprived it of much of its pleasurable force:

In a way, by transferring to the public imagination what they left to the private, we are the more Victorian—in the derogatory sense of the word—century, since we have, in destroying so much of the mystery, the difficulty, the aura of the forbidden, destroyed also a great deal of the pleasure. (213–14)

This rather romantic argument, however, is highly suspect. For one thing, it would seem to derive largely from a nostalgic male longing for the good old days when women stayed in their places, places that were determined by men. For another, this claim that the sexual pleasure of the Victorians may actually have exceeded our own is undercut by the almost ludicrously disappointing nature of the only explicit sexual encounters in the book. And finally, having been told how much pleasure the Victorians derived from sex, we are then immediately informed that the lack of sexual pleasure in the Victorian world contributed to a sublimation of sexual energies that allowed the Victorians to achieve great feats in other areas. For example, it is suggested that much of the force of the writing of Thomas Hardy resulted from the energies freed from the lack of consummation of his love for his cousin Tryphena. In short, Hardy's career is seen to consist largely of a process of direct sublimation of sexuality into textuality.

Again, all of these contradictions hopelessly undermine any attempt to reach a nonproblematic interpretation of Fowles's text. Moreover, these discussions of sexuality also have implications in the area of textuality. If we have demystified sexuality in our century by bringing it out into the open, then metafictional works such as *The French Lieutenant's Woman* have performed exactly the same operation on textuality. Fowles' text, by calling into question the assumption that our modern treatment of sexuality is superior to that of the Victorians (and vice versa), also questions whether the modern demystified narrative really represents such an advance over the Victorian model.

Fowles here is performing a precarious dance on the edge of an abyss, attempting to maintain his balance against the various pitfalls that threaten any work that attacks accepted notions of hierarchies and boundaries. In short, how does one overturn one set of hierarchies without setting up another (probably just as invidious) set of hierarchies in its place? This dilemma is one that Barthes recognized long ago in relation to the question of irony. Noting the way in which irony can become "a new stereotype," Barthes asks, "how can stupidity be pinned down without declaring oneself intelligent? How can one code be superior to another without abusively closing off the plurality of codes?" (*S/Z* 206).

Fowles's project in *The French Lieutenant's Woman* is precisely that of Barthes: he seeks to pin down the stupidity of the Victorians (which turns out largely to be our own stupidity as well) without declaring his own intelligence. Ultimately the only route through which such a project can be accomplished (if it can be accomplished) is through an appeal to infinity. Fowles's text reaches outward to other texts in a never-ending web of intertextual connections that makes it impossible to contain the meaning of his novel within the covers of the novel itself. Further, the paradoxes of the book's internal reflexive commentary and the narrator's many ambiguous statements and attitudes initiate an infinitely unstable oscillation of meaning that can never come to rest. In keeping with his theme of existential freedom, Fowles proposes no alternative dogma of his own, but merely seeks to subvert the kind of totalizing interpretations upon which all dogmas rely. This subversion is made particularly effective by the text's constantly employing the infinite ambiguity of sexuality as an analogue for the indeterminacy of the text itself. By suggesting parallels between the construction of his book and the way in which we construct our everyday reality, Fowles offers a powerful commentary on history and society.

Such direct "real-world" involvement in a text so avowedly metafictional would appear paradoxical. However, as I have shown, paradox is precisely the defining feature of *The French Lieutenant's Woman*. It may, in fact, be the defining feature of postmodernism in general. It is possible to read modernist literature as heir to the strictly defined categories and theological order of the Victorian world described by Fowles, so that the boundaries being transgressed by modernism can be defined with some precision. However, this oppositional model places modernism squarely in danger of falling into the position of "declaring itself intelligent" that Barthes decries. On the other hand (modernism having killed off God) postmodernism inherits a world of unstable and deconstructed boundaries. In order to carry out its transgressive function usefully it must work to restore at least partially (without nostalgia) the very boundaries that it calls into question.[10] Thus, postmodernism is fundamentally paradoxical, inherently involved in the "dance on the edge of an abyss" that I have associated with Fowles's text.[11]

From this point of view, *The French Lieutenant's Woman* becomes one of the paradigmatic transgressive texts of postmodernism, and is thus directly implicated in the many intense debates over the moral and ethical responsibility of postmodernism. The challenging of boundaries that occurs in postmodernism can be seen as generating interesting new directions in discourse and exciting new ways of approaching the world. Alternatively, it can be seen as kicking a dead horse, the restoration and subsequent questioning of boundaries in postmodernism being somewhat analogous to a boxer who holds up a wilting opponent in order to be able to inflict more punishment. Still, without the positing of boundaries against which to transgress, postmodernist and metafictional works are in constant danger of degenerating into empty formalism or even into parodies of themselves. I would suggest that the resistance to final interpretation that Fowles demonstrates in relation to both sexuality and textuality should not be construed as an attitude of nihilism, as a suggestion that all interpretation is pointless. Similarly, it should not be read as an endorsement of total interpretive anarchy, as a suggestion that any and all interpretations are just as good as any and all other interpretations. Fowles's invocation of specific, strongly defined discourses (Marxism, sexuality, poststructuralism, the Victorian novel) indicates the way in which meaning does not proliferate without limit within any text, but is restrained to run in certain "channels" made available by the discourses within which it operates.[12]

To view Fowles's book as either an instance of nihilism or of unrestrained proliferation of meaning (the same as no meaning) would simply be to endorse the Arnoldian distinction between culture and anarchy that the text effectively deconstructs. Fowles achieves ambiguity not through chaos or meaninglessness, but through paradoxical, undecidable, and nondialectical conflicts between clearly and specifically stated opposing forces, whether they be inside/outside, art/reality, truth/fiction, male/female, freedom/determination, nineteenth century/twentieth century, or Marxist history/bourgeois progress. His novel does not propose the dissolution of all boundaries. In fact, it depends for its effectiveness upon the interrogation of those boundaries, an interrogation that cannot occur unless boundaries exist. Similarly, it does not oppose interpretation, but in fact opposes the premature closing off of interpretation. The book suggests that the activities of reading and interpretation should participate in an endlessly ongoing process of textual and cultural examination and critique.

Obviously, my reading of *The French Lieutenant's Woman* leads to a significantly different view of its transgressive force than did my reading of *Mulligan Stew*. But what is there in these texts that makes for such a difference in effect? Actually, what leads to such different readings is not entirely in the texts. Transgression can never occur simply within a text; it must occur in the interaction between a text and its social and discursive surroundings. These surroundings include as an important element the reader of the text, so that in large measure it is fair to say that my readings of the two texts reach different conclusions because I have simply chosen to read them differently.

This conclusion, I hope, makes a point about the role of the reader in instilling a text with transgressive energies. But it raises an additional question of motivation. It seems entirely possible to conceive of a reader who would reach precisely the opposite conclusion, finding Sorrentino's text, with its avant-garde formal brilliance, to be transgressive, but finding Fowles's much more accessible text to be a mere pandering to the public appetite for romantic-stories-with-a-little-sex-thrown-in. Why did I read these texts the way I did?

I would be disingenuous if I did not admit that I read these texts differently partially to make a point about the different ways that it is possible to read texts. And I specifically choose to read Fowles's text as transgressive and Sorrentino's as not because on the surface it actually seems simpler to do it the other way around. But I also have specific motivations for my choice of reading strategies, reasons that address some of the fundamental questions concerning literary transgression that I explore in this study.

First of all, it is much easier to identify a legitimate target of transgression in Fowles's text than in Sorrentino's. Fowles inscribes the bourgeois ideology of progress and history-as-narrative directly in his text by presenting an effective simulacrum of a Victorian novel. But he disrupts the development of this novel at key points, having his narrator step outside the frame of the novel and remind the reader that what she is reading is a fiction constructed according to artificial conventions, not according to a reflection of "reality." As a result, the reader is effectively reminded that the narratives (literary or otherwise) she has encountered in the past were similarly conventional, however "natural" they might have appeared. Sorrentino's book disrupts these same narrative conventions, but so openly does so that the conventionality of narrative is taken as a given. Sorrentino's text can easily be read without the traditions of the conventional narrative being challenged, because they simply never come into play.

What does come into play in Sorrentino's text is the tradition of complex, difficult fiction inherited from modernism. But, written fifty years after the heyday of modernism, Sorrentino's is not a modernist text, but a parody of a modernist text. Its techniques, however sophisticated, are not new; they are quite familiar to any sophisticated reader who has been trained in the reading of modernist fiction. And it is precisely as such that they offer the reader a means for comfortably recuperating the text. Not only can a sophisticated reader deal easily with Sorrentino's textual strategies, but he can also congratulate himself for having done so. The text thus offers the reader a fantasy of mastery that is anything but transgressive.

It is helpful here to appeal to Althusser's notion of "interpellation": the process through which the ideologies inscribed in a text call out to the reader, offering him a specific subjective position which he can occupy within that ideology. In particular, this process proceeds by the positing of an "Absolute Subject" (for example, God) who serves as a model for the reader's subjectivity. In *Mulligan Stew*, this Absolute Subject is the knowing master, the sophisticated scholar who has read Joyce and Nabokov and the other texts parodied by Sorrentino, and who is thus knowledgeable enough not only to understand Sorrentino's allusions but to be able to decipher his complex framework of literary device. *The French Lieutenant's Woman*, on the other hand, seemingly offers the subjective position of the traditional bourgeois subject, particularly in its presentation of "realistic," self-identical characters with whom the reader can identify. But the narrator's metafictional intrusions disrupt this identification at critical junctures. This effect is particularly powerful in chapter 13 where, after a long initial section that is an effective imitation of a Victorian novel, the narrator announces the fictionality of his characters. Moreover, he suggests that he himself is losing control of those characters, which also undermines any attempt to identify with the narrator himself as a subjective center of the novel. The reader is thus left with no position that he can comfortably assume.

This interference in the process of interpellation is especially troubling (and effective) because it reveals that process at work, reminding us that all of the texts we read are constantly involved in such processes. The invocation of Althusser's Marxist perspective here shows that this troubling process has a social function and is more than a matter of individual *jouissance*. For example, Tony Bennett notes Terry Eagleton's Althusserian suggestion that conventional criticism seeks to smooth over the ideological contradictions in texts, thus preventing them from being troubling. In contrast, Bennett argues that Marxist critics should actively seek to read contradictions into texts, in an act of conscious political intervention (146). The kind of critical intervention proposed by Bennett can be performed on any text, though some texts work better than others. I am suggesting that Fowles's works better than Sorrentino's.

Finally, the questions of subjective positioning and of artistic technique suggest that some of the successful interventions that might be performed on these texts are feminist ones. One reason that I am privileging Fowles's more "popular" style over Sorrentino's more "sophisticated" technique is to challenge the notion that such distinctions between high and low art have any ultimate validity. Of course, to value Fowles more highly than Sorrentino strictly on the basis of artistic "merit," even if it goes against the usual direction of such distinctions, is not an improvement on the traditional high art–low art hierarchy. However, there are additional reasons for this distinction, related to the historical tendency to identify "low" art with the feminine.

In particular, Sorrentino's text, occupying the traditional male role of sophisticated text, does nothing to renounce that role. Gender is essentially a nonissue in *Mulligan Stew*. The only female characters who play an active role in the "plot" are the outrageous Berthe Delamode and Corrie Corriendo, temptresses extraordinaires. A typical description is:

Madame Delamode, with her slip off now, in bikini, her breasts monumental, my mouth was dry, Corrie Corriendo in jet-black corset and nylons, and with no panties, wearing black glossy heels of panting desire. (162)

There is nothing inherently wrong with such scenes; they in fact function as parodies of the representation of women as sex objects and thus potentially carry a positive message. The problem is that there is no hint of what this message might be, no presentation of a specific alternative vision. For example, the only "feminist" character in the book is the Susan B. Anthony who appears in the "Flawless Play Restored" section, described as a "belle of some balls" (178).

Balls, indeed. Anthony is depicted as a typical masculine feminist, with no use for men whatsoever. She declares her "political program" early in the section: "I long for a multiple clitoral orgasm without the intercession of the usual bore of a male organ! I long! I long!" She is then *carried off, her pelvis convulsing in time to the old Feltman's favorite, 'I'd Press My*

Thighs Together Ere I'd Kiss Your Greedy Lips'" (180, Sorrentino's emphasis). Again, this is all in good fun, and such scenes are almost necessitated by Sorrentino's attempt to update Joyce's "Circe." Only a rather vulgar feminist perspective would condemn such passages out of hand without exploring their textual functioning. For example, here it is obvious that Sorrentino's treatment of Anthony is a parody of offensive sexism. Sorrentino hints at his own awareness of such issues in various ways, such as having Anthony at one point tell another character: "Your sexism is the more reprehensible because it is unconscious" (187). Joyce, too, is writing against certain stereotypical visions of the feminine, but whereas Joyce effectively parodies those visions, Sorrentino ends up parodying (ineffectively) nothing but Joyce. Joyce presents his images of Bella Cohen as threatening female within a context that renders those images ironical, in a specific direction that indicates positive alternative visions. Sorrentino does not.[13] His book may not be anti-feminist, but it is certainly not pro-feminist, either.

In the case of *The French Lieutenant's Woman*, male fantasies of the feminine form the very core of the novel. Michael is right in suggesting that Sarah does not function as an overt image of a woman who breaks free of these fantasies. As she puts it: "The ideological nature of any perspective is undeniable and in this case the male perspective, which has been and still is dominant in western culture, brings to the novel all sorts of preconceptions and myths about women" (225). Sarah clearly remains inscribed within those preconceptions and myths. But I would suggest that, in the final analysis, Fowles's text, read transgressively, strikes a blow against those myths by revealing just how immanent they are and how difficult they are to escape. By making the ideology of such myths central in his novel, Fowles offers a point at which feminist critics can begin to expose those ideologies for what they are.

Michael herself decries the "undeniable absence of the issue of feminism or emancipation of women in *The French Lieutenant's Woman*" (226). In particular, she is concerned that there is no positive feminist voice in the novel. But I would suggest that she herself supplies that voice in her critique. Bennett suggests that Marxist critics should not look for Marxist voices in texts so much as they should seek to supply those voices themselves: "The task which faces Marxist criticism is not that of reflecting or of bringing to light the politics which is already there, as a latent presence within the text which has but to be made manifest. It is that of actively politicizing the text, of making its politics for it" (167–68). I would suggest that Bennett's comments hold true of feminist criticism as well. This is not to say that Marxist or feminist critics should ignore what they find to be objectionable or offensive in certain texts. It is simply to suggest that the task of criticism is not to judge texts, praising or condemning them for having the right or wrong ideologies. Rather, critics should seek to explore the ramifications of the effects produced in their readings within an ideological framework. In Chapter 5 I shall continue to explore this mode of reading by examining the uses of the motif of castration in a variety of literary texts. Such motifs lend themselves to vulgar and reductive readings of both psychoanalytic and feminist varieties, and it is easy enough in most cases to interpret them as a reflection of the author's fear of castration, and particularly of the feminine. Easy, but not very useful. I will seek more productive ways to read this motif.

"THE PENIS HE THOUGHT WAS HIS OWN":
CASTRATION AS LITERARY TRANSGRESSION

CHAPTER

5 ─────────────────────────────────

Castration itself does not function as one of the images that
Kristeva directly associates with the abject. Yet, given the horror
which it invokes and its explicit relation to physicality, castration bears a close relation to abjection. Especially within the
framework of Lacanian psychoanalysis, castration functions as
an image of loss, of the void that is at the heart of human existence. Most images of abjection (death, excrement, etc.) represent universal (if unpleasant) facts of human existence, but
castration occupies a special position among abject images because of its inherently dual, gender-coded nature. If the repression of abjection is related to the oppression of marginal groups,
then castration as abjection would seem to have a special resonance with the oppression of women, who have often been considered as both castrated and castrating, especially in psychoanalysis. Exploring the representation of castration in literary
works should provide fertile ground for transgressive readings
that expose the dynamics of this oppression.

Teresa de Lauretis argues that castration is the cardinal theme
of Italo Calvino's *If on a winter's night a traveler*, suggesting
that the various fragmented texts that appear in the book are
themselves castration images. Moreover, de Lauretis maintains
that Lotaria, the book's "feminist" character, is presented as a

threatening, castrating female, the implication of which is that Calvino is reacting to a perceived threat from the feminist sector. De Lauretis is herself highly (and rightfully) suspicious of the essentialism she sees embedded in psychoanalysis, but her diagnosis of Calvino at first seems based on a rather pedestrian application of the standard Freudian concept of castration anxiety. She indeed labels one bit of her textual evidence for the importance of castration in Calvino's book as "one of the classic 'Psychical Consequences of the Anatomical Distinction between the Sexes' described by Freud" (77).

It would be simple enough for de Lauretis to move from here to a reading of the presence of the castration motif in Calvino as a thoroughly conservative gesture, as an anxious reaction against the threat posed by feminism to traditional male power. But Calvino himself is perfectly aware of such interpretations and explicitly mocks them in his book. At one point he depicts a meeting of Lotaria's feminist reading group. In the meeting, literary buzzwords fly through the air in a virtuoso outburst of interpretive cliché:

"The polymorphic-perverse sexuality . . . "
"The laws of market economy . . . "
"The homologies of the signifying structures . . . "
"Deviations and institutions . . . "
"Castration . . . "

(91, Calvino's ellipses)

Perhaps the prominence of the castration theme in Calvino's text is not so much conservative as transgressive: it parodies both psychoanalysis and feminism as "official" modes of interpreting texts.[1] De Lauretis, showing less appreciation for the potential of Calvino's irony than she might, does not opt for this transgressive reading, which would see his depiction of Lotaria as an attack on stereotypical representations of the castrating feminist.[2] But de Lauretis is far too subtle and sophisticated a critic to settle for the simple conservative reading, either. For one thing, when she contrasts the objectionable depiction of male-female relations in *If on a winter's night* to a more acceptable example, she eschews the easy route of referring to a work by a woman writer, instead citing another story by Calvino. She thus eschews the insipid option of merely relating the theme of feminine threat in *If on a winter's night* to Calvino's personal psychology, a failing to which critics such as Gilbert and Gubar so often fall prey in their readings of male writers.

De Lauretis supplements the psychoanalytic implications of her reading of Calvino with cultural and semiotic ones, noting that Calvino's text "does not simply inscribe popular received wisdom but actually engages contemporary theories of signification" (79). In particular, she sees *If on a winter's night* as being symptomatic of a postmodernist crisis in signification. After Saussure, we all know that language is based on difference, and de Lauretis suggests that gender difference is paradigmatic of this effect. But (according to de Lauretis) feminism has deprived contemporary authors of an easy identification of woman as the Other, which translates into a threat to the ability to signify at all. Postmodernist writers thus often react against feminism, despite the fact that the two movements seem to have many common goals:

Because, I suggest, Woman is still the ground of representation, even in postmodern times. Paradoxically, for all the efforts spent to re-contain women in the social, whether by economic or ideological means, by threats or by seduction, it is the absent Woman, the one pursued in dreams and found only in memory or in fiction, that serves as the guarantee of masculinity, anchoring male identity and supporting man's creativity and self-representation. (82)

The phenomenon that de Lauretis describes here partakes directly of the Lacanian notion that the difference upon which language is based is grounded in the perception of gender difference acquired at the assumption of a subjective identity. In fact, her suggestion tends to make Lacan an extremely representative figure of postmodernism, playing much the same role often attributed to Freud in modernism. This Lacanian (or anti-Lacanian) slant in her argument places her emphasis on castration in an interesting light; "castration" can take on significantly different intonations within a Lacanian framework than within a conventional Freudian one. Moreover, de Lauretis's appeal to cultural and semiotic fields of information emphasizes that there are ways of reading the motif of castration outside of a psychonanalytic framework that can lead to considerably different interpretations.

One must apply psychoanalytic concepts to postmodernist texts with a great deal of caution (and irony), as the target of postmodernist transgression is often psychoanalysis itself. One thinks here of Vladimir Nabokov's famous definition of psycho-analysis as the "daily application of Greek myths to one's private parts." Indeed, Nabokov's mockery of psychoanalysis in texts such as *Lolita* and *Pale Fire* is emblematic of the effect I am describing. Consider his description of Humbert Humbert as he contemplates the murder of Claire Quilty, when he would have "pulled the pistol's foreskin back, and then enjoyed the orgasm of the crushed trigger: I was always a good little follower of the Viennese medicine man" (276). Nabokov is openly mocking Freud here, and any explication of this passage as something more than a parody of psychoanalysis inevitably blows up in the analyst's face. Sometimes, in postmodernism, an exploding cigar is just an exploding cigar.

Still, psychoanalysis can be used (at least analogically) to illuminate certain transgressive aspects of postmodernist texts. For example, from the point of view of Lacanian psychoanalysis, in which the "phallus" becomes a symbolic scepter of paternal authority, castration can be viewed as a transgression of that authority.[3] Donald Barthelme employs castration in this symbolic sense in *The Dead Father*. At one point the travelers (including the Father himself, his daughter Julie, and his son Thomas) reach an outpost of civilization only to find that the Father will not be allowed to enter without certain modifications. They are stopped by a guard who explains:

You'll have to deballock him and wipe your feet on the mat, said the man. . . . Do you need a deballocking knife? Scissors? Razor? Paper cutter? Shard of glass? Letter opener? Fingernail clippers? (134)

The Father, however, is less than enthusiastic at the man's generosity with his utensils, much to Julie's puzzlement:

Amazing how he holds on to his balls, said Julie, that is a curious thing, I don't understand it.
I understand it, said Thomas. (135)

As exemplified throughout *The Dead Father*, paternal authority (functioning as a trope for the authority of tradition in general) is a favorite target of postmodernist literary transgression. But an interpretation of all literary images of castration as transgressions against the Law of the Father would be just as simpleminded as interpreting them all as expressions of fear of being dominated by women. The motif is complex and multiply coded, and bears detailed study.

According to Lacan, for example, gaps, wounds, cuts, and other images of threat to bodily integrity open up an access to the Real Order and to the potential terrors of *jouissance*. Given Lacan's emphasis on the symbolic importance of the phallus, a wound to the physical genitalia might have even more significance. In particular, castration might be expected to be closely related to that dark side of jouissance that Julia Kristeva has described as abjection. Kristeva explores the topic of abjection in some detail in her book *Powers of Horror*. Although working from a largely Lacanian perspective, Kristeva also discusses social implications of abjection, relating it to the "demarcating imperative," the process through which societies base their identities on systems and hierarchies, particularly on the attempt to separate the "clean" from the "filthy" and thus to suppress abject images, which are associated with the latter (68). Abjection is thus at the heart of social systems, and literature that explores this topic has an especially subversive potential because it can "lay bare, under the cunning, orderly surface of civilizations, the nurturing horror that they attend to pushing aside by purifying, systematizing, and thinking" (210). Abject images in literature thus carry a powerful transgressive potential.

CASTRATION IN THE LITERARY TRADITION

Castration as a metaphor for the subversion of paternal authority considerably predates both postmodernism and Lacan. For example, there is a version of the myth of the Fall, popular in the Middle Ages, that depicts this original transgression in terms of the castration of the Father. In the *Romance of the Rose* Reason explains this motif, indicating that the fall of mankind began with the fall of Saturn, "whose testicles Jupiter, his hard and bitter son, cut off as though they were sausages and threw into the sea" (113).

Within a Freudian framework, the Oedipal reverberations of such images are rather obvious, and (given Freud's own emphasis on the significance of myth) it is not surprising that castration is a common mythic theme. However, in the Freudian model of the relationship between father and son what goes around comes around, and castration functions both as a figure of liberation from the power of the father and of anxiety over the loss of one's own power through paternal domination. Mythic representations of castration are thus often much more complex than the relatively transparent story of the castration of Saturn by Jupiter. For example, in an Egyptian myth with interesting feminist implications, the scattered body of the god Osiris is reassembled by his sister Isis, but she is unable to locate his severed phallus and is forced to manufacture an artificial substitute. Here, the male literally acquires his masculinity directly from the female, in precisely the movement that de Lauretis describes in a more symbolic sense.

Myths of castration often take the form of stories of self-mutilation. Frazer relates the myth of the Phrygian vegetation god Attis, who "unmanned himself under a pine-tree, and bled to death on the spot" (404). Attis here may have been following in his father's footsteps, since myth has it that his mother conceived "by putting into her bosom a pomegranate sprung from the severed genitals of a man-monster named Agdestis, a sort of double of Attis" (Frazer 406). Frazer suggests that the myth of Attis's self-mutilation is an attempt to account for the self-emasculation of the eunuch priests of the cult of the goddess Cybele. In fact, the priests of a number of pagan cults are given to self-castration, as Frazer notes. Of course, castration, self-inflicted or otherwise, is not the exclusive province of pagans. The example of the early church father Origen—not to mention the tradition of castrated choir boys—reminds us that genitalia can lead a precarious existence in Christianity as well.

In the Middle Ages castration (like so many other things) was felt to have great symbolic significance. Carolyn Dinshaw has discussed the significance of Chaucer's treatment of the Pardoner as a eunuch, noting the prevalence of castration as a medieval theme. For example, Abelard, a famous medieval castrato, "built his career as a Christian philosopher upon his castration" (Dinshaw 29).[4] In particular, Dinshaw sees castration as a metaphor for a particular kind of textuality. She discusses the way in which "medieval writers from Macrobius to Richard of Bury" imaged the fictional text as being "like a woman, extravagantly and seductively arrayed." These writers recommend the reading of texts via what Dinshaw calls a "heterosexual hermeneutic," a mode of reading in which the interpreter evades the seductions of the body of the text while at the same time stripping it of the garments of its material language and penetrating to the truth or spirit that lies behind the text (27–28). In opposition to this kind of drive for textual mastery, Dinshaw proposes the example of the "Pardoner's Tale," in which the physical fragmentation of the eunuch Pardoner is dramatized in the very language of his text. Dinshaw notes this characteristic of the Pardoner's language and suggests that it calls for an entirely different mode of reading: "The Pardoner enunciates the only possible strategy of using language in a postlapsarian world, cut off from primary wholeness and unity: he acts according to what I call the hermeneutics of the partial, or, for short, eunuch hermeneutics" (28).

Dinshaw's reading of castration in the "Pardoner's Tale" parallels de Lauretis's treatment of *If on a winter's night a traveler* in the relationship of textual incompleteness to castration. However, Dinshaw emphasizes the potential of the castration motif to subvert authority and totalization. Not that the Pardoner is himself an exemplar of transgression; he is essentially a conservative figure attempting to regain his lost wholeness through the fetishistic replacement of his lost genitals with his "relics."[5] But his use of language exposes the fragmentation that is at the heart of all language, allowing a conservative figure to perform a transgressive function, even if inadvertently.

Early literary treatments of the theme of castration and of sexual wounds in general often reflect a mythic or religious background, as Chaucer's selection of a cleric as his eunuch figure indicates. Thus Encolpius, the hero of *The Satyricon* of Petronius, is rendered impotent by the god Priapus for some unspecified offense. Having his virility momentarily restored by magic, Encolpius attempts to copulate with the goddess Circe, but is struck impotent once again, whereupon Circe angrily retaliates by having him whipped and spat upon. After this incident, Encolpius becomes so frustrated at the inadequate performance of his phallus that he contemplates chopping it off:

Three times I took the murd'rous axe in hand,
Three times I wavered like a wilting stalk

And curtsied from the blade, poor instrument
In trembling hands—I could not what I would.
From terror colder than the wintry frost,
It took asylum far within my crotch,
A thousand wrinkles deep.

(148)

So the recalcitrant organ is saved for the nonce. Later Encolpius
even adds a heroic dimension to his plight; because his impotence is attributable to his persecution by Priapus, he compares
himself to heroes such as Hercules and Ulysses who have also
been cursed by gods:

Now I too take my stand among these—
Over land and white Nereus' sea, I am hounded
By the mighty rage of Priapus of Hellespont.

(157)

Indeed, Sullivan points out "the parody of the *Odyssey* which
runs through *The Satyricon*" (19). In this vein, Petronius seems
to anticipate Joyce, with Encolpius's wanderings about the ancient world being highly reminiscent of Leopold Bloom's wanderings about Dublin in *Ulysses*. Note, moreover, how Encolpius's treatment by Circe anticipates the humilations of
Bloom at the hands of the Circean whoremistress Bella Cohen in
Joyce's "Circe" chapter.

Indeed, Bloom's temporary transformation into a female in
"Circe" can be read as a sort of castration. But the resemblance
between Petronius and Joyce on such points is not surprising,
given that both *The Satyricon* and *Ulysses* are closely related to
the transgressive tradition of Menippean satire. Works in this
genre quite frequently feature phallic imagery of various sorts,
including castration. In Rabelais's *Gargantua and Pantagruel*,
the birth of the giant Gargantua is (understandably) difficult for
his mother Grandgousier, who suggests to his father that "I wish
to heaven you had it cut off" to avoid such difficulties in the
future (51). Surprisingly, he gladly agrees to do so, whereupon
Grandgousier withdraws her request. But Rabelais (like Freud)
understands that castration has significance for both fathers and
sons. As Gargantua grows into boyhood, his nurses enjoy playing
with his member so much that they fight over it, one threaten-

ing to cut it off if she doesn't get her share. But she is quickly rebuked: "Cut it off. Why, that would hurt him, Madam. Is it your way to cut off childern's things? Why, then he'd be Master Short" (63).

In English literature, Laurence Sterne (a great admirer of Rabelais) partakes of this same Menippean tradition. Sterne is much more circumspect than Rabelais, working more by double entendre than by the outrageous directness of his French predecessor. But the idea of castration lingers constantly in the text of *Tristram Shandy*, whether it be in relation to Uncle Toby's unfortunate war wound or to Tristram's accidental "circumcision" by a falling window sash. Significantly, the text is also infused with a sense of problematic paternity. There are numerous hints that Tristram's parentage is suspect. Walter Shandy at one point wonders aloud who the tall Tristram "takes after." "I am very short myself," grumbles Walter. "You are very short," replies his wife, and the hint is clear, especially in light of the passage from Rabelais cited above (308). Hints of questionable parentage and of phallic inadequacy are intertwined throughout the text. Tristram, for example, tells us that "nothing was well hung in our family" (264). Even the family mare bears a progeny of suspicious paternity, and even the family bull is impotent.[6]

Richard Macksey has noted the way in which Sterne's treatment of paternity and castration addresses "topics central to Lacan's enterprise." Thus, *Tristram Shandy* is

an extended meditation on thwarted paternity and its
consequences, on a theory of reading that attends to the subversive
possibilities of signification, on proto-Freudian topics like the
primal scene, castration, and verbal wit, and supremely on a comic
narrative that elaborates the cross-implications of sexuality and
language—inscribed under a death's head. (1008)[7]

The examples of Sterne and his Menippean predecessors dramatically illustrate that the literary representation of castration and other phallic violence is certainly not new to the literature of our century. However, Macksey's mention of "proto-Freudian topics" in Sterne points to one important difference that must be taken into account in the interpretation of such episodes: modern writers write after Freud and are thus conscious of the Freudian significance of such topics. One significant difference between pre- and post-Freudian texts is that the latter often employ Freudian imagery in a direct attempt either to instantiate or to undermine Freudian interpretations.

CASTRATION AS ABJECTION
IN MODERN LITERATURE

During the nineteenth century, graphic, sexually related imagery was rare in Anglo-American literature, and when such imagery resurfaced in the twentieth century it was often with a specifically Freudian orientation. One result was that, with the exception of writers such as Joyce who carried on the Menippean tradition, the depiction of castration often became a matter for quite serious treatment, far different than the comic exuberance with which the technique was invested in the works of authors such as Petronius, Rabelais, and Sterne. William Faulkner's treatment of Joe Christmas in *Light in August* is illustrative of this development, although even Faulkner's use of castration as an image of abjection occurs in a context with certain carnivalesque overtones. Christmas is himself in many ways an exemplary figure of transgression. He both commits heinous acts and has them committed upon him. Moreover, he is characterized by a fundamental and irreducible ambiguity. When we first see him he is presented as a mysterious and somewhat sinister stranger, though a highly ambiguous one:

He looked like a tramp, yet not like a tramp either. His shoes were dusty and his trousers were soiled too. But they were of decent serge, sharply creased, and his shirt was soiled but it was a white shirt, and he wore a tie and a stiffbrim straw hat that was quite new. . . . He did not look like a professional hobo in his professional rags, but there was something definitely homeless about him. (63)

None of these contradictions will be resolved as the book proceeds. We never learn with certainty whether Christmas is black or white, villain or victim, homosexual or heterosexual, leading Martin Kreiswirth to call Christmas a "virtual walking oxymoron" (63). The foreshadowing of the role that Christmas will play in the novel becomes more explicit when the men at the mill begin to discuss his absurd name. "Did you ever hear of a white man named Christmas?" asks the foreman, and the name seems to carry ominous tones of danger:

there was something in the sound of it that was trying to tell them what to expect; that he carried with him his own inescapable warning, like a flower its scent or a rattlesnake its rattle. (29)

Even this passage carries a note of ambivalence: the image of the rattlesnake is combined with the image of a flower, creating two decidedly different effects.

The height of abjection in *Light in August* occurs when Faulkner's proto–storm trooper Percy Grimm fatally shoots Christmas, then sexually mutilates him as he dies:

when they saw what Grimm was doing one of the men gave a choked cry and stumbled back into the wall and began to vomit. Then Grimm too sprang back, flinging behind him the bloody butcher knife. "Now you'll let white women alone, even in hell," he said. (439)

Again, this scene is open to multiple interpretations. While the castration motif here bears little similarity to the way it is used in the Menippean tradition, it does participate in another consciously literary mode, the strain of Southern Gothic that runs through so much of Faulkner's work.[8] This scene also seems calculated to trigger a strong reader response. Michael Millgate suggests that the story of Christmas is specifically constructed to elicit reader involvement:

But the great and unifying strength of the book remains its most obvious one: the sheer force and passion of its presentation of Joe Christmas, the quintessential victim, and the way in which we, like all the characters in the book, are irresistibly swept into the vortex of Christmas's restless life and agonising death. (137)

Many commentators have also noted the symbolic significance of Christmas's name, seeing him as a figure of Christ. His mutilation thus partakes of some of the mythic tradition of the castrated god. Robert Slabey argues that the story of Christmas is directly related to myths of death and regeneration, seeing Christmas as a figure of Adonis (77–81).[9] Slabey thus notes that the wounding of Adonis by a boar "is always a symbolic castration if not an anatomical one" (78). Moreover, Frazer links

Adonis to Attis, suggesting that Attis "was to Phrygia what Adonis was to Syria" (403).

Myths of death and rebirth are closely related to the motif of ritual crowning and uncrowning that is central to Bakhtin's conception of the carnival.[10] Indeed, Kreiswirth has suggested that *Light in August* epitomizes the polyphonic novel described by Bakhtin: "*Light in August* thus keeps both the individual voices and the silences between those voices inexhaustibly present. It is the kind of truly polyphonic structure that Bakhtin sees as the special province and the ultimate goal of the novel as a genre" (78). This identification with the polyphonic novel suggests a potential political force. For example, Grimm stands as a clear image of the totalitarian mentality, and his mutilation of Christmas is a clear link between sadism and authoritarianism.[11] Millgate hints at a political orientation when he argues that the theme of the book is "the demand of organised society and organised religion that the human individual act in strict accordance with prescribed abstract patterns" (127–28). Irving Howe sees a similar social statement in the novel, arguing that it is "Faulkner's most sustained confrontation of modern society" (62). And Richard Pearce notes that the book dramatizes the demands of a society in which "there is no compromise between being Negro or white, 'Christian' or immoral, heterosexual or homosexual" ("Faulkner's One Ring Circus" 272). In short, it effects a transgression of the kinds of fundamental categories upon which the power structure of modern society is based.

Faulkner's contemporary, Ernest Hemingway, uses the shock effect of phallic violence to confront the evils of the religious repression of sexuality in his short story "God Rest You Merry, Gentlemen." Set at Christmas time for increased effect, the story concerns a young boy obsessed by sexual guilt of religious origins who decides to castrate himself, but doesn't quite know just what castration entails. As a result of this ignorance, he cuts off his penis and bleeds to death, à la Attis. Hemingway's story gains a great deal of power from this motif, and the link between its Christmas setting and Faulkner's Joe Christmas may not be entirely devoid of significance. As the example of Origen indicates, Christianity and genitalia have long been at odds, even as God himself stands as the most potent phallic authority of all. Indeed, Hemingway makes a special point of emphasizing the symbolic significance of the date on which this mutilation occurs:

"On Christmas day, too," Doctor Wilcox said.
"The significance of the particular day is not important," Doc Fischer said.
"Maybe not to you," said Doctor Wilcox. (396)[12]

Probably the best-known presentation of "castration" as commentary on man's condition in the modern world occurs in Hemingway's story of the wartime emasculation of Jake Barnes in *The Sun Also Rises*, though Barnes (like the boy in the above story) has lost his penis rather than his testicles. The significance here again seems highly symbolic, both in terms of psychological characterization of Barnes and in terms of a commentary on the barren emptiness of life in post–World War I Europe. Hemingway is conceivably echoing Sterne (without the comic orientation) in the use of this motif, but the most obvious echo is of T. S. Eliot's *The Waste Land*. Eliot's poem can be interpreted in many ways, but he himself indicates in his published notes to the poem that it is based on the Grail legend as described in Jessie L. Weston's book, *From Ritual to Romance*. This legend has various forms, but basically deals with a land that is ruled by a Fisher King who has suffered a sexual illness or wound rendering him impotent. As a result, the land itself has become barren and sterile, a waste land. The only hope for salvation lies in the possibility that a questing knight (after perhaps undergoing various ordeals) will appear to ask the meaning of the Grail and the Lance, whereupon the Fisher King will be healed and the land returned to fertility.[13] Jake Barnes, sexual cripple and fisherman extraordinaire, can certainly be identified by the reader with the Fisher King, despite Hemingway's claim to have gotten the idea of the sexual wound from his own personal observations during World War I:

I wondered what a man's life would have been like after that if his penis had been lost and his testicles and spermatic cord remained intact. I had known a boy that happened to. So I took him and made him into a foreign correspondent in Paris and, inventing, tried to find out what his problems would be when he was in love with someone who was in love with him and there was nothing they could do about it. (Baker 745)

The use of sexual violence as an metaphor for abjection extends to postmodernist texts as well, and no discussion of this subject would be complete without mention of William S. Burroughs, the postmodern master of abjection. Burroughs's *Naked Lunch* is particularly filled with examples of shocking sexual violence, perpetrated against both sexes, but more often on males (especially boys) than on females. The notorious Orgasm Death Gimmick is perhaps the most shocking example of all. In this gruesome scene, a young boy is sodomized and hanged, causing him to have an erection. He is then raped and cannibalized:

Mark reaches over with a sharp knife and cuts the rope, catching Johnny as he falls, easing him onto his back with Mary still impaled and writhing. . . . She bites away Johnny's lips and nose and sucks out his eyes with a pop. . . . She tears off great hunks of cheek. . . . Now she lunches on his prick. . . . Mark walks over to her and she looks up from Johnny's half-eaten genitals, her face covered with blood, eyes phosphorescent. (97, Burroughs's ellipses)

It would be easy enough to read this scene as a depiction of feminine threat, with Mary playing the role of castrating, devouring female in a rather literal way, but one should not be too hasty in interpreting this passage. Again, the critic who would leap to this sort of simplistic interpretation would make himself a potential target of Burroughs's satire. After all, excessive literalization is a favorite satiric device of writers such as Jonathan Swift. Burroughs himself characterizes the Orgasm Death Gimmick as Swiftian social satire, claiming in his introduction to *Naked Lunch* that this scene is intended "as a tract against Capital Punishment in the manner of Swift's *Modest Proposal*" (xliv). Matters are complicated still more in that this passage occurs not at the principal narrative level of the text, but within a fantastic pornographic movie set inside the text. Still, the boundaries between this inset film and the surrounding narrative are quite nebulous. As David Lodge points out, the bizarre nature of this movie is no different in character from the text in general, so that "when we come to the Orgasm Death Gimmick, no norms have been established by which its nauseating grotesquerie can be measured and interpreted in the way intended by Burroughs" (38). In fact, as Brian McHale notes, the effect of Burroughs's mode of presentation of this scene has more to do with the general ontological confusion of the text than with either satire or pornography (116–7).

Burroughs is heeding a general movement toward more and more shocking and graphic depictions of transgressive violence in modern literature.[14] With Faulkner and Hemingway behind him, Burroughs must go farther in order to achieve startling effects. Not only is he writing in a period after modernism made it difficult for formal experiments to appear shocking, but he is also writing in the wake of World War II, when the Nazi death camps demonstrated a real-world horror that fiction would be hard-pressed to match. Yet Burroughs's suggestion that the Orgasm Death Gimmick is an allusion to Swift indicates that this scene follows a literary tradition. Moreover, the depiction of such horrors within a movie embedded in the text closely parallels another instance of the dark side of the Irish literary imagination: the similar nightmare scenery of Joyce's "Circe" chapter, a play embedded in *Ulysses*.[15] Indeed, the hanging of the croppy boy in "Circe" anticipates Burroughs quite closely:

The assistants leap at the victim's legs and drag him downward, grunting. The croppy boy's tongue protrudes violently. . . . He gives up the ghost. A violent erection of the hanged sends gouts of sperm spouting through his deathclothes on to the cobblestone. . . . [Rumbold] undoes the noose . . . he plunges his head into the gaping belly of the hanged and draws out his head again clotted with coiled and smoking entrails. (484–85, Joyce's italics)

The Orgasm Death Gimmick, then, can be read in many ways: as an allusion to both Swift and Joyce, as a commentary on capital punishment, as a satire against oversimplistic reading, and as a metafictional commentary on the uncertain boundaries between fiction and reality.

Graphic phallic violence on a more realistic level occurs in John Irving's *The World According to Garp*, where the illicit episode of fellatio between Michael Milton and Garp's wife ends in disaster for the former when Garp inadvertently crashes his car into theirs:

Helen's mouth was snapped shut with such force that she broke two teeth and required two neat stitches in her tongue. At first she thought she had bitten her tongue off, because she could feel it swimming in her mouth, which was full of blood. . . . It wasn't her tongue, of course. It was what amounted to three quarters of Michael Milton's penis. (268)

Irving's offhand presentation endows this episode with an oddly distant quality (which is further increased by Milton's not being a likable character). Reader reaction to Milton's fate is also tempered by the fact that, in the same accident, Garp's small son Duncan is seriously injured, including the loss of an eye.[16] And the episode is made still less affecting by contrast to the story of Ellen James, an eleven-year-old girl who is raped and then has her tongue cut out Philomel-style by her attackers.

CASTRATION AS SELF-CONSCIOUS TROPE

Irving's presentation of Michael Milton's unfortunate accident within the context of the rape of Ellen James and the injury to Duncan Garp is emblematic of a turn in more contemporary texts toward the self-conscious use of castration images as a literary trope. The seemingly inappropriate casualness of the language with which this scene is described calls attention to the language itself and to the fictionality of the narrative. It is as if the reader is being pulled in two directions at once, being drawn into closer identification with the text through the character of the action being narrated, but being distanced from the text by the unemotional tone of the narration itself.

David Hayman describes this sort of effect as "double-distancing," seeing it as one of the principal techniques that distinguish modern literature from the literature of previous eras. He cites as particularly illustrative of this technique the work of the Marquis de Sade, whose texts are "simultaneously over- and underdistanced, works that eschew middle distance, preferring to oscillate boldly between cool intellection and heated engagement" (Re-Forming the Narrative 23). Although Hayman does not pursue the social and political implications of double-distancing, he does note how this movement tends to break down the distinction between centers and margins, between the accepted and the excluded, noting that Samuel Beckett's use of this technique "has established, thematically as well as formally, the centrality of the excluded" (42).

This breaking down of barriers is obviously central to literary transgression. It also directly recalls Kristeva's suggestion that texts of abjection call attention to what societies have excluded and suppressed in order to define themselves. But Hayman's analysis of the work of writers such as de Sade, Beckett, and Lautréamont indicates the extent to which the use of images of abjection (such as castration) has become a self-conscious literary device in modern literature. There is, in fact, a danger that such images will become so conventionalized as to be deprived of any real political impact. Again, it is useful here to consider the mechanism that Bakhtin refers to as "canonization": the process (a form of objectification) by which literature appropriates and subsumes social voices, turning them into a merely literary language divested of dialogic force (*Dialogic Imagination* 417–18). Much of the turn toward more and more graphic depictions of abject scenes in recent literature (such as in Burroughs) can then be attributed to a desire to overcome this conventionalization and to restore some of the emotional effect of such scenes.

Irving's offhand presentation of Michael Milton's accident can be interpreted as an attempt to defamiliarize the event by describing it in surprising language, thereby restoring some of the shock effect. Irving's language is reminiscent of Robert Coover's deadpan mode of narration in "The Marker," one of the "Seven Exemplary Fictions" in his *Pricksongs and Descants*. In a text filled with parodic representations of all sorts of primal terrors, the story's main character, Jason, marks his place and puts down a book he is reading in order to make love to his seductive wife. He turns out the light and climbs into bed, but something doesn't seem right; a police officer and four assistants suddenly burst into the room to find that he (much to his own surprise) is making love to a long-dead corpse. Disgusted with the abjection of Jason's necrophilia, the intruders "hold him up against the table and the police officer, without ceremony, pulls Jason's genitals out flat on the tabletop and pounds them to a pulp with the butt of his gun" (91). Then, as if that weren't enough, the officer adds insult to injury by thumbing through Jason's book and allowing the marker to fall out, losing his place.

Even with this ironic ending, and even with the generally comic tone, it would be ever so easy to critique Coover's story as anxious and conservative. Jason's wife, significantly, is nameless, beautiful and affectionate, a perfect sex object. Her transformation into a corpse reveals a secret horror of the physical that associates everything feminine, especially feminine sexuality, with abject images of death and decay. The intrusion of the police into the scene and the subsequent mutilation of Jason's genitals reveal the terror associated with yielding to the lures of the feminine, as well as the guilt associated with sexuality in general.

And so on. But such interpretations are a little too obvious, and in the end they are impoverishing, leaving out much that is interesting about the story. Does Jason's name indicate a parodic link to the quest myth? What are we to make of the role of the book that Jason is reading in the story? What about the fact that at the end of the story Jason seems more concerned about losing his place in his book than about the sad condition of his genitalia?[17] Does not the police officer's expression of disgust at Jason's necrophilia place him in the position of a reader who would be disgusted at Coover's presentation of such a scene? The whole story can be read as an allegory of reading, as a satire on the desire that propels readers through plots. In this case, the lost book marker and the pulped genitals both function as emblems of lost textual mastery, whether the text being mastered is a book or a woman. And if (as I suggested in my comments on Fowles) the structure of the traditional narrative plot parallels the movement of the male sex act, then the surprising turn taken by Jason's lovemaking becomes a reflexive commentary on the way in which stories such as Coover's disrupt the reader's expectations associated with conventional laws of realistic plot structure. Thus Coover, in keeping with his highly metafictional mode, takes advantage of (and parodies) the canonization of castration into a literary trope and uses the motif as a commentary on the nature of his own text, much in the same manner as does Calvino.

This use of castration as a trope for a certain kind of textuality goes back to the Middle Ages, as Dinshaw has shown. But it is an especially common postmodern motif. For example, in addition to Calvino and Coover, we have the case of Salman Rushdie's Saleem Sinai, the narrator of *Midnight's Children*. Sinai begins to fragment and split apart as the narrative progresses, mirroring the fragmented condition of the narrative itself. And this fragmentation is quite literal: cracks propagate through his bones as he physically begins to disintegrate. Rushdie also gives the motif a specifically political twist, suggesting that Sinai's dissolution arises from the split between India and Pakistan. Rushdie suggests that Sinai falls apart because he is "abandoning consciousness, seceding from history" (420).

In keeping with the dual physical and political nature of Sinai's fragmentation (and with the clear influence of *Tristram Shandy* on Rushdie's text), his fate also includes castration at the hands of the minions of the Widow, India's sinister Prime Minister. In fact, all 430 of the remaining Midnight's Children, male and female, are rounded up and sterilized or castrated to prevent them from producing offspring who might eventually become a political problem. Rushdie's description of the actual operation is quite direct and to the point:

They were good doctors: they left nothing to chance. Not for us the simple vas- and tubectomies performed on the teeming masses; because there was a chance, just a chance that such operations could be reversed . . . ectomies were performed, but irreversibly: testicles were removed from sacs, and wombs vanished for ever. (523)

Again, it would be easy to see the Widow (a thinly veiled version of Indira Gandhi) as a typical representation of the threatening, castrating female. However, this surgical procedure is carried out on women as well as men, and is administered by the evil (male) Major Shiva, Sinai's alter ego.[18] The sterilization of Sinai and his fellows is more usefully interpreted in political than in psychological terms, especially as the Children of Midnight were all born simultaneously with the birth of the Indian Republic, making them figures of the new nation and making their surgeries emblematic of (among other things) the scission between India and Pakistan that figures so prominently in Rushdie's work.[19] In Sinai's case, the castration is also a symbol of the inadequacy of his narrative, and in particular of the incompleteness of our representations of history.

In a manner very similar to *Midnight's Children*, the text of Pynchon's *Gravity's Rainbow* fragments in conjunction with the scattering of the central character, Tyrone Slothrop. Slothrop's disintegration is also related to the motif of the sexual wound. For example, it is hinted throughout the book that Slothrop received in infancy some sort of experimental Pavlovian conditioning at the hands of the sinister Dr. Laszlo Jamf. Just what that conditioning was never becomes clear, but it seems linked with Slothrop's genital functioning. Indeed, there are hints that Slothrop's genitalia may have been somehow surgically altered, or perhaps even replaced entirely by a synthetic apparatus composed of the mysterious Imipolex G.

Slothrop's story is obviously intended as an allegory of the twentieth-century predicament in general, though the general ontological confusion and overdetermination of the book make precise interpretation of the allegory difficult. There is, for example, a clear Freudian aspect to Slothrop's misfortunes, and the association of the phallus with law and authority could also lead to a variety of Lacanian interpretations as well. Note, for example, Pynchon's use of the "penis of commendation" as a symbol of approval by recognized authority (516). However, Pynchon self-consciously complicates any Oedipal interpretations of Slothrop's plight. In a sort of parodic reformulation of the Oedipal situation, we discover the complicity of Slothrop's father in the sexual experiments that were performed on the infant. It is not sons who murder fathers in *Gravity's Rainbow*, but vice versa:

there is a villain here, serious as death. It is this typical American teenager's own Father, trying episode after episode to kill his son. And the kid knows it. Imagine that. So far he's managed to escape his father's little death-plots—but nobody has said he has to keep escaping. (674)

This particular symbolic aspect is echoed many times throughout the book, in which parents often appear as sinister figures in relation to their children. Mothers in the Zone turn out to be anything but objects of sexual desire, and the family triangle leads to a never-ending cycle of frustration and repression:

The Oedipal situation in the Zone these days is terrible. There is
no dignity. The mothers have been masculinized to old worn
moneybags of no sexual interest to anyone, and yet there are their
sons, still trapped inside inertias of lust that are 40 years out of
date. The fathers have no power today and never did, but because 40
years ago we could not kill them, we are condemned now to the
same passivity, the same masochist fantasies they cherished in
secret, and worse, we are condemned in our weakness to
impersonate men of power our own infant children must hate, and
wish to usurp the place of, and fail. . . . (747, Pynchon's ellipsis)

Thus, the Oedipal (or anti-Oedipal) theme is linked to the
general (paranoid) idea of determination and conditioning that
functions throughout *Gravity's Rainbow*. In this vein, Pirate
Prentice receives a secret message from Them that only becomes visible when coated with semen, and finds that They
have thoughtfully supplied a pornographic picture corresponding exactly to his innermost sexual fantasies to aid him in sum-
moning up the requisite fluid. The implications are ominous:

Like every young man growing up in England, he was conditioned
to get a hardon in the presence of certain fetishes, and then
conditioned to feel shame about his new reflexes. Could there be,
somewhere, a dossier, could They (They?) somehow have managed
to monitor everything he saw and read since puberty . . . how else
would They know? (71–72, Pynchon's ellipsis)

Slothrop's penis, then, becomes an emblem for the loss of
personal freedom in a modern society that is controlled by vast,
impersonal forces. These forces seek to take away all privacy and
personal freedom, even down to very personal things. Slothrop
cannot even be sure that his penis is his own, as symbolized by
the inserted song "The Penis He Thought Was His Own":

But They came through the hole in the night,
And They sweet-talked it clear out of sight—
Out of sight . . .
Now he sighs all alone,
With a heartbroken moan,
For the pe-nis, he thought-was, his, owwwwn!
(217, Pynchon's ellipsis)

On the surface, this motif would appear to validate strikingly Lacan's notion of the phallus as always already lost. But Pynchon's explicitness renders any such interpretation superfluous, and the clear social and political implications of Slothrop's predicament far exceed any interpretation that relies strictly on the centripetal framework of the Oedipal family.

The links between Slothrop's sexual conditioning and larger trends in twentieth-century society are also strengthened by the fact that his erections are somehow keyed to the arrival of German rockets in World War II London. It should be emphasized, however, that it is impossible to recover the true "meaning" of Slothrop's condition (or of its relation to the rockets) from Pynchon's text. In fact, much of the symbolism involving Slothrop's penis contributes to little more than a textual wild-goose chase on the part of the reader, who is tantalized by information that can never be fully converted to understanding. Once again, the incompleteness symbolized by castration is related to an inability to achieve interpretive mastery of the text.

The technological threat to freedom (and especially to fertility and sexual potency) is represented by the mysterious relationship of Slothrop's penis to the synthetic Imipolex G. However, this aspect of Pynchon's phallic allegory is even more explicitly represented by the limericks inserted in the middle portion of the book, almost all of which deal with unfortunate encounters between male genitalia and various technological contraptions. For example, we have:

There once was a fellow named Ritter,
Who slept with a guidance transmitter.
    It shriveled his cock,
    Which fell off in his sock,
And made him exceedingly bitter.
              (334)

These limericks make Pynchon's point about the dehumanizing (and desexualizing, which may be the same thing) effects of technology very directly, but at the same time their blatant fatuousness undermines any simple interpretation of his message. Thus, the limericks embody Pynchon's most common techniques for undermining the interpretation of his allegory: making it overexplicit, and making it silly.

Not only does *Gravity's Rainbow* provide a wealth of instances of the allegorical use of phallic violence, it also provides many examples of the use of such violence for shock and for comic effect as well, adding to the complication of interpreting the allegory. In terms of shock effect, many scenes in the book can rival Burroughs at his best (or perhaps worst), and indeed one can detect a possible influence of Burroughs in many scenes. The most notoriously abject sexual imagery in the *Rainbow* probably occurs in the graphic episode of coprophagia and sexual humiliation between Brigadier Pudding and Katje Borgesius (as Domina Nocturna) (232–36). But in terms of specific violence directed against male sex organs, the detailed surgical description of the castration of Major Marvy (who is mistaken for Slothrop) has to take the prize:

Muffage decides to dispense with shaving the scrotum. He douses it first with iodine, then squeezes in turn each testicle against the red-veined and hairy bag, makes the incision quickly and cleanly through skin and surrounding membranes, popping the testicle itself out through the wound and welling blood, pulling it out with the left hand till the cords hard and soft are strung visible under the light. . . . he severs them at the proper distances from the slippery stone, each incision then being bathed in disinfectant, and the two neat slits, side by side, finally sutured up again. The testicles are plopped into a bottle of alcohol. (609)

As in the case of Irving's Michael Milton, the shock here is ameliorated by Marvy's unlikable nature, and by a certain relief that it was Marvy and not Slothrop who went under the knife. Like Nabokov, Pynchon makes a point of being overexplicit in his symbolism: the authoritarian Major Marvy, the male chauvinist pig extraordinaire, was mistaken for Slothrop because he was wearing Slothrop's pig costume. This pig costume also gives a carnivalesque twist to the whole episode that, combined with the carnivalesque nature of the text in general, makes it highly subversive.[20]

The theme of castration and phallic violence is often treated comically in postmodernist texts. In *Willie Masters' Lonesome Wife* William H. Gass presents an extended burlesque centered around Ivan's discovery of his own penis baked inside a roll that his wife Olga presents him for breakfast. Gass explains:

Actually, it doesn't matter how this scene is played, for this is what
they call a naturally humorous situation. It's what you want to try
for: a naturally humorous situation. Now a fellow finding his penis
baked in his breakfast roll like a toad in a biscuit—that's a
naturally humorous finding, the very heart of a naturally humorous
situation, and he could say: say, I think I've found my penis baked
in this roll like a toad in a biscuit, and everyone would laugh.
(pages unnumbered)

Gass's playfulness has its ominous aspects, however, particularly the atmosphere of sexual aggression that pervades his little
book. This aggression is especially effective because it is largely
aimed at the reader, who is both seduced and abused by the
lonesome wife. Indeed, what is interesting about Gass's use of
the motif of seduction and castration is what it tells us about
the desire of the reader and of the impossibility of gaining phallic mastery over a text.

In Steve Katz's *The Exagggerations of Peter Prince*, the very
title is a phallic pun, and phallic shenanigans abound. For example, when Peter Prince is captured by tribesmen in Ethiopia, he
awakes to find himself tightly bound and suffering a considerable pain in the groin area. Naturally, he suspects the worst:

"They didn't do that to me," he said aloud, startled at the pitch of
his own voice, and he was afraid to move his hand down to his
testicles to see if they had snipped them off. (11)

Fortunately for Peter Prince, all is well, however, and in fact
what his captors have done is to perform certain procedures that
will actually enhance his sexual performance:

they took it on themselves to cultivate his virility, which they
pitied, because they thought his penis small by their standards,
hardly a phallic trophy, like one of a small boy. They stretched it
with splints and rubbed it with the pitch from the Zegba. . . . The
treatments did work, making of Peter Prince's medium-sized
member a large, nobby showpiece, somewhat discolored, but
impressive; and his endurance improved too. (62–63)

And speaking of showpieces, later in the book we are presented with the encounter between cameo character Linda Law-

rence and her lover who attempt to have intercourse through a small aperture between the men's and women's restrooms at her office. Unfortunately, the penis involved here grows to such monstrous size that the partition between the rooms is splintered, and withdrawal from the women's room becomes impossible. The trapped member is "thick as a strand of George Washington Bridge," and poor Linda is forced to camouflage it from prying eyes by papering it with pages from a Saul Bellow novel (260–62).

Katz's description of this impressive phallus bears a family resemblance to Coover's presentation of man with "a doodang about five feet long" who "wraps it around his leg or carries it over his shoulder" (135). Such phallic grotesquerie participates in a traditional Menippean motif. Rabelais, for example relates the story of an ancient people who ate of a magic fruit, causing all manner of swelling and growth. In particular, some

> grew in the length of that member which is called Nature's
> labourer, so that it grew marvellously long, big, stout, fat, lusty, and
> proud, after the ancient fashion, so much so that men made use of
> it as a belt, twisting it four or five times round the body. (172)

Indeed, the motif goes back at least as far as Petronius, whose Encolpius enviously encounters a young man who "had such enormous sexual organs that you'd think the man was just an attachment to his penis. What a man for the job! I think he starts yesterday and finishes tomorrow" (103).

Such connections highlight the element of carnival that inheres in most postmodernist representations of explicitly phallic imagery, a resurgence of the Menippean energies of much earlier works. Indeed, most examples of postmodern use of the motif seem to have much more in common with Petronius and Rabelais than with the more abject images of Faulkner and Hemingway. An especially direct link between the castration motif and the Bakhtinian carnival occurs in Angela Carter's *Nights at the Circus*. Carter's presentation of the "dance of the buffoons" is one of the most carnivalesque scenes in literature, and all the more so because of the generally transgressive nature of the text in which it appears. In this dance a group of circus clowns performs all manner of bizarre and sacrilegious acts in "celebration of the primal slime" (125). Among other things the ritual includes a parody of the Last Supper, with Buffo, the head clown, cast as Christ and being served a cauldron of "fish soup" that turns out to contain "all manner of rude things—knickers, lavatory brushes, and yard upon yard of lavatory paper" (124). Importantly, all of this carnivalesque energy is specifically linked to castration and phallic grotesquerie:

A joey thrust the vodka bottle up the arsehole of an august; the august, in response, promptly dropped his trousers to reveal a virile member of priapic size, bright purple in colour and spotted with yellow stars, dangling two cerise balloons from the fly. At that, a second august, with an evil leer, took a great pair of scissors out of his back pocket and sliced the horrid thing off but as soon as he was brandishing it in triumph above his head another lurid phallus appeared in the place of the first, this one bright blue with scarlet polkadots and cerise testicles, and so on, until the clown with the shears was juggling with a dozen of the things. (124)

Here, the cyclic recurrence of erection and amputation can be directly linked to the motif of crowning and uncrowning that so centrally informs Bakhtin's description of the carnival. As such, it also helps to explain why the motif of castration plays such a central role in fertility myths, with their emphasis on cycles of death and rebirth. The castration motif, despite its abject aspects, has much to do with the spirit of carnival and with the transgression of boundaries in general, and an emphasis on these kinds of relationships is much more interesting than an insipid appeal to vulgar psychoanalytic cliché.

Still, even without an overt reliance on the "truth" value of psychoanalytic models, there is much to the feminist argument that males might metaphorically see woman as bearing not a phallus but a bleeding wound, thus functioning as an image and reminder of the threat of castration. Within the dynamics of the social repression of abject images (of which castration is one), this correlation of woman with castration points toward a view of woman not only as Other, but as threatening and disgusting Other who must be circumscribed and subjugated at all costs. Moreover, the Freudian model of the castration complex implies that the Law of the Father is maintained within the family through violence and terror, a suggestion that serves as a comment on patriarchal society in general. Carter employs a number of abject (though often subtle) images of castration in her earlier book, *The Magic Toyshop*, in a movement that Palmer astutely interprets as a demonstration of the "violence at the heart of the patriarchal family unit" (184).

Indeed, feminist readings, far from being universally banal, have produced some of the most exciting transgressive effects in all of criticism. There is, for example, much room for feminist exploration of one particular form of "castration," the motif in which a man is transformed by some means or other into a woman. Cheryl Herr, for example, has noted the way in which Leopold Bloom's temporary transformation into a woman in "Circe" helps to reveal the artificiality of conventional gender roles, which in turn destabilizes our notions of individual identity in general:

From the notion that there's no "natural" or "nonalien" gender, *Ulysses* posits that there is no human nature in the ordinary sense of the term and no inner being that one struggles to understand, develop, or fulfill. Rather, *Ulysses* shows us cultural codes mingling in the minds of each character to the effect that the character— whether known through dialogue, thoughts, or action—is properly constructed as a narrative event. (154)

Herr's reading of Joyce is an excellent illustration of positive and productive criticism, as opposed, for example, to the entirely negative reading given this episode by Sandra Gilbert. Gilbert, on the other hand, has done an excellent job of finding transgressive energies in Virginia Woolf's use of a similar technique of gender transformation in *Orlando*. According to Gilbert, the ease with which Orlando changes sex shows a conception of gender as mere costume, and "feminist modernist costume imagery is radically revisionary in a political as well as a literary sense, for it implies that no one, male or female, can or should be confined to a uni-form, a single form or self" ("Costumes" 196). Indeed, I would argue that conventional gender boundaries are so fundamental to the structure of society and its institution that an attack on such boundaries represents one of the most subversive gestures available to a work of literature. As such, perhaps one should not be too hasty in dismissing the transgressive potential of any work (such as Joyce's "Circe") that seems to call these boundaries into question.

The phallus has been installed, especially in psychoanalysis, as the most fundamental gender boundary of them all, so that attacks on the phallus, whether metaphorical or literally physical, have much to do with the transgression of gender boundaries. The male with incomplete genitals is deprived of a principal signifier of his difference from the feminine. Yet the castrato is not female, either; his gender position is ambiguous. This situation is well illustrated by Balzac's *Sarrasine*, which centers on Sarrasine's infatuation with la Zambinella, a "woman" opera singer who turns out to be a castrato. The uncertain gender of la Zambinella has a way of infecting Balzac's entire text, which is filled with images of gender transgression.

One could argue that a literal castration such as la Zambinella has undergone reinforces essentialist notions of gender, as it is only after surgical removal of the phallus that la Zambinella is able to cross gender boundaries. However, it is interesting to note that the castrated singer seems able to float freely between the masculine and the feminine merely by changing costume— the implication being that it is only a misplaced emphasis on the phallus that holds conventional gender boundaries in place to begin with. Roland Barthes's reading in *S/Z* of the castration motif in this story also emphasizes the symbolic aspect of castration. Barthes suggests that the story is indeed structured around castration, but that in this case castration is not a matter of biological gender. The characters of the story divide not along lines of male and female, but according to the roles they play as castrating or castrated, active or passive. Most importantly, Barthes notes that the castrato himself does not necessarily fall in the camp of the castrated: "he is the blind and mobile flaw in this system; he moves back and forth between active and passive: castrated, he castrates" (36).

Barthes's reading of the symbolic function of castration in *Sarrasine* is somewhat reminiscent of de Lauretis's semiotic interpretation of the significance of castration in *If on a winter's night a traveler*. However, the situation of la Zambinella, in which gender becomes merely a matter of costume, also brings to mind recent feminist discussions of the artificiality of gender by critics such as Gilbert and Gubar. Of course, modern medical technology has made it possible to change gender in even a literal, physical sense, and the castration of la Zambinella prefigures this fact, which often surfaces in postmodernist texts. For example, *The World According to Garp* features Roberta Muldoon, a former NFL tight end who has been surgically made female; the contrast between traditional views of the feminine and traditional views of NFL tight ends adds symbolic resonance to Muldoon's situation. Perec makes the symbolism of the sex change even more explicit in *Life: A User's Manual* with the story of singer Sam Horton, who undergoes an operation transforming him into "Hortense." In a sort of reversal of the situation of la Zambinella, the woman "Hortense" retains her masculine voice, which has a decidedly unsettling effect on her audiences. If gender boundaries can be so easily transgressed, then boundaries in general must be unstable. As a result, " 'Hortense' quickly became the incomparable symbol of the fragility of all things" (182).

Perhaps because of the availability of sex change operations (as well as the growing feminist challenge to conventional gender stereotypes), the motif of gender reversal has become quite prominent in recent literature. In Gore Vidal's *Myra Breckinridge*, a surgical sex change of the title character from male to female leads to a complete reversal of gender signs, with the existing gender system remaining entirely intact.[21] Thomas Berger's *Regiment of Women*, on the other hand, presents a futuristic dystopia in which the characters remain of the same gender, but the gender system is itself inverted, with women assuming traditional male roles, and vice versa.[22]

Most effectively transgressive among these science-fiction works are those that challenge the very basis of gender difference, rather than merely exploring modifications to or reversals of the existing system. Ursula K. Le Guin's *The Left Hand of Darkness*, for example, is a science-fiction exploration of a distant planet on which all of the inhabitants are thoroughly androgynous, with social implications of considerable relevance to our own world. Even more effective is Samuel R. Delany's postulation of a future society (*Triton*) in which sex-change operations are quite common, and in which the real complexity and diversity of sexual orientations is fully accepted.[23] In the society of *Triton*, for example, names are totally gender-nonspecific, so that people will not have to change names if they change genders. Further, this society recognizes "forty or fifty basic sexes, falling loosely into nine categories" (117). Perhaps most effective of all these interrogations of gender is Angela Carter's *The Pas-*

sion of New Eve, with its switches not only of physical sex (including surgical castration), but of gender roles, and its allusive interrogations of the gender orientations of much of Western literature. The result, as Suleiman argues, is a thorough reformulation of our notions of gender, acting to "expand our notions of what it is possible to dream in this domain, and thereby criticize all dreams that are too narrow" (27).

Carter's text owes an obvious debt to Woolf's *Orlando*, which can be taken as a sort of retroactive Ur-text of all such modern investigations of gender boundaries.[24] The free-floating gender of Orlando has clear symbolic significance, as feminist critics have been quick to point out, and the specificity of the feminist viewpoints of authors such as Woolf and Carter adds greatly to the transgressive potential of their work. But I would argue that one can respect this specificity while still emphasizing the family resemblances among works such as those of Woolf and Carter and of the male writers surveyed in this chapter. The topoi of castration and of gender transformation have great potential for the subversion of oppressive social and political boundaries, and there is much to be gained by highlighting that potential.

WHAT'S THE DIFFERENCE?: THE CARNIVALIZATION OF GENDER IN VIRGINIA WOOLF'S **ORLANDO**

CHAPTER

6 _____

Among the many fascinating scenes in Virginia Woolf's *Orlando* is one in which the title character meditates on mortality while browsing (literally) through the bones of his ancestors in the family crypt:

"Nothing remains of all these Princes," Orlando would say,
indulging in some pardonable exaggeration of their rank, "except
one digit," and he would take a skeleton hand in his and bend the
joints this way and that. (71)

This morbid musing is especially illustrative of *Orlando* as a whole, because it not only engages in a dialogue with literary tradition, but with two traditions at once. For one thing, Orlando has been driven to such thoughts of death and decay because of his rejection by a woman, the Russian Princess Sasha. As such, his meditations engage and parody the long-standing Western tradition of associating women with such images. But the scene also clearly echoes the gravedigger scene in *Hamlet*, itself a participant in a central Menippean motif.[1]

The multivocal dialogue in Woolf's crypt scene is characteristic of *Orlando*'s engagement with literary and cultural tradition.

The specific dialogue here with Menippean satire highlights the strong affinities between *Orlando* and that tradition, especially as it has been described by Bakhtin. Indeed, *Orlando* is of key importance to those who would seek to utilize Bakhtin's work in the interest of feminist criticism. In a now-famous essay, Wayne Booth lauds Bakhtin for providing a means of bringing ideology into criticism without dogmatism. Yet, turning to Bakhtin's reading of Rabelais, he finds a striking lack of any interest in a genuine feminine perspective on the part of both Bakhtin and Rabelais:

The truth is that nowhere in Rabelais does one find any hint of an
effort to imagine any woman's point of view or to incorporate
women into a dialogue. And nowhere in Bakhtin does one discover
any suggestion that he sees the importance of this kind of
monologue, not even when he discusses Rabelais' attitude toward
women. (165–66)

Still, feminist critics have found Bakhtin increasingly useful as a resource in recent years, particularly because his theories of dialogism lend themselves to a critique of the kind of authoritarian discourse often associated with the patriarchal tradition. *Orlando*, by bringing gender so prominently into view, illuminates the feminist potential in Bakhtin's work. The voices engaged in dialogue in *Orlando* are often of different gender. At the same time the boundaries of gender itself are challenged, carnivalized, and exposed as arbitrary social constructions.

In many of the social and intellectual constructions of Western society, gender difference becomes the paradigm of all difference, and the separation between the genders can be taken as the prototype for all social systems of categorization. Moreover, it becomes a model for social hierarchies as well: women in this scheme assume the subservient position of the Other against whom men can be defined and against whose lack men can experience fantasies of wholeness and plenitude. Indeed, gender is one of the fundamental criteria used to define social typologies. As a result, one would expect a great deal of transgressive potential in *Orlando*'s questioning of traditional notions of gender boundaries. Hélène Cixous explains the centrality of gender difference to human social systems:

In fact, every theory of culture, every theory of society, the whole conglomeration of symbolic systems—everything, that is, that's spoken, everything that's organized as discourse, art, religion, the family, language, everything that seizes us, everything that acts on us—it is all ordered around hierarchical oppositions that come back to the man/woman opposition, an opposition that can only be sustained by means of a difference posed by cultural discourse as "natural," the difference between activity and passivity. ("Castration" 44)

Cixous here echoes Barthes's reading of *Sarrasine*, as well as pointing toward the recent emphasis on blurring of conventional gender boundaries in the work of critics such as Gilbert and Gubar. Perhaps the classic modern illustration of such transgressions of gender boundaries is *Orlando*. Gilbert and Gubar emphasize that *Orlando* changes gender as easily as one might change clothing, while remaining otherwise rather unaffected, "and this not because sexually defining costumes are false and selves are true but because costumes are selves and thus easily, fluidly, interchangeable" (*No Man's Land* 344). Woolf's book thus mounts a direct challenge to conventional notions of identity and to the hierarchies with which those notions are associated.

GENDER AND GENRE: **ORLANDO** AS POLYPHONIC NOVEL

If Orlando as a character continually oversteps the categorical boundaries of gender, it is equally true that *Orlando* as a book refuses to settle within the categorical boundaries of genre. Indeed, at first glance it would seem that genre criticism is particularly ill-suited to the discussion of *Orlando*, because its genre is so uncertain. After all, attempts at taxonomy and classification partake of exactly the sort of masculine drive toward totalizing systems that Woolf's book attacks and ridicules. *Orlando* is radically antigeneric. But this antigeneric quality of the book is precisely why genre criticism is so valuable. Much of modern genre theory—especially that strain beginning with the work of the Russian formalists and running through the work of Mikhail Bakhtin—has emphasized the way in which a "genre" can be not a fixed form, but a field of conflict upon which new forms can parody and replace old ones.[2] In a recent study, Alastair

Fowler suggests that it is the essence of the literary to modify genre conventions: "For to have any artistic significance, to mean anything distinctive in a literary way, a work must modulate or vary or depart from its generic conventions, and consequently alter them for the future" (*Kinds of Literature* 23).

Actually, Fowler's model of genre subversion is a rather conservative one relative, say, to Bakhtin, and he himself explicitly parallels it to Eliot's notion that all literary works modify the literary tradition when they appear. Still, Fowler's insistence on the cardinal importance of change to the very definition of genres indicates the particular relevance of genre studies to works (such as *Orlando*) that derive much of their effect from the subversion of genre conventions. After all, the point of such subversion is largely lost if one does not recognize what is being subverted. As Tzvetan Todorov points out in relation to genre transgressions of this kind, "[f]or there to be a transgression, the norm must be apparent" (8).

Todorov is speaking here specifically of the transgressive potential of the fantastic, a genre that obviously has much to do with *Orlando*, although Woolf's book also contains a strong element of allegory, which Todorov would exclude from the fantastic. But recognizing the essentiality of genre subversion is also fundamental to Bakhtin's conception of the novel, and here it is informative to note that Woolf herself was consistently adamant that conditions in the modern world demanded new literary forms. She was particularly convinced that women writers needed to seek new modes of expression that went beyond the "man's sentence" of "Johnson, Gibbon, and the rest" (*Room* 79). Encouraged by the achievements of the great nineteenth-century women novelists, Woolf saw the novel as the genre within which these new forms and modes could be expected to develop:

There is no reason to think that the form of the epic or of the
poetic play suits a woman any more than the sentence suits her.
But all the older forms of literature were hardened and set by the
time she became a writer. The novel alone was young enough to be
soft in her hands. (*Room* 80)

This notion of the novel as an open-ended and evolving genre is quite reminiscent of the model of the novel put forth by Bakhtin. However, Bakhtin's privileging of the novel, in conjunction with his polemic against poetry, indicates potential difficulty in viewing the novel as the ideal form for feminist expression. What Bakhtin is writing against is the traditional literary hierarchy that would classify poetry as "high" art and the novel as "low." Within such a hierarchy, it becomes clear that one reason women turned to the novel as a means of expression in the nineteenth century was simply that the novel was seen as a marginal site of discourse that patriarchal society allowed women to inhabit because it was not "serious" or "important." Thus women, even while adopting the novel as a form, were forced to work against this perception in order to be taken seriously. Woolf herself wonders elsewhere in *Room* whether even the novel will provide an adequate vehicle for future feminist expression, and in a diary entry (July 27, 1934) she shows a great deal of ambivalence toward the form: "That cannibal, the novel, which has destroyed so many forms of art will by then have devoured even more. We shall be forced to invent new names for the different books which masquerade under this heading" (quoted in Richter 7).

Woolf's metaphor of the novel as cannibal, even if slightly sinister, is again reminiscent of Bakhtin's characterization of the novel as a form that absorbs other genres into itself in its continual process of evolution. In light of her musings on innovative forms such as those in *A Room of One's Own* it is also significant that Woolf was composing her most generically enigmatic work at the same time as *Room. Orlando* is so enigmatic that until recent feminist interventions it had been largely ignored by critics as a fanciful aberration in Woolf's career.

The centrality of genre subversion to *Orlando* can be seen in the prevalence of criticial attempts to pin it down by labeling its genre. John Graham, for example, suggests that *Orlando* is difficult to classify because of its mixed tone of comedy and seriousness, but finally opts to consider it a fantasy, although a flawed one that fails to "follow to the end the laws of its literary nature" (110). J. J. Wilson, on the other hand, takes a somewhat different view of the "literary nature" of *Orlando*, arguing that an emphasis on the elements of fantasy in the book largely misses the point, and that *Orlando* is an "anti-novel" in the tradition of *Tristram Shandy*. But *Tristram Shandy*'s own genre is somewhat problematic, and in this vein, Harvena Richter suggests that *Orlando* (along with *Between the Acts*) can be considered an "anatomy" as outlined by Northrop Frye (7n).[3] Avrom Fleischman agrees, arguing that the distinctive generic feature of *Orlando* is its encyclopedism, a characteristic seen by Frye as being central to the anatomy (Fleischman xi–xii). And finally Beverly Ann Schlack avoids the temptation to identify *Orlando* with any given genre, but simply opts for pluralism, noting that the work is a hybrid form that "combines biography, history, fantasy, fiction, poetry, and allegory. It resembles, in passing, the quest novel, the picaresque novel, satire, the fairy story, the feminist pamphlet, the *Bildungsroman*, and a history of English literature told in metaphors" (77).[4]

Schlack's pluralistic perspective is in many ways well advised, and within the contemporary climate one might add magic realism to this list, as *Orlando* serves as a forerunner of the many recent texts in that mode. But given the above catalogue of characteristics (the seriocomic tone, the importance of parody, the elements of the fantastic, the mockery of novelistic expectations, the encyclopedic form, and the inclusion of elements from a wide variety of genres) one could also simply say that *Orlando* is a novel. Moreover, from the point of view of Bakhtin it is not an aberrant work at all, but exemplary of the best features of the novel tradition.[5] While it may be true that *Orlando* (like *Tristram Shandy*) is an anti-novel, it is also true that Bakhtin's work calls into question normal distinctions between inside and outside, between proper and improper, so that the marginalized anti-novel in fact becomes curiously pivotal to the novel tradition. Thus, if it is true that nineteenth-century society marginalized the novel in such a way as to associate it with the feminine, then it is also true that Bakhtin's attempts to recuperate the novel have an interesting feminist potential, despite Bakhtin's own apparent lack of interest in gender issues.

The kinds of novels privileged by Bakhtin are directly linked to the tradition of Menippean satire (i.e., of the anatomy), which is itself closely identified with encyclopedism, so that the identification of *Orlando* as a Bakhtinian novel is at first glance largely a reiteration of the genre identifications made by Fleischman and Richter. However, Bakhtin's understanding of the social and political implications of the Menippean form brings special force to the consideration of *Orlando* in this way. As Bakhtin has stressed, it is the essence of the Menippean satire to be a satire of *something*, to provide a concrete response to its specific contemporary social, political, and historical moment. Menippean satire is not merely a formal technique, but is primarily an attitude toward the world. Moreover, it is an oppositional attitude, directed *against* specific targets. To Bakhtin the novel is a special genre, unique in its contemporaneity, its contact with everyday life, its close connection with extraliterary genres.

Important to Bakhtin's conception of the novel is the idea of the carnival, and it is obvious that carnivalesque elements play a large role in *Orlando*.[6] Julia Kristeva discusses the highly carnivalesque character of many novels that derive primarily from Bakhtin's Second Line, which she refers to as "subversive," or "polyphonic" novels, noting their close affinity with Menippean satire. "Carnivalesque," however, does not connote frivolity. "The laughter of the carnival is not simply parodic; it is no more comic than tragic; it is both at once, one might say that it is serious" ("Word" 50). She writes that "Menippean discourse develops in times of opposition against Aristotelianism, and writers of polyphonic novels seem to disapprove of the very structures of official thought founded on formal logic." In the subversive novel, "identity, substance, causality and definition are transgressed so that others may be adopted: analogy, relation, opposition, and therefore dialogism and Menippean ambivalence" (55–56).

Kristeva's discussions of the seriousness of carnival indicate that the whimsically comical *Orlando*, as a novel informed by the Menippean tradition, may be quite serious as well. In *Problems of Dostoevsky's Poetics* Bakhtin begins his list of the central characteristics of Menippean satire by noting that the comic element is generally quite important in this genre (114), and obviously comedy plays a large role in *Orlando*, probably more so than in any other of Woolf's novels. Woolf herself described the book as a "joke," and subsequent critics have frequently regarded it as a work of slight substance, largely due to its lack of high seriousness. However, Bakhtin's work reflects recent theory that calls into question the traditional hierarchical privileging of seriousness over play. One of the ways in which such a questioning takes place is through the intermingling of comic and serious effects within a single work; Bakhtin notes that the seriocomic nature of Menippean satire is linked to the typical ambivalence of the carnival (*Problems* 132). *Orlando* has its serious as well as its comic elements, and Graham has argued that the mixture of comedy and seriousness in the work was a flaw that "vitiated the artistic integrity of the book" (112). On the other hand, one might consider Robert Langbaum's suggestion (discussing Mann, Yeats, and Shakespeare) that "tragicomedy" is perhaps the "complete or ultimate vision" available to a work of art, and that it is the "characteristically modern style" (177, 184).

Graham's opposition to the combination of seriousness and comedy in a single work is an old one (dating in English literary criticism at least as far back as *Orlando*'s erstwhile contemporary Sir Philip Sidney), but Bakhtin's insights allow us to see that this combination is not necessarily a flaw at all. Rather, it is simply one of the many ways in which normal hierarchical distinctions are abolished in this subversive book. Minow-Pinkney points out that Woolf's various contradictory comments on the playfulness of *Orlando* describe an ultimate seriousness that grew out of an initial playful impulse, the effect being an overturning of the usual assumption that seriousness is primary, "affirming instead the primacy of play" (117). Judy Little also emphasizes the seriousness of the comedy in *Orlando*, arguing that Woolf's novel mockingly reveals the way in which so many of our accepted "truths" are actually culturally constructed illusions:

And the things that she identifies as illusions are not simply the manners and dress of an age, but those large cultural codes which a less radical comedy would identify as truth and norm. *Orlando* perceives the rhetorically constructed "nature" of love, and the verbal politics that (en)gender the "nature" of the sexes. (190–91)

Many critics have argued the transgressive potential of comedy and play in feminist discourse. Cixous, for example, affirms the power of laughter: "Laughter that breaks out, overflows, a humor no one would expect to find in women—which is nonetheless surely their greatest strength because it's a humor that sees man much further away than he has ever been seen" ("Castration" 55).[7] Interestingly, this motif of the view from a great distance is a common one in Menippean discourse, as exemplified in works such as Lucian's *Icaromenippus*. Viewing *Orlando* within the framework of Menippean satire (and its heir the polyphonic novel) supports recent efforts by Little and others to identify *Orlando* as a work with strong political potential.

Bakhtin cites *Icaromenippus* as an example of how Menippean satire is often informed by "a special type of experimental fantasticality . . . which results in a radical change in the scale of the observed phenomena of life" (*Problems* 116). In *Orlando* the principal phenomenon that is made to appear radically different by a fantastic change in perspective is gender itself. Todorov has characterized the fantastic as a mode informed by ambiguity and hesitation in meaning: "The fantastic is that hesitation experienced by a person who knows only the laws of nature, confronting an apparently supernatural event" (25). Thus Orlando's gender transformations are truly (and doubly) fantastic: not only is the reader unable to reach a final explanation for his/her changes in gender, but that gender itself remains indeterminate.

An appeal to the tradition of Menippean satire also helps to show that the fantastic elements of *Orlando*, like the elements of play, are more than mere whimsy. Minow-Pinkney, for example, classifies the book as a "fantasy" and notes the inherently transgressive nature of fantasy as a form: "*Orlando* . . . shows the nature of fantasy itself, which I take to be the transgression of boundaries as a play with the limit, as a play of difference" (122). Minow-Pinkney's analysis is expressly informed by the work of Bakhtin, and particularly by Rosemary Jackson's reinscription of Bakhtin's reading of the fantastic. Jackson links the fantastic both to political subversion and to the forbidden desire that psychoanalysis sees in the unconscious mind. Noting the way in which the fantastic can challenge our normally comfortable assumptions about the nature of "reality," she labels the fantastic "the literature of subversion" and notes that "[f]rom Hoffmann and German Romanticism, to the modern fantastic in horror films, fantasy has tried to erode the pillars of society by un-doing categorical structures" (176).

In short, Woolf's playfully fantastic anti-biography is not stupid stuff at all, but an effective assault on contemporary social conventions. To understand the feminist impulse behind *Orlando*, one must also appreciate the close parallelism between this novel and its companion volume, *A Room of One's Own*. Not only were the two works composed during the same period of time, but they both express very similar feminist philosophies. Indeed, *Orlando* can be read virtually as a direct novelization of the ideas presented more discursively in *Room*. Jane Marcus has invoked Bakhtin in her analysis of the discourse of *Room*, arguing that Woolf's discourse in this pair of reworked lectures is "triologic," composed of the voices of Woolf, her audience for the talks on which the book is based, and the readers of the book.[8] It thus "invents human intercourse on a model of female discourse, as a conversation among equals" (155–56). The point is that Woolf thus breaks down the normal (male) authoritarian structure of the lecture as a form, in which the speaker as the subject-who-is-presumed-to-know dispenses wisdom to his relatively passive audience.

Woolf's revision of the lecture form thus also involves a direct assault on the unity of the conventional subject. In the beginning of *Room*, for example, she announces that she will employ an "I" with a fluid deixis, pointing first to one subject, then another, but never settling into a representation of a fixed, stable speaker: " 'I' is only a convenient term for somebody who has no real being . . . call me Mary Beton, Mary Seton, Mary Carmichael or by any name you please—it is not a matter of any importance" (*Room* 4–5).

In Bakhtinian terms, then, the two "lectures" that went into the making of *Room* are in fact parodies of lectures. *Orlando*, meanwhile, serves as a very similar parody of another traditional male authoritarian form, the scholarly biography. The book is subtitled "A Biography," and it includes a variety of scholarly accoutrements, such as a mock preface, several photographs of Orlando at various stages in his/her life, and a concluding index. The book's narrator is a putative biographer who sometimes steps outside the frame of the narration to present us with reflexive meditations on the art of biography. Biography, *Orlando* teaches us, is an art, not science, more a matter of constructing a narrative than of compiling a transparent representation of the "truth." For example, during the Puritan Revolution, numerous records were destroyed, posing significant problems in documentation: "We have done our best to piece out a meagre summary from the charred fragments that remain; but often it has been necessary to speculate, to surmise, and even to make use of the imagination" (119). This example is quite specific, but it also stands as a sort of mini-allegory mocking the pretensions of biographers and historians who would claim to be able to reconstruct the past accurately.

As Graham points out, Woolf's parody of biography in *Orlando* also represents a more general parody of "the absurdities of the whole approach to things which she considered typically masculine" (107). Indeed, just as *Room* deals extensively (and often acerbically) with the question of the male literary tradition, the discourse of *Orlando* is constructed largely from a patchwork of parodies of various styles in that tradition.[9] It is no accident that of eight literary predecessors acknowledged in the book's mock preface, only one (Emily Brontë) is female. Clearly, then, the discourse of both *Room* and *Orlando* is extensively dialogic in the Bakhtinian sense. In fact, much of the power of both works derives from the way in which Woolf subverts the male literary tradition with its own discourse.

Woolf anticipates Gilbert and Gubar in *Room* when she complains that patriarchal domination of language left nineteenth-century women writers without a suitable means of literary expression. She notes that the woman, attempting to write, would discover that the very structure of the sentence was antipathetic to her nature, that "there was no common sentence ready for her use. . . . That is a man's sentence; behind it one can see Johnson, Gibbon and the rest. It was a sentence that was unsuited for a woman's use" (79–80). Woolf is similarly writing within the restrictions of a patriarchal linguistic environment, but in *Room* she makes the most of that disadvantage, getting considerable mileage from her parody of the male lecture form and from her parodic allusions to male writers, both literary and scholarly.[10] In *Orlando* she takes this kind of parody even farther, attempting to initiate a subversive dialogue with the "man's sentence" of the literary tradition through her explicit depiction of gender-related issues. The most obvious of these dimensions concerns the androgynous nature of the book's protagonist, but the book in fact conducts a subversive dialogue with the male tradition throughout.

THE DIALOGICS OF GENDER: WOOLF AND BAKHTIN

Woolf's literary explorations of gender issues have provided fertile material for a number of feminist discussions in recent years. For example, her now-famous call for a "woman's sentence" anticipates the attempts of French feminists such as Hélène Cixous to develop *l'écriture féminine*, and Gilbert has described Woolf as a "crucial feminist predecessor of Cixous" ("Introduction" xv). On the other hand, as I have suggested elsewhere, there is much in Woolf's project to suggest that her concept of a "woman's sentence" can be read not as an attempt to propose an alternative order of feminine discourse so much as to propose effective ways in which women can speak within the existing order ("Nothing"). This phenomenon is well illustrated by the striking passage in *Mrs. Dalloway* in which Woolf presents her singing "battered old woman." This mysterious, archetypal figure is introduced as "a frail quivering sound . . . with an absence of all human meaning," singing an inarticulate song that sounds like "ee um fah um so / foo swee too eem oo—" Moreover, she is suitably timeless and androgynous, "the voice of no age or sex." She "stood singing of love—love which lasted a million years . . . the old bubbling, burbling song, soaking through the knotted roots of infinite ages" (122–23).

Both Woolf and Cixous envision the ideal feminine language-user as a nameless singer, and surely this battered old woman is a personification of that vision. Indeed, Gilbert sees this old woman as being among Woolf's "most striking female artists" ("Woman's Sentence" 218). But has Woolf here really created an effective example of a rhythmic, musical woman's discourse that completely breaks free of the restrictions of patriarchal language and tradition? Not necessarily. For one thing, J. Hillis Miller has argued rather convincingly that Woolf is in fact transforming the words of "Allerseelen," a song by canonical male composer Richard Strauss, in the construction of this passage ("*Mrs. Dalloway*" 190). For another, a close reading of the passage reveals that it may be not so much an explosion of radical feminine discourse as an instance of masculine fantasy—or (since Woolf is a woman) a feminine fantasy of a masculine fantasy.

It is important to recognize the style of indirect discourse in which *Mrs. Dalloway* is constructed. Although there is a sort of presiding narrative consciousness that at times seems to be in control of the narration of the book, the vast majority of the text is constructed as a collage of zones in which the consciousnesses of different characters influence the narration. This effect is similar to what Bakhtin calls "character zones" (*Dialogic Imagination* 320), though in Bakhtin the style itself would usually change from one consciousness to the next (as in, say, Joyce), whereas in *Mrs. Dalloway* the style remains virtually unchanged regardless of which character is currently in control of the narration. Usually in *Mrs. Dalloway* the voice of a single character is dominant, although in some cases it is difficult to identify the controlling character, especially during transitions from one character zone to another when multiple character voices are "active." In the case of the "battered old woman" passage, however, it is clear that we at least begin in the consciousness of Peter Walsh. Walsh is lost in thought about Clarissa Dalloway, then suddenly "[a] sound interrupt[s] him; a frail quivering sound, a voice bubbling up without direction" (122). The next three pages then present the song of the timeless old woman (with no indication of a shift in narrative consciousness), after which Walsh gives her a coin and departs in a taxi. The woman's song then ends, and the narration transfers to the consciousness of Rezia Warren Smith.

Given that the particularly evocative details of the old woman's song are supplied primarily by Peter Walsh, she then becomes not an archetypal woman artist, but a typical male fantasy of the eternal nourishing mother. Walsh, in fact, is given to such stereotypical fantasies, as demonstrated earlier in the book when he sees a young woman and is instantly transmogrified into a daring buccaneer. He follows the girl home, engrossed in fantasies of adventure and male conquest, but then she simply enters her house and is gone. He is brought back to reality. It was simply "invented, this escapade with the girl" (81).

If the battered old woman is similarly invented, if she is in fact an inscription of Peter Walsh's male fantasy, then one is naturally led to suspect that Woolf in this passage is similarly inscribed within male language. And in a sense she is. However, Bakhtin's theories of parody aid our understanding that even though the old woman may be singing a song from the male canon, she is singing it in a context so different from the male canonical one that a new light is cast on Strauss. Such parody, of course, would be impossible in a discourse that escaped the bounds of male language entirely; parody requires the presence of a specific target and of an interaction with that target. The effect here is to set up a dialogue that questions the validity of

traditional hierarchies that by definition value the musical pro-
ductions of a Strauss more highly than those of an old woman by
a train station.[11]

The entire episode is seemingly narrated from within a narrative zone dominated by Peter Walsh, but such zones are inherently dialogic. They are never dominated completely by the
voice of a character. Rather, they are zones of dynamic interactions of the voice of the dominant character with the voices of
the author, narrator, and perhaps of other characters as well.
Thus, we read this scene from the male point of view of Peter
Walsh, but it is possible to detect a feminine viewpoint as well.
The strangeness of this scene indicates the inability of the patriarchal viewpoint ever to control language completely. Indeed,
the poetic nature of the language in this section seems beyond
the range of Walsh himself, and figures of anonymous female
singers play an important role in Woolf's work that far transcends the fantasies of Peter Walsh.

In short, it is impossible to relate the language of this passage
directly to either gender. The language is dialogic, and in particular the relationship between the genders is dialogized. Woolf
consciously strives for this effect. In *A Room of One's Own*, for
example, she explains that the artist must seek to integrate the
points of view of both genders:

It is fatal to be a man or woman pure and simple; one must be
woman-manly or man-womanly. . . . Some collaboration has to take
place in the mind between the woman and the man before the act
of creation can be accomplished. Some marriage of opposites has to
be consummated. (108)

Relatively little attention has been paid to the dialogic or
carnivalesque aspects of Woolf's discourse (although Marcus has
invoked Bakhtin in her analysis of the discourse of *Room* as a
parody of the male lecture, as I noted earlier). Meisel, while not
citing Bakhtin, sees a similar dynamic at work in Woolf's relationship to Pater, noting that she turns Pater's work "into the
basis of a female vision to rival and overturn it, guerilla or sabo-
teurlike, by blowing up the enemy camp from within, using its
own weapons" (241). Indeed, such dialogues with male tradition
are a typical Woolf strategy, as shown by her dialogue with
Strauss in the song of the battered old woman. Woolf's work,

like that of so many modernists, is highly allusive.[12] Moreover, the vast majority of her allusions are to male writers, though it is also true that the male writer to whom she refers most is Shakespeare, whom she sees as a figure of androgyny.[13] Anne Herrmann has recently produced a book-length study of Woolf and German writer Christa Wolf from a Bakhtinian perspective. Herrmann discusses such items as Woolf's dialogic relationship to her fictional predecessor Judith Shakespeare, as well as noting Woolf's subversive interaction with the male literary tradition. She suggests that the response of both Woolf and Wolf to the dominant literary culture "lies in breaking with a literary tradition by totally immersing herself within it, at once appropriating and interrogating it" (2).

Alice Fox has also noted the way in which Woolf employs allusions to male writers in *Room* as a means of subverting the male tradition and thereby making a feminist statement. For example, Woolf's references to Milton are openly sardonic. "In both *Three Guineas* and *A Room*, then, by invoking Milton, Woolf asks her readers to think of the extra measure of frustration that women must feel, whether their field be literature or religion, simply because they are women" (Fox 150). In *Orlando* Woolf carries on an even more effective subversive dialogue with the male literary tradition. Indeed, *Orlando* is largely a history of literature, but it is history with a decidedly feminist twist, even though it deals almost exclusively with male literature. In the eighteenth century, for example, Orlando is so fortunate as to travel in the most fashionable of circles, to have access to tea parties featuring the most prominent (male) wits of the day.[14] And yet she finds this society oddly disappointing. For example, there is her troubling encounter with Alexander Pope:

He turned to Orlando and presented her instantly with the rough draught of a certain famous line in the "Characters of Women." Much polish was afterwards bestowed on it, but even in the original it was striking enough. . . . really she felt as if the little man had struck her. (214)

And struck her he had, the line no doubt containing Pope's notorious pronouncement as to the absolute lack of character in most women. In her typical fashion, Woolf employs an analogy to the male literary tradition in order to emphasize the exclusion of women from that tradition. But Woolf does not stop at this negative comment on the male attitude toward women. Instead, she presents a feminine alternative. Orlando takes to the streets and meets Nell, who is "of the tribe which nightly burnishes their wares" (216). And, despite her own aristocratic background, Orlando finds the company of Nell preferable to that of such masculine wits as Pope, Addison, and Lord Chesterfield, and ends up joining the "society" of Nell and her fellow prostitutes in a gesture toward feminine solidarity. The preference for these marginal feminine figures over the greatest masculine wits of the day represents a typical Bakhtinian inversion of hierarchies, except that the issue of gender is added to the usual ones of social class. Indeed, the dialogic interaction between genders in Woolf's writing directly participates in her carnivalesque assault upon strictly defined boundaries between the genders.

Woolf uses this episode to take an additional shot at male scholars. Noting that male students of women have concluded that "women are incapable of any feeling of affection for their own sex and hold each other in the greatest aversion," Woolf's biographer-narrator opts to "merely state that Orlando professed great enjoyment in the society of her own sex, and leave it to the gentlemen to prove, as they are very fond of doing, that this is impossible" (220). Of course, one is reminded here of Woolf's browsings in *Room* through the many volumes on women that have been written by men. Moreover, in *Room* she decries the lack of depiction of relationships among women in literature and suggests the potentially radical force of even so simple a sentence as "Chloe liked Olivia" (86).

There are dialogic elements in all of Woolf's novels, as witnessed by her frequent use of the "character zone" technique of free indirect style. There are scattered examples of overt carnivalization as well, such as in the pageant of *Between the Acts*. But *Orlando* contains the greatest concentration of carnivalesque energies in all of Woolf's fiction, as well as her most direct assault on fixed gender boundaries. These energies are manifested in numerous ways, such as the explicit inclusion of a carnival, the one conducted on the frozen River Thames in the early days of the rule of King James (34–36).[15] In addition, the novel conducts carnivalesque interrogations of language itself, as well as providing a subversive challenge to conventional notions of gender and individual identity.

Orlando's linguistic subversion includes highly literal heteroglossic mixtures of languages. For example, Orlando meets and becomes enamored of a Muscovite Princess at the carnival on the frozen Thames, but finds that this princess cannot speak English. So he and she (or she and he—both partners are of rather ambiguous gender) converse in French instead: "He was seldom far from her side, and their conversation, though unintelligible to the rest, was carried on with such animation, provoked such blushes and laughter, that the dullest could guess the subject" (41). This scene conveys that there are modes of expression other than official ones, whether they involve the use of foreign languages, or the languages of blushes and laughter. The effect is reminiscent of Patricia Yaeger's discussion of the prevalence of bilingual heroines in Charlotte Brontë:

The point is to make the dominant discourse into one among many possible modes of speech. By placing this discourse in contradiction the woman writer begins to rescript her available language games, to locate multivocality as one site of transformation for women's own writing and productivity. (41)

This motif of lovers speaking an alternative language of their own reappears when Orlando and her usually absent husband Marmaduke Bonthrop Shelmerdine are forced to communicate by telegraph and thus to develop their own private "cypher language which they had invented so that a whole spiritual state of the utmost complexity might be conveyed in a word or two without the telegraph clerk being the wiser" (282). In *Orlando* Woolf repeatedly emphasizes the inherent multiplicity of language, suggesting that there is no one language of truth. Thus, Orlando fails when he attempts to describe the grass and the sky in scientifically precise language, only to find that poetry interrupts his efforts, arising in his mind in a manner analogous to Kristeva's description of the irruption of the semiotic in the symbolic:

"The sky is blue," he said, "the grass is green." Looking up, he saw that, on the contrary, the sky is like the veils which a thousand Madonnas have let fall from their hair; and the grass fleets and darkens like a flight of girls fleeing the embraces of hairy satyrs from enchanted woods. "Upon my word," he said (for he had fallen into the bad habit of speaking aloud), "I don't see that one's more true than another. Both are utterly false." (102)

Note, however, that all of the alternative languages in *Orlando* are embedded in a matrix of relatively conventional discourse with which they dialogically interact, even as that matrix itself subtly parodies the language of scholarly biographies. Orlando herself explicitly emphasizes that even poetic language does not arise simply from the mind of its creator, but in dialogic tension with other languages: "Was not writing poetry a secret transaction, a voice answering a voice?" (325).

But if, as Lacan has emphasized, the human subject is constructed in and by language, then these assaults on the integrity of monologic language should have incontestable implications for the traditional notion of the stable, autonomous self as well. Indeed, Woolf's attack on conventional models of subjectivity is the most subversive element in *Orlando*, and she mounts this attack on several fronts. She attacks the sovereignty of the ego in her emphasis on anonymity. In *Room*, she praises Shakespeare for having transcended his personal passions in his writing:

All desire to protest, to preach, to proclaim an injury, to pay off a score, to make the world the witness of some hardship or grievance was fired out of him and consumed. Therefore his poetry flows from him free and unimpeded. (*Room* 58–59)

She continues this emphasis in *Orlando*, as the title character mediates on

the value of obscurity, and the delight of having no name, but being like a wave which returns to the deep body of the sea; thinking how obscurity rids the mind of the irk of envy and spite; how it sets running in the veins the free waters of generosity and magnanimity; and allows giving and taking without thanks offered or praise given: which must have been the way of all great poets. . . . Shakespeare must have written like that, and the church builders built like that, anonymously, needing no thanking or naming. (104–5)

Orlando's emphasis on the generosity that is embodied in anonymity, on the way in which namelessness embodies a willingness to give without the expectation of receiving anything in return, is another link between Woolf and Cixous. This emphasis on giving is central to Cixous's distinction between masculine and feminine modes of discourse. To Cixous, the masculine emphasis on ownership, related to a fear of castration, results in a libidinal economy of give-and-take, in which giving is always associated with debt and nothing is to be given without the expectation of something in return. The consequence of this economic model is a masculine discomfort with both giving and receiving:

For the moment you receive something you are effectively "open" to the other, and if you are a man you have only one wish, and that is hastily to return the gift, to break the circuit of an exchange that could have no end. ("Castration" 48)

Similarly, the male author insists on having his name attached to his text, on receiving credit for his work, because "[i]f a man spends and is spent, it's on condition that his power returns" (50). Women, in contrast, lack the typical masculine castration anxiety, and can therefore be comfortable with generosity and anonymity:

Unlike man, who holds so dearly to his title and his titles . . . woman couldn't care less about the fear of decapitation (or castration), adventuring, without the masculine temerity, into anonymity, which she can merge with, without annihilating herself: because she's a giver. (Cixous, "Laugh" 259)

Meanwhile, in *Room* Woolf celebrates the contributions of the anonymous artist, suggesting that "Anon, who wrote so many poems without signing them, was often a woman" (51). She explores the figure of Anon at great length in a late essay by that title, noting particularly the primal qualities of Anon as a nameless singer, dating back to the silence of the primeval forest:

The voice that broke the silence of the forest was the voice of Anon. Some one heard the song and remembered it for it was later

written down, beautifully, on parchment. . . . Everybody shared in
the emotion of Anons [sic] song, and supplied the story. Anon sang
because spring has come; or winter is gone; because he loves; because
he is hungry, or lustful; or merry; or because he adores
some God. Anon is sometimes man; sometimes woman. ("'Anon'"
382)[16]

Woolf here depicts a fantasy of an ancient, pre-linguistic forest
filled with song that bears some obvious parallels to the more
up-to-date Lacanian psychoanalytic fantasies of the primal, pre-
linguistic Imaginary stage of the infant privileged by Cixous and
Kristeva. Woolf also prefigures Lacan in her emphasis on the
multiple and split nature of the psyche. We are told, for example,
that Orlando "had a great variety of selves to call upon" (309). In
particular, Woolf relates the multiplicity of the self to the passage of time, to the notion that a given individual undergoes
many transformations of self in the course of a lifetime:

For if there are (at a venture) seventy-six different times all ticking
in the mind at once, how many different people are there not—
Heaven help us—all having lodgment at one time or
another? . . . these selves of which we are built up, one on top of
another, as plates are piled on a waiter's hand, have attachments
elsewhere, sympathies, little constitutions and rights of their own.
(308)

This relationship between the fragmentation of time and the
fragmentation of the self directly recalls Fredric Jameson's diagnosis of late consumer capitalism as producing "schizophrenic"
subjects. To Jameson, the schizophrenic is characterized by loss
of temporal connection in language use. Moreover,

he or she does not have our experience of temporal continuity
either, but is condemned to live a perpetual present with which the
various moments of his or her past have little connection and for
which there is no conceivable future on the horizon. In other
words, schizophrenic experience is an experience of isolated,
disconnected, discontinuous material signifiers which fail to link
up into coherent sequence. The schizophrenic thus does not know
personal identity in our sense, since our feeling of identity depends
on our sense of the persistence of the "I" and the "me" over time.
("Postmodernism" 119)

Jameson is here speaking of a trend he finds characteristic of postmodernist literature, and indeed examples such as the scattering of Tyrone Slothrop in *Gravity's Rainbow* or the fragmentation of Saleem Sinai in *Midnight's Children* tend to bear out his analysis. Woolf herself presents us with a more literal schizophrenic in the person of Septimus Smith in *Mrs. Dalloway*. And Orlando undergoes a similar schizophrenic destabilization of the temporal continuity of the self:

Nothing could be seen whole or read from start to finish. What was seen begun—like two friends starting to meet each other across the street—was never seen ended. After twenty minutes the body and mind were like scraps of paper tumbling from a sack and, indeed, the process of motoring fast out of London so much resembles the chopping up small of body and mind, which precedes unconsciousness and perhaps death itself that it is an open question in what sense Orlando can be said to have existed at the present moment. Indeed we should have given her over for a person entirely dissassembled. (307).[17]

Woolf's attacks on the stable autonomous self in *Orlando* often have vaguely Marxist intonations, as in her anticipation of Jameson here. But Woolf's attacks on the subject are most striking in her treatment of Orlando's gender. Ostensibly, Orlando is born (in the sixteenth century) a boy. Woolf calls attention to his gender in the very first sentence of the book: "He—for there could be no doubt of his sex, though the fashion of the time did something to disguise it—was in the act of slicing at the head of a Moor which swung from the rafters" (13). Indeed, Orlando's warlike play in this initial abject scene does seem a typically male entertainment, despite the temptation to interpret his swordplay with the decapitated head as an image of castration. But this declaration of Orlando's gender is highly ironic: there is in fact a great deal of doubt about his sex, and the entire fabric of the text is permeated with images of ambiguous gender.

When Orlando falls in love with the Muscovite Princess he begins to call her Sasha, which is rightly a boy's name, emphasizing that Sasha's gender is highly uncertain. Sasha first appears as Orlando sights "a figure, which, whether boy's or woman's, for the loose tunic and trousers of the Russian fashion served to disguise the sex, filled him with the highest curiosity" (37). And even as a romance begins to develop, Sasha remains of ambiguous gender, going about, for example, "booted like a man" (59). But Sasha sails away on a Russian ship amid the bizarre and surrealistic breakup of the frozen Thames. Orlando, heartbroken, "hurled at the faithless woman all the insults that have ever been the lot of her sex. Faithless, mutable, fickle, he called her; devil, adulteress, deceiver" (64).

Orlando's stereotypical condemnation of femininity is parodic, of course, not the least because of his own ill-defined gender. Later, Woolf pokes additional fun at male stereotypes of the feminine as a harpylike Archduchess Harriet amorously pursues Orlando with such determination that he is forced to have himself sent away as the Ambassador Extraordinary to Constantinople in order to escape her advances. Thus, not only does he flee the threat of the feminine, but he does so by escaping to the exotic East, that mysterious land of exotic (and erotic) adventure.[18] After various escapades in this highly appropriate setting, Orlando falls into a trance and is visited by an additional troop of feminine stereotypes, the Ladies Purity, Chastity, and Modesty, after which he awakens to discover that a remarkable transformation has taken place:

He stretched himself. He rose. He stood upright in complete nakedness before us, and while the trumpets pealed Truth! Truth! Truth! we have no choice left but confess—he was a woman. (137)

Orlando learns of this change while viewing himself/herself naked in a mirror, but finds it all surprisingly unaffecting:

Orlando looked himself up and down in a long lookingglass, without showing any signs of discomposure, and went, presumably, to his bath. . . . Orlando had become a woman—there is no denying it. But in every respect, Orlando remained precisely as he had been. The change of sex, though it altered their future, did nothing whatever to alter their identity. (138)

The ease with which Orlando accepts this transformation has brought the praise of critics such as Gilbert and Gubar, and with good reason. Not only does it strike a blow against biological essentialism, but it also gives the lie to any notion (such as the

Lacanian one) that would find gender differentiation to be at the heart of human identity.

Orlando's transformation is aided further as she spends the initial period afterwards in the company of a band of gypsies who themselves seem to pay little attention to gender identity. It is only when she returns to English society, with its strictly enforced code of gender difference, that she begins to realize "with a start the penalties and the privileges of her position" (153). And, having had the subject of gender brought to her attention, her unique perspective on such matters makes it possible for her to see the silliness of so many of the interactions between the sexes:

> And here it would seem from some ambiguity in her terms that she was censuring both sexes equally, as if she belonged to neither; and indeed, for the time being she seemed to vacillate; she was man; she was woman; she knew the secrets, shared the weaknesses of each. (158)[19]

To make matters even more confused, upon her return to England Orlando finds that her new gender does not exempt her from the advances of the Archduchess Harriet, because it turns out that this worthy was secretly the Archduke Harry all along. Indeed, society in general often seems to have flip-flopped in its attitudes toward Orlando because of her change in gender, regardless of how unchanged she might otherwise be.

Woolf gets a great deal of satiric mileage out of her depiction of the ways in which society treats Orlando differently because she is now ostensibly a woman though still the same person. Perhaps the most effective of these satires concerns the difficulty that Orlando has in assuming her property, as the change in gender renders her identity legally open to question. But the difficulties are solved by legal decree: she regains her estates (or at least the right to pass them on to her male heirs) and her gender is decided "indisputably" to be female (255). Woolf here not only takes some specific shots at English property laws, but also makes explicit the artificial and conventional nature of gender boundaries; Orlando's gender is not a matter of biology, but of official pronouncement within the laws of England.

But Orlando's gender remains highly uncertain despite this legal pronouncement and despite the biological fact that she later bears a child. Her husband Shel (who presumably ought to know) suspects that Orlando is really a man, just as Orlando suspects that Shel is really a woman. In this highly transgressive book, legal and biological boundaries simply will not hold. The specificity of the boundaries that are transgressed in the book endows it with a great deal of political force, and *Orlando* gains energy from the way in which it turns the discourse of the male tradition against that tradition. This mode of feminist transgression through parodic appropriation of male discourse is one with great potential, and one that is extensively used by feminist successors to Woolf such as Monique Wittig and Angela Carter, whose work I shall discuss in the next two chapters.

But this kind of transgression raises a question. How is one to determine when a woman writer is effectively using male language against the male tradition and when she is actually endorsing male language, perhaps being so inscribed within the domination of such language that she can write no other way? Elaine Showalter puts the question nicely: "And in mimicking the language of the dominant, how can we guarantee that mimicry is understood as ironic—as civil disobedience, camp, or feminist difference rather than as merely derivative?" (369). Showalter argues (no doubt correctly) that, regardless of the transgressive potential of "mimicry," feminists must also seek genuinely feminine modes of expression. However, such alternative means of expression are themselves in danger of degenerating into an empty formalism that loses sight of its real political targets. Meanwhile, in *Orlando* Woolf offers an obvious answer to the question of assuring that the transgressive use of dominant discourse will be read as ironic: she embeds that discourse in a textual fabric itself so saturated with irony that it would be virtually impossible to interpret it any other way.[20] She employs her simulacrum of the dominant discourse to describe specific content (such as the fluidity of Orlando's gender) that undermines the ideology on which this discourse is based and that is powerfully antithetical to any nonironic use of such discourse. Woolf thus maps out transgressive strategies of both form and content that are later employed to good effect by writers such as Wittig and Carter. By doing so she provides for such writers the strong feminine predecessor her own lack of which she so thoughtfully explored in the twin texts *Orlando* and *A Room of One's Own*.

WOMEN IN LOVE AND WAR:
LESBIANISM AS SUBVERSION
IN THE FICTION OF MONIQUE WITTIG

CHAPTER
7

Feminism has proved in recent years to be a tremendously energetic transgressive force in literary theory and criticism. Not
only has the feminist movement produced a number of fresh and
exciting new perspectives from which to view literature, but it
has also provided incontestable arguments for the political significance of literature. A number of feminist theorists have emphasized the strongly linguistic basis of patriarchal oppression,
and the obvious implication of this emphasis is that the resistance to patriarchy must occur on largely linguistic grounds
as well. In order to be effective, such struggles must occur
throughout the full range of discourses upon which patriarchal
society has based its power. Such "official" discourses as the
languages of science, technology, philosophy, and religion have
contributed to the oppression of "unofficial" viewpoints, and
they form natural targets for this subversive project. However, it
is in literature, with its (presumably) greater susceptibility to
innovation and its suasive potential to redefine the ways in
which we envision ourselves and our institutional structures,
that the greatest possibility for linguistic subversion may reside.

Feminist critics have convincingly argued that, in literature,
the political stakes are high indeed. It comes as no surprise,
then, that many of the leading figures in the feminist struggle to

redefine language have been literary critics, literary artists, or both. For example, Hélène Cixous (herself a novelist and literary critic) optimistically proclaims the subversive potential of feminist literature when she declares: "A feminine text cannot fail to be more than subversive. It is volcanic; as it is written it brings about an upheaval of the old property crust, carrier of masculine investments; there's no other way" ("Laugh" 258).

To Cixous, the voice of the woman, raised loudly enough, will automatically shatter the patriarchal tradition, like Günter Grass's Oskar Matzerath demolishing a pane of glass. Unfortunately, that tradition has all too often shown itself to be less like delicate crystal and more like one of those resilient science-fiction monsters that simply absorb the energies of all attacks launched against them, growing increasingly powerful as those attacks become more and more intense. Susan Rubin Suleiman has described this absorptive ability of the patriarchal establishment: "Like modern capitalism, modern patriarchy has a way of assimilating any number of subversive gestures into the 'mainstream,' where whatever subversive energy they may have possessed becomes neutralized" (11). Indeed, Cixous herself has often been cited as a prime example of the dangers of this kind of assimilation, with any number of commentators observing that *l'écriture féminine* remains thoroughly inscribed within traditional male views of the feminine.[1]

How, then, does one attack the patriarchal monster? In science fiction one might attempt to isolate the beast from all sources of energy until it runs down of its own accord. In feminism the analogous strategy would be to follow the suggestion of de Lauretis in her discussion of Calvino and to present women "who simply have no interest in men or men's desire" (77). This approach would seem to be the one employed by lesbian feminists such as Monique Wittig; presumably, lesbians avoid feeding any new energy to the patriarchy by simply cutting men out of the circuit of desire. Elaine Marks makes a strong case for the resultant subversive potential of lesbian feminism, suggesting that "[t]here is no person in or out of fiction who represents a stronger challenge to the Judeo-Christian tradition, to patriarchy and phallocentrism than the lesbian-feminist" (369). She argues that, because of the absence of male figures in the text, "the most subversive voices of the century" are to be found in lesbian texts (370). She further suggests that the narrator of Wittig's *The Lesbian Body* is "the most powerful lesbian in literature. . . . She is, in fact, the only true anti-Christ, the willful assassin of Christian love" (376). Finally, Marks concludes that "[n]o one since Sappho has made a greater contribution to lesbian intertextuality than Monique Wittig" (377).

Wittig's texts do have enormous subversive potential, particularly because of the specificity of her political position not only as a lesbian feminist, but also as a Marxist. Unfortunately, Marks's description of Wittig's texts as foreclosing the male presence makes Wittig sound as if she is putting her head in the sand, ostrichizing women by ostracizing men, hoping that the problem of the patriarchy will go away while she simply pretends that it doesn't exist. In the world of political reality, however, oppressors are not so cooperative. And even in the world of literary texts subversion is only possible in the presence of a norm against which that subversion is directed. In the case of patriarchal oppression one might legitimately argue that the norm is all too painfully apparent because of the exigencies of life in the world as it presently stands. Following this line of argument, one could maintain that the target of Wittig's subversion is all the more conspicuous by its very absence from her texts.[2] However, there is no need to defend Wittig's project from charges of "ostrichism" in this way, because in truth the voice of patriarchal authority is not at all absent from her texts. Wittig's lesbian texts are effectively subversive not because of their elimination of the male viewpoint, but precisely because the patriarchal tradition maintains a strong presence in those texts. (It is, however, a presence that is significantly transformed by the power of the lesbian context in which it appears.) In *Les Guérillères* Wittig depicts an explicit confrontation with the masculine tradition, as a group of women warriors mount a violent revolution to overthrow the rule of patriarchy and establish a new order based on feminine principles. In *The Lesbian Body* Wittig depicts the relationships among a group of lesbians who live on a secluded island where even all of the animals are female. But even here her writing practice confronts the masculine tradition, both in the way her techniques echo male authors and in her parodic use of masculine texts as intertextual fodder for the construction of her own texts.

Commentators have tended to suggest that Wittig's lesbian texts achieve their subversive effects through the totality of their break with male tradition. Wittig herself, in her introductory note to *The Lesbian Body*, describes that text as being among those that are in "total rupture with masculine culture, texts written by women exclusively for women, careless of male approval" (*Lesbian Body* 9). This rupture allows Wittig to avoid the kind of appropriation by the patriarchal monster that she sees occurring in the work of Cixous. Nevertheless, even in such a condition of "total rupture" there exists an interface across which there is a possibility of ideological exchange. I agree that Wittig's dialogues with traditional myth, with the conventions of genre, and with the structure of language itself have a significant subversive potential. In all of these cases, however, this subversion is achieved through dynamic interaction with male voices that are present in the text.

Returning one last time to my metaphor of the energy-eating monster, let me note that another of the traditional science-fiction strategies for attacking such a creature is to avoid feeding it any new energy and instead to employ a sort of high-tech jujitsu, inducing the monster to expend its existing energies by turning them against itself. This technique is also often employed in the field of literature, where the subversion of a target text or tradition by turning its own discursive energies against it traditionally goes by the name of parody. I would like to suggest, concentrating particularly upon *Les Guérillères* and *The Lesbian Body*, that Wittig's lesbian texts are effectively subversive primarily because of the powerful way in which they parody and thus transform the patriarchal tradition in literature.

There is a scene in *Les Guérillères* in which Wittig provides us with an excellent description of her use of materials from the patriarchal tradition in the development of her subversive project. In this scene Wittig's women warriors gather together various implements of culture and toss them onto an immense pyre which they then set ablaze. They then dance about with carnivalesque exuberance as these reminders of the past go up in flames. The destruction, however, is not complete; there is still something left to be built upon:

When the fire has burnt down, when they are sated with setting off explosions, they collect the débris, the objects that are not consumed, those that have not melted down, those that have not disintegrated. They cover them with blue green red paint to reassemble them in grotesque grandiose abracadabrant compositions to which they give names. (*Guérillères* 73)[3]

The "grotesque grandiose abracadabrant compositions" of this passage clearly include Wittig's own texts, and the transformative reassembly of the leftovers of the past in the production of these compositions corresponds quite closely to the way in which Wittig employs literary tradition in her writing. These transformations may be seen to be of several types, but for purposes of simplicity in discussion they can be divided into three basic categories. First and most specifically, Wittig's texts initiate dialogues with specific works of the past, and in particular with various traditional myths. Second, her texts enter more broadly into a potentially subversive exchange with the literary tradition through their parodic inversion of the conventions of established genres. Finally, Wittig's texts attack the patriarchal tradition at the level of language itself, thereby calling into question basic assumptions about what language means and the way it relates to the speaking subject.

Wittig's works sometimes refer to specific literary texts of the past, as when the poem appearing near the end of *Les Guérillères* clearly parodies one by Mallarmé (Durand 74). However, her specific cultural references are more often to various myths, in keeping with the generally mythic quality and "atmosphere of archetypal forces at work" that pervades her own texts (Durand 73). Wittig generally employs these traditional myths with a great deal of transformative ironic distance. She also chooses her myths carefully. In *The Lesbian Body*, a primary mythic pattern is the Egyptian story of Isis and Osiris, and the fragmentation of Wittig's text itself is directly related to the fragmentation of the body of Osiris.[4] This choice is highly strategic: the Isis–Osiris myth deals directly with the issue of the fragmentation of the body and has a strongly feminist orientation. In this myth the female Isis comes to the rescue of the male Osiris by gathering and reassembling his fragmented body; moreover, at least according to one version of the myth, Isis is unable to recover one key part of that body, the phallus, whereupon she manufactures an artificial replacement in order to complete the process of reassembly. Wittig takes this version of the myth one step further, doing away with the phallus entirely and making Osiris a woman. The myth thus becomes a sort of anti-Lacanian allegory concerning the demystification of the phallus in the development of human subjectivity.[5]

The Isis myth is also relevant to Wittig's own project of reassembling the fragments of patriarchal culture sans that dominant phallus. Wittig employs more traditionally male myths to good effect, generally by repeating them in such a way as to privilege the feminine. For example, the women of *Les Guérillères* find in their "feminaries" a guide to the cycle of the legends of the Holy Grail and conclude that the Grail itself can be interpreted as a symbol of the vulva. However, it should be noted that the women later abandon the cult of the vulva that dominates their society in the early pages of *Les Guérillères*, concluding exactly midway through the book that "they must now stop exalting the vulva. They say they must break the last bond that binds them to a dead culture" (*Guérillères* 72). In short, they have discovered that their privileging of the vulva leaves them thoroughly inscribed within male fantasies of the feminine. In this light, the exaltation of the vulva in the first half of *Les Guérillères* might be taken as a parodic jab at Cixous, Luce Irigaray and others who have proclaimed the virtues of the feminine body as a (w)hole.[6] Indeed, the "feminaries" themselves, which have generally been interpreted as privileged sacred books of Wittig's society of women, seem to be undercut.[7]

Wittig's most common feminization of traditional myths, especially in *The Lesbian Body*, involves the recasting of those myths with female heroes. Thus, this text features figures such as Ulyssea, Achillea, Zeyna (a female Zeus, complete with lightning bolts), Archimedea, and even "Christa the much-crucified" (*Lesbian Body* 35). Crowder correctly sees this strategy as formidable, suggesting that Wittig's rewriting of cultural myths in the female voice is radically subversive, and that her feminization of male names causes radical shifts in the perspective from which those myths are viewed (130). The replacement of such a staunchly patriarchal figure as Ulysses (being awaited by a patiently faithful Penelope) with a female counterpart has great potential for redefining our traditional notions of gender roles. There is a great deal of dialogic tension in Wittig's appropriation of male names, however; there is always a constant threat that the force of the patriarchal tradition will overwhelm Wittig's own discourse. But it is just this tension that adds transgressive energy to Wittig's writing.

Wittig's ironic reinscriptions of traditional myths not only confront the male mythic tradition head-on, they also participate in important trends in modern literature. The "mythic method" has been one of the stays of both modernist and postmodernist literature, and it is characteristic of modern literature to approach its mythic sources with a considerable amount of irony. Wittig's ironic inversions of traditional myths would seem, in a formal sense at least, to be well within the mainstream of modern literature. Recognizing Wittig's similarity to this largely male mainstream, however, actually increases the transgressive potential of her work by creating a dialogue between Wittig's lesbian feminist point of view and the more traditional points of view of her male counterparts. Suleiman offers as evidence of the radicalism of one of Wittig's "rewritten, feminized versions of classical and Christian myths" the fact that the Golden Fleece is described in *Les Guérillères* as "one of the designations that have been given to the hairs that cover the pubis" (20).[8] But Wittig is doing far more here than parodying a male myth. This use of the Golden Fleece closely parallels Wittig's depiction of the Holy Grail as a symbol of the vulva, so that this passage again targets both the male tradition and the particular brand of feminist discourse represented by women such as Cixous. The association of the Golden Fleece with "the hairs that cover the pubis" is quite well established in the male tradition, so much so that this association is even parodied in male texts. Consider the case of Donald Barthelme's *The Dead Father*, in which the title character completes his cross-country quest with Thomas and Julie only to find nothing waiting for him but a grave:

No Fleece? asked the Dead Father.
Thomas looked at Julie.
She has it?
Julie lifted her skirt.
Quite golden, said the Dead Father. Quite ample. That's it?
All there is, Julie said. Unfortunately. But this much. This where life lives. A pretty problem. As mine as yours. I'm sorry. (218)

Both Barthelme and Wittig here take on the traditional patriarchal form of the quest myth as the target of their respective ironies. However, Wittig's critique is the more forcefully transgressive of the two because of the leverage gained from her political position. In Barthelme there is a sense that the rule of the father is being ended only so that he can pass the crown to his son, perpetuating patriarchal ideology. Wittig, on the other hand, attempts to effect a radical break in this patriarchal order of succession by having her female guerillas usurp the throne.

This depiction of the quest myth as an allegory of sexual desire for the body of the woman is not unusual in modern literature. In fact, one could argue that even so archetypal a text as Homer's *Odyssey*, itself one of the specific targets of Wittig's parodies, is based on precisely this motif, in which the homeward-bound Ulysses participates in a quest with the body of Penelope as prize. James Joyce, that most prominent of all modern reinscribers of Homer, makes extensive use of this motif. Further, he takes the additional step of conflating myth with science, suggesting that the quest myth functions not only as a representation of sexual desire, but also as an image of the desire that drives scientific research. Thus Joyce's Leopold Bloom (a.k.a. Dr. Luitpold Blumenduft) is both an ironic refiguration of Ulysses and an amateur scientist-type whose inquiring mind wants to know all sorts of things, including the secrets of gynecology. He muses, for example, on the implications of such anatomical facts as "Three holes all women" (*Ulysses* 234). This link between sexuality and scientific curiosity is even more explicit in *Finnegans Wake* where the scientific theorizing of the boys Dolph and Kevin (a.k.a. Shaun and Shem) in the "Nightlessons" section turns into a fantasy of lifting the apron of ALP to explore the secret regions of their mother's body:

Outer serpumstances being ekewilled, we carefully, if she pleats, lift by her seam hem and jabote at the spidsiest of her trickkikant (like thousands done before since fillies calpered. Ocone! Ocone!) the maidsapron of our A.L.P., fearfully! till its nether nadir is vortically where (allow me aright to two cute winkles) its naval's napex will have to beandbe. (297.7–14)

Psychoanalysis has also made this connection between science and sexuality. Freud, in his discussion of Leonardo da Vinci, suggests that not only da Vinci but scientists in general derive much of the energy for their professional investigations from a sublimation of sexual desire, a phenomenon that Freud sees as growing out of infantile researches into the question of where babies come from (Freud 27–29). Indeed, Joyce's brothers immediately turn their researches to this very question, pondering the apparent unfathomability of exactly how it was that they were produced through the union of HCE and ALP, through "the elipsities of their gyribouts those fickers which are returnally reprodictive of themselves. Which is impassible" (298.16–18). It is likely, in fact, that Joyce's parodic treatment of this theme is specifically directed at Freud, as psychoanalysis functions as a principal target for his parodies at various points in the *Wake*. Thus Joyce's parodic technique is able to slay two sacred patriarchal birds with a single subversive stone, poking demystifying fun simultaneously at science in general and at Freud's analysis of the scientific impulse.[9]

Wittig, like Joyce (and like any number of other modern writers, Vladimir Nabokov perhaps being the most obvious), also singles out psychoanalysis as a target of her parody.[10] She indicates her opinion of psychoanalysts in *Lesbian Peoples: Material for a Dictionary*, referring to them as "traffickers in the unconscious" (157). Wittig opposes psychoanalysis for two reasons. First, psychoanalysis traditionally posits heterosexuality as a norm from which homosexuality is measured as deviant and inferior. Second, through its emphasis on timeless psychological essences as embodied in the universality of the Oedipal drama, psychoanalysis is unable to deal with the realities of the political drama of history. Crowder notes the way in which Wittig dismisses traditional family structures in favor of the bonds of lesbian lovers in *The Lesbian Body*, the result being the "absence of the Freudian/Lacanian unconscious" from that text (125). This escape from traditional family structures also results in an escape from the Oedipal triangle, which is fundamentally based upon recognizing and accepting sexual difference. As Wittig points out, "the discourse of psychoanalysis . . . builds on the a priori and idealist concept of sexual difference, a concept that historically participates in the general discourse of domination" ("Paradigm" 119).

Wittig also parallels Joyce in gaining additional subversive energy through the conflation of science and myth. For example, by including the story of Archimedes in the list of male myths called into question in *The Lesbian Body*, she strikes a demystifying blow against the patriarchal authority of science-as-truth. When Archimedea begins with her hydraulic experiments in time-honored male scientific empirical fashion, Wittig's narrator deflates the pretensions of those proceedings with a carnivalesque burst of laughter:

you cause m/e to observe that a body immersed in a liquid sustains a vertical thrust directed from below upwards, that m/y dearest is manifest to anyone who spends three-quarters of the day plunged in water . . . you say that you have discovered therein a fundamental law of our physical universe, at these words I can no longer contain m/y laughter, I sink therefore, I emerge to thank the Blessed One the thrice august since you woman of little faith do not think of so doing. (*Lesbian Body* 159–60)

Roland Barthes has noted the conservative function that myth usually plays in society, suggesting that myth opposes the possibility of change by presenting itself as already complete and hiding the contingency of its own historical development (*Mythologies* 117). Traditional science similarly presents itself as a preexisting totality. By attacking structures such as science and myth and showing that they could have been otherwise, both Joyce and Wittig have selected particularly apt targets for their subversive projects. Furthermore, the inscription of science and psychoanalysis within the general mythic atmospheres of *Finnegans Wake* and of *The Lesbian Body* suggests that perhaps science, psychoanalysis, and myth function in similar ways, laying claim to a privileged access to truth by obscuring that they developed in specific historical contexts. Through her attacks on traditional structures of authority such as those embodied in myth, science, and psychoanalysis, Wittig shows that her texts do not inhabit some hermetically sealed female territory, but instead initiate powerful and productive dialogues with the voices of male tradition. That her technique of mythic reinscription so closely resembles that of male authors such as Barthelme and Joyce adds further energy by bringing those voices into the dialogue as well.

Wittig's use of myth is particularly forceful in its specific orientation toward gender issues. Commentators such as Higgins, Rosenfeld, and Shaktini have noted the way in which Wittig's central emphasis on the Isis–Osiris myth renders her work powerfully feminist. And the use of this myth in itself opens specific dialogues. Among Wittig's feminist predecessors, for example, Virginia Woolf makes extensive use of Egyptian myth, with a special emphasis on the importance of Isis as a female figure.[11] Moreover, as both Margot Norris and Bonnie Kime Scott note, the Isis–Osiris story forms one of the most important sources of mythic material for *Finnegans Wake*.[12] Norris suggests that Isis's gathering of the fragments of Osiris (who, in typically Joycean fashion, is conflated in the *Wake* with that other famous figure of fragmentation, Humpty Dumpty) functions as a mirror of the way in which Joyce composed the *Wake* itself through the accumulation of bits and pieces of diverse materials (67–69).

In fact, the Isis–Osiris myth is essential to a number of male texts, and the fragmentation associated with the sparagmos of Osiris might be taken as a quite general metaphor for the functioning of many modern texts, ranging from *Ulysses* and *The Waste Land* to the jigsaw-puzzle structure of Georges Perec's *Life: A User's Manual* and the various physically dismembered books represented in Calvino's *If on a winter's night a traveler*. This emphasis on formal fragmentation in modern texts obviously participates in the various contemporary critical discussions of techniques such as montage, collage, and bricolage in modern art. Gregory Ulmer goes so far as to suggest that "collage is the single most revolutionary formal innovation in artistic representation to occur in our century" (86). Collage is not so much a twentieth-century innovation as Ulmer here indicates (and he himself admits that it has ancient roots); nonetheless, his point concerning its importance in modern art is well taken.[13]

Ishmael Reed's *Mumbo Jumbo* is a classic example of the modern fragmented text, and it is significant that he devotes thirty pages of this relatively brief book to his own ironic retelling of the Isis–Osiris myth (161–91). Moreover, his book, which can be read as an ironic inversion of *The Waste Land*, features a central "Text" that is distributed piecemeal around the country among fourteen holders.[14] This Text is in turn a metaphor for Reed's own highly fragmented text.

Thomas Pynchon's *Gravity's Rainbow* is another highly fragmented modern text, and it has been pointed out that the scattering of Tyrone Slothrop in the *Rainbow* can be related to the sparagmos motif.[15] I might add that Pynchon even plays on the favorite feminist version of the myth: one of the principal mysteries of the book concerns the exact nature of Slothrop's penis, which may (or may not) have been replaced by a synthetic substitute while he was still a child. Pynchon employs this motif in a complex and sophisticated way, using it simultaneously to parody the psychoanalytic emphasis on castration anxiety and to comment ironically on man's sense of helplessness in the modern world. Moreover, by having Slothrop wander over post–World War II Europe in search of the secret of his questionable organ (and of the blatantly phallic 00000 rocket), Pynchon inverts the motif of the quest for the vulva, making it instead a quest for the phallus.

Wittig, then, is far from being alone in her use of the myth of Isis and Osiris. But again, Wittig's use of the myth is far more specific in its implication than is the use of the same myth in authors such as Reed and Pynchon. In both of these latter authors, the myth becomes a sort of generalized symbol of fragmentation, with multiple textual, cultural, and psychoanalytic significances. Multiple interpretations are available in Wittig's text as well, but her particular perspective lends a special weight to the Isis–Osiris myth as an allegory of the subversion of phallic domination.

Wittig also participates in a long literary tradition in her reinscription of traditional myths through gender reversals. Woolf's *Orlando* is the obvious modern predecessor here. But as Linda Hutcheon points out, parody is generally characterized by ironic reversals, and gender reversals are among the most obvious ways to achieve such effects. Hutcheon notes that Byron's *Don Juan* gains much of its energy by having women chase after the title character in a reversal of the traditional gender roles associated with the Don Juan story. Even among the ancient Greeks, Euripides effectively parodied Aeschylus and Sophocles in his *Medea*, where he supplanted the traditional male protagonist with a woman and replaced the usual collection of (male) elders and suppliants with a female chorus ("Modern Parody" 88).

Wittig's reversals of the genders of traditional mythic figures have much in common with a general emphasis on gender reversals (especially as manifested in depictions of transvestism) that Sandra Gilbert and Susan Gubar, among others, have noted to be widespread in modernist literature. Gender reversals are essential to the works of women writers such as Woolf, Barnes, and Angela Carter. Moreover, gender reversals are also employed by male writers such as Lawrence, Eliot, and Joyce, often to potentially subversive ends, despite Gilbert's arguments that only women can use the transvestism motif successfully. Pynchon is especially reminiscent of Wittig when he feminizes the name of Oedipus, making Oedipa Maas the protagonist of *The Crying of Lot 49*.[16] Again, there is an effective political message embodied in this switch of gender. As Cathy Davidson notes, "Oedipa challenges the cherished myths of a male-dominated society, assumptions which, in their way, comprise a Sphinx as implacable as the female figure encountered by her mythic namesake" (50).

Pynchon's technique of gender reversal in *Lot 49* parallels that of Wittig in more ways than one. His particular choice of the Oedipus figure as a mythic model irresistibly initiates a dialogue with psychoanalysis, and in a text where the only psychoanalyst actually present is an insane ex-Nazi named Dr. Hilarius, that dialogue cannot avoid being parodic.[17] Moreover, Pynchon's novel is largely a parody of the genre of detective fiction, with the nontraditional move of making the detective-protagonist female a component of that parody. In the Oedipus myth (and indeed in most of Western culture) the woman is seen not as a solver of riddles, but as a poser of mysteries. The Sphinx is, after all, a female, but in *Lot 49* it is the female Oedipa who seeks to unravel the riddle posed by the male Pierce Inverarity. Pynchon himself calls attention to this transgression against the traditional form of the mystery in the motel-room scene, in which Oedipa and Metzger play "Strip Botticelli." In this game, Oedipa is to ask questions toward a prediction of the outcome of the movie *Cashiered*, which they are watching on television and in which Metzger had starred as a child actor. Every time she receives an answer from Metzger she must remove an article of clothing, and if she fails to guess the outcome correctly she must yield up her body to Metzger as the prize.

Oedipa prepares herself for the game by donning a prodigious array of garments, parodying the traditional Western myth of the woman who is cloaked in mystery and whose secrets (especially the secrets of her body) must be revealed only gradually and with difficulty. The mockery of this convention is strengthened by the slapstick manner in which Oedipa is finally undressed and "seduced." Overcome with alcohol, she collapses

so weak she couldn't help him undress her; it took him 20 minutes, rolling, arranging her this way and that, as if she thought, he were some scaled-up, short-haired, poker-faced little girl with a Barbie doll. She may have fallen asleep once or twice. She awoke at last to find herself getting laid. (42)

The image of Metzger here as a "little girl" emphasizes the theme of gender transgression, and indeed it must be remembered that the role of Sphinx in this game of riddles is played by Metzger; he knows the answer that Oedipa is only trying to guess. Moreover, in the end Oedipa (like Oedipus) does solve the riddle correctly, so it is not Oedipa's body that winds up as prize, but Metzger's: "'You won me,' Metzger smiled" (43).

Pynchon's refusal to conform to the expectations of the detective story points to a larger role of generic subversion throughout *Lot 49*. Wittig's similar attacks on the conventions of genre are a primary weapon in her transgressive arsenal. Hélène Vivienne Wenzel notes the way in which Wittig refuses to confine herself to genres that have traditionally been available to women, but instead "appropriates and inverts those traditional male genres that have held the power to shape and reflect their language and their reality." Wenzel goes on to suggest that each of Wittig's four books subverts and redefines a specific traditional genre: *The Opoponax* creates a female version of the *Bildungsroman*; *Les Guérillères* parodies the traditional epic poem; *The Lesbian Body* parodies the "Song of Songs" from the Bible, as well as all of Western mythology; and *Lesbian Peoples: Material for a Dictionary* redefines the conventions of the dictionary form (284–85).

Again, Wittig chooses her targets carefully. Her attacks on the epic are particularly effective because, as Bakhtin has argued, the epic is the ultimate authoritarian genre, presenting itself as a completed form and as a vehicle for the transmittal of the authority of the past. The events of the epic exist in an ideal past time that is strictly sealed off from any dialogue with the present. "In the past, everything is good; all the really good things . . . occur only in this past. The epic absolute past is the single source and beginning of everything good for all later times as well" (*Dialogic Imagination* 15). As the genre of sacrosanct and supposedly unchallengeable authority, inherently opposed to the possibility of change, the epic is a natural target for subversion. It is also the patriarchal genre par excellence. Christa Wolf conducts a similar assault on the epic tradition in *Cassandra*, her feminist reinscription of the *Iliad*. In an essay published with the novel, Wolf explains the appropriateness of the epic as a feminist target: "The epic, born of the struggles for patriarchy, becomes by its structure an instrument by which to elaborate and fortify the patriarchy" (296).

Durand presents a fuller discussion of the way in which *Les Guérillères* attacks and subverts the tradition of the epic, arguing that Wittig "takes 'feminine' attitudes and uses them in the supremely male epic tradition so as to mock the concepts of both and to show the singleness of being human" (77). But Wittig's subversion of the epic goes far beyond the mere infusion of feminine attitudes into this traditionally male genre. By writing in present tense, Wittig thrusts her epic material into the realm of the contemporary, destroying the absolute distance of a inaccessible epic past and forcing the epic into a dialogue with the historical contingency that it traditionally denies.[18] Wittig also attacks the monoglossic purity of the epic form, inserting into *Les Guérillères* a number of other genres as well. At times she steps out of the epic frame entirely, directly presenting tutorial tracts of contemporary feminist theory. For example, she diagnoses the way in which men have traditionally dominated language and used their power of naming to define women:

The women say, the men have kept you at a distance, they have
supported you, they have put you on a pedestal, constructed with
an essential difference. . . . They say, in speaking they have
possessed violated taken subdued humiliated you to their heart's
content. They say, oddly enough what they have exalted in their
words as an essential difference is a biological variation. They say,
they have described you as they described races they called inferior.
(*Guérillères* 100–102)

Wittig also inserts two lyric poems in her epic framework, and often presents her epic material in a lyrical mode of discourse. This mixture of two seemingly incompatible genres undercuts the authority of both, and once again Wittig is able to attack multiple simultaneous targets.[19] Indeed, the subjective orientation implied in the traditional lyric is as much anathema to Wittig as is the patriarchal authority implied in the epic. Within Wittig's Marxist perspective, such individuality merely leads to an isolation and alienation of individuals that works directly against the possibility of any effective mass political action. Therefore, she attempts to redefine the lyric as a means of expression of class, rather than individual consciousness. This attempt is evidenced in that the protagonist of *Les Guérillères* is generally described as "the women," i.e., as the community rather than as any discrete individual.[20] This redefinition of the lyric is continued in *The Lesbian Body*, and Crowder suggests that Wittig's most subversive gesture in this text is her direct attacks on the conventions of Western love poetry: "The poet's task is to transform via metaphor lips into rubies, eyes into jewels, breasts into snow. Implicit in such metaphor is the rejection of the actual woman as inadequately desirable" (121). In short, the apotheosis of the (female) loved one in traditional male poetry involves a gesture of contempt for the body and a desire for an idealization that denies the physical reality of the woman. But in Wittig eyes are eyes and breasts are breasts. By emphasizing in concrete terms the body itself, in all its physicality, Wittig strikes a vigorous blow at poetic tradition and helps to demonstrate the antifeminist bias of such poetry.[21]

Genre, like myth, is a natural target for any project that seeks to subvert the dominant ideological structures of society. Fredric Jameson, echoing Bakhtin, has emphasized the way in which genres are not innocent, but in fact arise in direct response to ideological forces in their historical moments.[22] These ideologies then become "hardened" as generic forms become fixed (much as myths become fixed). An attack on the authority of a genre amounts to a confrontation with the ideologies embedded in that genre as well, because

a genre is essentially a socio-symbolic message, or in other terms, that form is immanently and intrinsically an ideology in its own right. When such forms are reappropriated and refashioned in quite different social and cultural contexts, this message persists and must be functionally reckoned into the new form. (*Political Unconscious* 141)

Genre subversion is one of the most effective ways in which literature can make an effective political statement because the ideology inherent in genre presents a well-defined target for transgression. Wittig's attacks on traditional notions of genre are thus effectively conceived. However, these attacks, formidable though they may be, again place her in direct dialogue with the mainstream of twentieth-century literature. One need only think of Joyce's ironic treatment of the epic in *Ulysses*, Woolf's parody of the scholarly biography in *Orlando*, and William Carlos Williams's dialogue with the lyric tradition in poems such as "The Red Wheelbarrow" and "This Is Just To Say" to see that the reorientation of traditional genres forms a major trend in modern literature.[23] Jameson suggests that both modernism and postmodernism are inherently antigeneric, and even goes so far as to suggest that, within the context of late consumer capitalism, no work can be considered true art *unless* it mounts an attack on traditional notions of genre:

With the elimination of an institutionalized social status for the cultural producer and the opening of the work of art itself to commodification, the older generic specifications are transformed into a brand-name system against which any authentic artistic expression must necessarily struggle. (*Political Unconscious* 107)

It is true that contemporary culture, in which it seems virtually impossible to sustain the idea of a "pure" genre, is particularly susceptible to Jameson's analysis here. However, the transformation of genre is in fact a much broader and more ancient phenomenon than Jameson indicates. As I discussed in Chapter 6, much of modern genre theory (especially Bakhtin's work on the novel) sees genre not as a fixed form but as a field for conflict and evolution.

Wittig, then, has not redefined literature through her attacks on traditional genres. She has simply done what novels are supposed to do, if we accept the description of the novel provided by Bakhtin. As with her use of myth, Wittig is able to achieve subversive effects in her treatment of genre not because she avoids the use of male forms, but precisely because she meets those forms head on, appropriating and reaccentuating them for her own purposes. On a more fundamental level, she employs the same strategy with language itself. All Western languages

have been defined by male-dominated societies, but as Rosenfeld points out, French is a language that is even more male-
oriented than most, adding new significance to Wittig's encounter with the language itself (235). Suleiman notes the way in
which Wittig categorically rejects the notion (à la Cixous or
Irigaray) of a woman's language that is somehow apart from that
of men. To do so would merely be to play into the hands of the
patriarchy, ceding to it the power inherent in the dominant language. Thus instead of attempting to develop some radically
different feminine form of discourse Wittig generally opts to
employ the male-oriented French language in a relatively conventional way, electing to seek subversive effects by subtly reaccentuating that language from within. Crowder notes Wittig's
belief that "[t]o abandon language because it presently reflects
masculinist structures is to abandon transformation of all sexist
structures in favor of a marginal women's culture." She then
explains that Wittig's works,

> while extremely daring in form, are very lucid, controlled, and
> correct in grammar and vocabulary. She rarely indulges in the puns,
> wordplay, and neologisms characteristic of writers trying to create a
> new language. Her nonfiction is a model of almost classical essay
> style and clarity. (127)[24]

This does not mean, however, that Wittig fails to interrogate
existing linguistic structures profoundly. Indeed, she is intensely aware of the role that language plays in perpetuating the
system of sexual difference that she sees as being responsible for
the historical oppression of women. What we need, she suggests,
is a language that is free of gender designations entirely: "Hu-
mankind must find another name for itself and another system
of grammar that will do away with genders, the linguistic in-
dicator of political oppositions" ("Paradigm" 121).[25]

Wittig's project of redefining language proceeds on several
fronts. *Lesbian Peoples: Material for a Dictionary*, for example,
begins a project of redefining the words of language in a way that
attempts to escape the narrow bounds of denotation, thus initiating an attack against the Western tradition that words are
related to meanings in transparent and representational ways.
This attack on the transparency of language continues in the
novels, where Wittig consistently calls attention to the mate-

riality of language as medium. Her treatment of naming is representative of this technique. Naming is the prototype of the masculine symbolic use of language in general; it presents in the most obvious form the traditional theory of language as representation. The naming of objects represents an attempt to circumscribe and control those objects within language. We are named before we can speak, labeled in language before we can choose our own labels. As Lacan points out, "the subject, too, if he can appear to be the slave of language is all the more so of a discourse in the universal movement in which his place is already inscribed at birth, if only by virtue of his proper name" (*Écrits* 148).

Feminists such as Woolf and Cixous have attempted to evade the tyranny of male naming through a privileging of anonymity. Wittig, however, once again chooses the tactic of head-on assault, abrogating this tyranny by appropriating the authority of naming for her own use. In *Les Guérillères* the text is frequently interrupted with lists of the names of the various women warriors. Besides their obvious function as parodies of the traditional epic catalogue, these lists of names amount to a declaration of independence from male linguistic domination.[26] The women wield their own names like swords, announcing that they now control their own linguistic destinies, just as in *The Lesbian Body* the names of the parts of the body are enumerated as a declaration that the women now control their own bodies.

Wittig's feminization of the names of mythical male heroes in *The Lesbian Body* obviously appropriates the authority of naming. Shaktini notes the foregrounding of naming in this text:

Although the process of naming is largely unconscious for us, Wittig's frequent use of the word "nom" (name)—which appears twenty-seven times—heightens our consciousness of the power of the illocutionary process while also making us aware that naming implies the point of view of the namer. (38)

Partially, as Shaktini also notes, this emphasis on naming provides another link to the Isis myth, as Isis was the goddess of words and of naming. Isis also magically tricked the sun-god Ra into revealing his secret name (Higgins 161). Indeed, in *The Lesbian Body* names take on a talismanic significance, as witnessed by the motif of the secret name that resounds throughout the text. The narrator of the book repeatedly stresses the interdiction against uttering the name of the loved one: "*I* call to you, you unnameable unnamed, she whose name *I* may not utter she whose unnameable name pronounced by m/e makes the wasps leave their hives . . . not once *I* swear to you will *I* utter your name" (*Lesbian Body* 46, translator's italics). Naming is an act of power, an act of control. It is also an act of distancing. In *If on a winter's night a traveler*, Calvino also refuses to speak the name of his central character, referring to him simply as "the Reader":

This book so far has been careful to leave open to the Reader who is reading the possibility of identifying himself with the Reader who is read: this is why he was not given a name, which would automatically have made him the equivalent of a Third Person, of a character. (141)

Similarly, Wittig's narrator refuses to speak the name of the loved one, because such an act of naming would place the loved one in third person and identify her as Other, weakening the lesbian bond. Though Wittig's lesbian women seek to seize control of their own names, they reject the notion of appropriating the names of others, particularly of loved ones. These women refuse to seek the domination of the other that naming implies, opting instead for a relationship of mutuality that leaves each fully in control of her own name and her own identity, even if that identity is also inextricably related to that of the community.

Higgins additionally notes that the motif of the taboo name reflects the conflict between speech and silence that she sees as paramount in *The Lesbian Body* (163). This conflict is presented particularly directly in the episode in which the women awake to find that all the vowels have inexplicably disappeared from their language. This newly transformed language presents difficulties in pronunciation for the loved one that the narrator greets with high hilarity:

The novel effect of the movement of your cheeks and mouth the difficulty the sounds have in making their way out of your mouth are so comical that I choke with laughter, I fall over backwards, m/y tears stream, I am increasingly overcome by laughter. (*Lesbian Body* 104)

This episode of the disappearing vowels emphasizes the materiality of language in an obvious way. Higgins notes how this episode privileges writing over speech: writing can function without vowels much more readily than can speech. Moreover, she sees an additional link here to the Isis–Osiris myth: "Like Osiris, language has been dismembered. The human body and the communicative function of oral speech die and are resurrected as writing" (165). I also suggest that this carnivalesque de-privileging of the oral represents another jab at Cixous, who has repeatedly emphasized the importance of music and of the voice in women's writing.[27]

Probably the most striking way in which Wittig foregrounds language itself as a battleground upon which to confront the oppression of patriarchy is her innovative use of pronouns. I have already noted the shift from third person plural to first person plural pronouns at the end of *Les Guérillères*. Even more striking is the practice, followed throughout *The Lesbian Body*, of printing all first-person pronouns (je, moi, etc.) divided by a slash after the first letter.[28] In her introductory note to the book, Wittig explains that she employs this technique to emphasize how women are forced to function within the confines of a patriarchal language that is fundamentally alien to them:

If in writing je, I adopt this language, this je cannot do so. J/e is the symbol of the lived, rending experience which is m/y writing, of this cutting in two which throughout literature is the exercise of a language that does not constitute me as subject. J/e poses the ideological and historic question of feminine subjects. (*Lesbian Body* 10–11)

A useful analogy here is the suggestion by Emile Benveniste that the use of the first-person pronoun allows the speaking subject to generate his own subjectivity in language:

It is in and through language that man constitutes himself as a *subject*, because language alone establishes the concept of "ego" in reality, in *its* reality which is that of the being. . . . Language is possible only because each speaker sets himself up as a *subject* by referring to himself as *I* in his discourse. . . . Language is so organized that it permits each speaker to *appropriate to himself* an entire language by designating himself as *I*. (224–26, Benvenistes' emphases)

To Benveniste, this appropriation of language must be continually renewed, and the subject is dynamically constituted through his participation in actual speech acts. Wittig would appear to agree with this position, but Benveniste's heavy use of masculine pronouns here may be telling.[29] For a woman, the access to language is not so easy, "a generic feminine subject can only enter by force into a language which is foreign to it" (*Lesbian Body* 10). Wittig's feminine subject, like the subject of Benveniste, is constituted through participation in language, but she indicates the increased difficulty of this constitution for women by slashing first-person pronouns to indicate her sense of exclusion at being a feminine subject constituted within a language designed by and for men.[30]

But the sense of alienation noted by Wittig here has been recognized before, and not just by feminists.[31] Rimbaud's famous statement that "je est un autre," for example, indicates a similarly problematic view of the selfhood indicated by first-person speech. Wittig's clearest predecessor here, though, is Woolf, whose impatience with "the damned egotistical self" often takes the form of an interrogation of the functioning of the first-person pronoun.[32] For example, she notes the overshadowing presence of the self of the author in traditional male texts:

But after reading a chapter or two a shadow seemed to lie across the page. It was a straight dark bar, a shadow shaped something like the letter "I." . . . One began to be tired of "I." (*Room* 103)

In her own texts, Woolf seeks to avoid this shadow of the male "I," as in the opening of *A Room of One's Own* (discussed in Chapter 6). This effect becomes even more pronounced in *The Waves*, where through most of the text she employs six different, constantly alternating, first-person narrators, so that the continual switching from one speaker to another problematizes the association of the "I" of the text with any specific speaking subject. The effect of such continual shifts in deixis is to call into question the nonproblematic relationship that Benveniste sees between use of the first-person pronoun and the generation of subjectivity. Wittig's slashing of those pronouns has much the same effect.

Critical commentary on Wittig's writing tends to emphasize the radically innovative nature of her texts, a nature that invests those texts with subversive force. These commentaries, despite their general tone of admiration, are often put off by the highly political nature of Wittig's project. Many critics view Wittig's writing as a mechanical re-presentation of her political views. Through my emphasis on Wittig's technical similarities with other modern writers, I have suggested that she employs standard literary techniques that have been widely used by both male and female writers of the twentieth century. Thus, in terms of actual writing strategies, she remains well within firmly established territory. I do not discount Wittig's achievement as an artist, but emphasize how her political statement is made within a specifically literary context. She produces not novelized politics, but politicized novels. Appreciating Wittig's dialogue with the literary tradition contributes greatly to understanding the mechanisms through which her novels achieve their subversive effects. The striking impact of her work cannot be explained in terms of any formalistic descriptions of her language or texts. It is only when one considers the lesbian context within which she writes, a context that empowers traditional writing strategies with renewed subversive energy, that one begins to understand the way in which she is truly exploring an undiscovered country. Wittig, as a lesbian feminist with Marxist inclinations, writes from a viewpoint intensely situated within the contemporary political climate. She writes against particular targets that themselves occupy highly charged positions in this climate. This combination of perspectives, of a well-defined political position from which to speak and specific political targets to speak against, gives her work the special sense of orientation that accounts for its uniquely subversive effects.

Attempting to achieve subversive transgression within a literary text that does not first clearly posit the boundaries that are being transgressed would be pointless, on the order of attempting to play tennis without a net. In Wittig's case it might be more like playing tennis without balls; the particularly sexual nature of her transgressions adds greatly to their impact. But to be politically effective, any literary transgression must have a strong communal element. The subversive effects achieved by a literary text must involve not only private emotional reactions, but public responses as well, interrogating the broad social conventions that underlie political practice, thereby calling into question the hierarchies and institutions that promulgate these conventions and that are in turn made possible by them.

I noted in my discussion of Sorrentino (Chapter 3) Allon White's concern that this emphasis on the social and the public is lacking in much of modern (post-Romantic) literature, which has come more and more to rely upon the terror and abjection of subjective experience (especially sexuality) to achieve its transgressive effect. Foucault's comments on sexuality as an arena for transgression, however, show how sexuality itself is largely determined by public discourse, indicating that effective political force can be achieved in works that emphasize sexuality. Wittig's lesbian texts similarly formulate sexuality as a domain of transgression. In Wittig's texts, gender issues are always specifically couched in terms of class and ideological struggle. She suggests that the fundamental difference between categories of individuals is not some essentialized notion of gender, as psychoanalysis might have it, but "a difference belonging to a political, economic, ideological order."[33] Therefore, "[h]eterosexuality is a cultural construct designed to justify the whole system of social domination based on the obligatory reproductive function of women and the appropriation of that reproduction" ("Paradigm" 115).[34] Wittig effectively employs this insight in her fictional texts, harnessing the transgressive energies that are inherent in sexuality not in the service of subjectivized experience but of a socialized and communal political statement.

ABJECTION AND THE CARNIVALESQUE: TRANSGRESSION IN **NIGHTWOOD** AND **NIGHTS AT THE CIRCUS**

CHAPTER

8 _____

On the very first page of Djuna Barnes' *Nightwood*, we are given a description of the "military beauty" of Hedvig Volkbein and told that the rotund belly of her husband Guido was marked with "the obstetric line seen on fruits." The reversal of traditional gender-coding in the language of these descriptions sets the tone for the remainder of the book, which challenges not only conventional boundaries between the genders, but also the fundamental distinctions between dominant and marginal culture, human and animal, cleanliness and filth. The various boundary transgressions in *Nightwood* gain energy, to be sure, from the book's transgressive structure and language, but they derive even greater force from the images of abjection throughout the text. All of the characters (and the text itself) seem on the edge of terror and hysteria, all fighting desperately to push back the horror and corruption that lurk just out of sight, constantly threatening to burst into view.

In contrast, Angela Carter's *Nights at the Circus* is, on the surface at least, a zany, lighthearted romp. Yet Carter's book, like Barnes's, is a veritable compendium of images of transgression. Carter's strategy is to approach these transgressions in carnivalesque fashion, writing in the best Menippean tradition. But carnivalesque laughter can be deadly serious; its funny, wild, exuberant, and vastly entertaining surface notwithstanding, *Nights at the Circus* has a dark side as well. A comparison of *Nightwood* and *Nights at the Circus* thus illustrates the dynamic connection between the celebration of the carnival and the terror of the abject.

ABJECTION AS TRANSGRESSION IN **NIGHTWOOD**

Nightwood's transgressions begin at the formal level of its digressive structure and unusual language. Stephen-Paul Martin, for example, has offered the book as a paradigm of what he terms the "feminine imagination" in literature, as one of a number of innovative modern works that "ask us to create and nurture them, to give them shape over time in the parts of our imaginations that make new forms" (9). Indeed, much of Barnes's writing in *Nightwood* anticipates contemporary French feminist discussions of women's writing. On the other hand, one should also keep in mind that Barnes's work participated in a larger movement of avant-garde artists in the thirties. The philosophy of these artists, heavily influenced by the work of Joyce and again anticipating feminist thinkers such as Cixous, can be summarized from the statement offered by Eugène Jolas describing the philosophy of his journal transition: "The poet who gives back to language its pre-logical functions, who re-creates it as an orphic sign, makes a spiritual revolt" (cited in Gluck 22).

Nightwood's refusal to conform to traditional narrative conventions led Joseph Frank to use it as his principal example in his highly influential discussion of "spatial form" in modernist literature. According to Frank, modernist authors such as Eliot, Pound, Proust, Joyce, and Barnes construct their works not as temporal progressions, but as simultaneous wholes. These authors "ideally intend the reader to apprehend their work spatially, in a moment of time, rather than as a sequence" (9). However, Frank's analysis is recuperative, informed by the organic tendencies of the New Criticism. The works with which he deals radically violate the conventions of nineteenth-century realistic narrative, so Frank introduces the concept of spatial form in an attempt to tame these transgressive texts by producing a new paradigm to which they can be shown to conform. As Alan Singer succinctly puts it in his discussion of *Nightwood*, "Spatial form criticism fails to elucidate modernist texts because it merely substitutes space for time as the principle of coherence" (48).[1]

But from the point of view of a transgressive reading, it is precisely the lack of coherence that endows *Nightwood* with some of its most subversive energies. Not only does the overall plot defy conventional development, but the structure of Barnes's writing challenges the paradigm of coherence more locally as well. Even the typical structure of Barnes's individual sentences is highly transgressive, refusing to conform to the model of the "man's sentence" identified by Woolf. Consider a representative example:

Three massive pianos (Hedvig had played the waltzes of her time with the masterly stroke of a man, in the tempo of her blood, rapid and rising—that quick mannerliness of touch associated with the playing of the Viennese, who, though pricked with the love of rhythm, execute its demands in the duelling manner) sprawled over the thick dragon's-blood pile of rugs from Madrid. (5)

Such sentences refuse to conform to the metonymic paradigm of the traditional sentence, being composed of a paratactic collection of clauses that present digression within digression rather than progressive movement.[2]

Perhaps the most obvious attacks on coherence in the linguistic structure of *Nightwood* occur in the speeches of the inimitable Dr. Matthew-Mighty-grain-of-salt-Dante-O'Connor. O'Connor's speeches dominate the book, yet, as Singer points out, his discourse has a strangely decentered quality, being indistinguishable from the discourse of the narrator (60). In a sort of inversion of Bakhtin's notion of the character zone, O'Connor's speech dissolves into the fabric of the text even as he himself emerges as its most spectacular character. As a result, O'Connor's speeches have an inauthentic quality that reinforces his status as pathological liar. But the authenticity of identity itself is also called into question by O'Connor's discourse, as well as by numerous developments in the book as a whole. As the Duchess asks Felix Volkbein, "Am I what I say? Are you? Is the doctor?" (25).

The transgressive nature of O'Connor's discourse comes through not only in his use of fantastically hyperbolic language and in his refusal to conform to the principles of verisimilitude, but also in his constant tendency toward digression. "I have a narrative, but you will be put to it to find it," he tells Nora Flood, and the same might be said of Barnes as well (97). Indeed, O'Connor is at his most digressive (and transgressive) in direct conversations with interlocutors such as Felix and Nora. The latter attempt to carry on conventional conversations, asking questions or making comments and expecting answers, but the doctor is totally uncooperative, generally offering responses that seem only marginally related to what has been said to him. For example, after his lengthy description of that abject region known as the "night," Nora asks him how he lives at all with such knowledge:

"Ho, nocturnal hag whimpering on the thorn, rot in the grist, mildew in the corn," said the doctor. "If you'll pardon my song and singing voice, both of which were better until I gave my kidney on the left side to France in the war—and I've drunk myself half around the world cursing her for jerking it out—if I had it to do again, grand country though it is—I'd be the girl lurking behind the army, or up with the hill folk, all of which is to rest me a little of my knowledge, until I can get back to it. Misericordia, am I not the girl to know of what I speak?" (90)

O'Connor's characterization of himself as a "girl" here is a reference to his homosexuality, which is only one of the many instances of the transgression of traditional gender roles in this book.[3] The book is filled with instances of gender transgression, involving virtually every character who appears. In some ways even more striking than Dr. O'Connor is the enigmatic Robin Vote, who floats through the book as a sort of personified Lacanian *objet a*, the illusive and ungraspable object of the heterosexual desire of Felix Volkbein and of the lesbian desires of Nora Flood and Jenny Petherbridge. Robin constantly dresses in boys' clothing (as O'Connor is prone to wear women's clothing and makeup, especially in the privacy of his room) and she is referred to as "a girl who resembles a boy" (136).

But Robin (who, like O'Connor, can be read as a reflexive representation of Barnes's own ungraspable text) exhibits a much more radical transgression than mere cross-dressing or homosexuality. She calls into question the very definition not only of male or female, but even of human, as she straddles the boundary between human and animal. She is compared to a "beast turning human" (37), and perhaps the most memorable scene in the book occurs at the end when Robin, on all fours, indulges in a barking and growling match (with sexual overtones of bestiality) with Nora's dog (169–70).

Barnes reinforces the central figures of Dr. O'Connor and Robin Vote by embedding them in a text that is filled with images of transgression against the norms of polite society. For example, there is the carnivalesque collection of characters who frequent Nora's salon:

It was the "paupers" salon for poets, radicals, beggars, artists, and people in love; for Catholics, Protestants, Brahmins, dabblers in black magic and medicine. (50)

One of the important images of marginality and transgression in *Nightwood* is Felix Volkbein, who (like Leopold Bloom) is born of a Jewish father and Christian mother, which places him in the marginal position of being regarded as Jewish by Christian society but not by Jewish law.[4] Felix, however, aspires to a more central social position. He is obsessed with the aristocracy and longs to be one of them, attempting to pass himself off as a baron, complete with bogus coat of arms and fake portraits of prominent ancestors. But he is also fascinated with the marginal figures who populate the circus; he frequents their dressing rooms and becomes "for a little while a part of their splendid and reeking falsification" (11). Indeed, these circus performers function as a carnivalized version of the aristocracy that Felix so admires, taking on titles of their own:

There was a Princess Nadja, a Baron von Tink, a Princepessa Stasera y Stasero, a King Buffo and a Duchess of Broadback: gaudy cheap cuts from the beast life, immensely capable of that great disquiet called entertainment. (11)

This Duchess of Broadback, whose muscular heaviness makes her title quite apt, is an especially interesting figure. Her actual name is Frau Mann, which adds to the hint at gender transgression in her powerful build. Barnes's description of Frau Mann emphasizes the Frau's problematic gender, as well as suggesting transgression of the boundary between the animate and the inanimate:

She seemed to have a skin that was the pattern of her costume: a
bodice of lozenges, red and yellow, low in the back and ruffled over
and under the arms, faded with the reek of her three-a-day control,
red tights, laced boots—one somewhat felt that they ran through
her as the design runs through hard holiday candies, and the bulge
in the groin where she took the bar, one foot caught in the flex of
the calf, was as solid, specialized and as polished as oak. The stuff
of the tights was no longer a covering, it was herself; the span of
the tightly stitched crotch was so much her own flesh that she was
as unsexed as a doll. (13)[5]

In *Nightwood* it is difficult to classify with certainty the gender of virtually any of the characters. Felix Volkbein is the only prominent character in the book who seems openly heterosexual, yet the object of his affections is the boyish Robin Vote and he consistently displays feminine characteristics. In this book, the conventional boundaries that society erects to compartmentalize human existence simply will not hold, and it is from this fact that it gains its atmosphere of pure terror. Without the protection of these boundaries we are brought face to face with the death, corruption, and filth that are integrally a part of human life but that our social structures are designed to repress. Barnes writes long before Kristeva's work on abjection, but she understands this effect very well. She has Dr. O'Connor explain it to us:

"Man is born as he dies, rebuking cleanliness. . . . So the reason for
our cleanliness becomes apparent; cleanliness is a form of
apprehension; our faulty racial memory is fathered by fear. Destiny
and history are untidy; we fear memory of that disorder." (118)

O'Connor's acknowledgement of the untidiness of history is one that runs throughout *Nightwood*. The book does not, as Frank would have it, represent a modernist attempt to escape the nightmare of history through spatial form. What Barnes seeks to evade is not history, but narrative, which attempts to efface the messiness of genuine history by reformulating it into sanitary narrative packages. One might argue, in fact, that it is traditional realistic narrative that is spatial, because it seeks to present events as being related in a natural, organic fashion while works like *Nightwood* disrupt this illusion of narrative wholeness, acknowledging the contingent and aleatory character of real events.[6]

The tone of abjection in *Nightwood* is reinforced by O'Connor's messy vision of history, as well as by the liberal selection of abject images scattered throughout the text. Even in the innocence of childhood, horrors lurk in the margins. They appear, for instance, in many traditional children's stories, especially fairy tales, which often reveal the violence and terror at the heart of social institutions, particularly those (such as the family) that have most to do with sexuality. Nora Flood realizes as much when she enters Dr. O'Connor's squalid bedchamber and sees him sitting in bed in full drag: "It flashed into Nora's head: 'God, children know something they can't tell; they like Red Riding Hood and the wolf in bed!'" (79).[7]

Nightwood contains a number of images of death and corruption, such as O'Connor's memory of seeing a decapitated horse during the war (127).[8] There are also grotesqueries such as O'Connor's story of the girl with no legs who is carried off, raped, and abandoned by a sailor who is fascinated by her physical defects. O'Connor sees this story as an allegory of love in general, noting that this incomplete girl can still suffer complete pain: "I tell you, Madame, if one gave birth to a heart on a plate, it would say 'Love' and twitch like the lopped leg of a frog" (26–27).

These links between amputated limbs and love continue throughout the text, and indeed O'Connor relates his memory of the decapitated horse to the kind of painful memories that linger after love is gone (127). In *Nightwood* there is always an abject core to every experience, especially love, as indicated by the implied sexual encounter between Little Red Riding Hood and the wolf (which foreshadows that of Robin Vote and Nora's dog). All of the lovers in the book suffer horrible agonies of the spirit, summed up by O'Connor's declaration: "Love, that terrible thing!" (75).[9]

It comes as no surprise, then, that lovers are among the tortured outcasts who inhabit that strange, fantastic region of transgression that Dr. O'Connor refers to as the "night" in the bizarre "Watchman, What of the Night?" chapter. This land of dark abjection, O'Connor tells us, is inhabited by marginal misfits who cannot function in the light of day of normal society, by "those who turn the day into night, the young, the drug addict, the profligate, the drunken and that most miserable, the lover who watches all night long in fear and anguish" (94). O'Connor's long description of the "night" clearly echoes Eliot's "unreal city" and the "Nighttown" of the "Circe" chapter of *Ulysses*, and all three partake of Freud's discussions of the unconscious and of dreams. But perhaps the best literary analogue to O'Connor's collection of nighttime misfits is the disinherited "preterite" who functions so prominently in the work of Thomas Pynchon. For example, when Oedipa Maas wanders through San Francisco at night in *The Crying of Lot 49*, she meets a collection of homosexuals, strange children, failed revolutionaries, rejected lovers and other marginal figures who could have stepped right out of the pages of *Nightwood* (117–24).[10]

Lot 49 resembles *Nightwood* in a number of ways, many of which may not be coincidental. Dr. O'Connor, after all, is a native of the same San Francisco that Oedipa tours. Pynchon's book is also fundamentally informed by a constant threat of some unknown (and perhaps unspeakable) danger, of the possibility of "intrusions into this world from another" (124). Associating *Lot 49* with *Nightwood* suggests that the vague terror lurking in the margins of Pynchon's book is precisely the abjection that has been repressed by official society.

Pynchon enhances the atmosphere of terror in his book by including within it an authentically horrendous Jacobean revenge play, *The Courier's Tragedy*. He may have learned this technique from Eliot, who used it to such good advantage in *The Waste Land*. Eliot himself recognized a similar intertextual dynamic at work in *Nightwood*, describing it as possessing a "quality of horror and doom very nearly related to that of Elizabethan tragedy" (Introduction xvi). He might have just as well indicated Jacobean tragedy; the air of corruption and decadence that pervades Barnes's text is very Jacobean in character, though there are few overt allusions to Jacobean works.[11] One potential allusion occurs in Dr. O'Connor's rumination on the relationship of Nora Flood and Robin Vote: "Nora will leave that girl some day; but though those two are buried at opposite ends of the earth, one dog will find them both" (106). The direct referent here would seem to be the sinister dog who roams *The Waste Land*, causing a voice to warn: "O keep the Dog far hence, that's friend to men, / Or with his nails he'll dig it up again!" (*Collected Poems* 55).

Eliot's own poem here invokes the tradition of Jacobean tragedy by referring directly to Webster's *The White Devil*, in which a funeral dirge warns: "But keep the wolf far hence, that's foe to men, / For with his nails he'll dig it up again." In both cases what will specifically be dug up is a corpse, but the fear that these buried corpses will return functions as a representation of the more general way in which society "buries" reminders of abjection (of which death and corruption are primary), hoping that they will not resurface.

The sinister dog who will find both Nora and Robin obviously prefigures the final view of Robin Vote as "dog-woman" in *Nightwood*. Indeed, Barnes's use of this motif exhibits an astonishing intertextual and intratextual richness. The lines from Webster link Barnes's dog imagery to Jacobean tragedy, but also to the wolf from Little Red Riding Hood. Eliot's transformation of the wolf into a dog may have been influenced by *The Satyricon*, which brings in the intertextual associations of Menippean satire, and appropriately so: in the midst of the "Watchman" chapter O'Connor relates how he was once tempted to steal a volume of Petronius from Jenny Petherbridge (104).[12] Finally, Eliot's use of the dog as a symbol of terror echoes the similar practice by Joyce, as in the dog that Stephen watches nuzzling a canine corpse on the beach in the "Proteus" section of *Ulysses*:

a rag of wolf's tongue redpanting from his jaws. . . . The carcass lay on his path. He stopped, sniffed, stalked round it, brother, nosing closer, went round it, sniffling rapidly like a dog all over the dead dog's bedraggled fell. . . . then his forepaws dabbled and delved. Something he buried there, his grandmother. He rooted in the sand, dabbling, delving, and stopped to listen to the air, scraped up the sand again with a fury of his claws, soon ceasing, a pard, a panther, got in spousebreach, vulturing the dead. (38–39)[13]

Gilbert and Gubar acknowledge that Barnes parallels Eliot and Joyce here, though they prefer to read her work as "a revisionary response to male modernists" (*No Man's Land* 361). In fact Barnes, Eliot, and Joyce are all making much the same point here, though admittedly from different perspectives, with the darker visions of Eliot and Barnes contrasting with the comic ironies of Joyce. Their misunderstanding of these alignments accounts for the bewilderment that Gilbert and Gubar experience when attempting to interpret the final scene of *Nightwood*, leading them to label Robin's encounter in the ruined chapel with Nora's dog as "the most enigmatic scene in the book" (361). In truth it is the clearest scene in the book, the point at which all of the book's images of abjection culminate and come together.

Robin's behavior in this scene dramatizes the return of the animality that polite society (represented by the chapel setting) has attempted to repress as filthy and vile, but which is too integral a part of human nature to be completely repressed. Animals emerge amidst the messiness of birth, then shit, piss, fuck, and die—precisely the kinds of realities that institutions such as the church are designed to obscure. And one of the ways that the institutions do so is by identifying such physical processes with marginal groups (including women) and then rejecting those groups as inferior. Religion thus makes the ideal counterpoint to abjection, as indicated by O'Connor's earlier remark that "[t]he Bible lies the one way, but the night-gown the other" (80). And the dog makes an ideal counterpoint to religion through reference to the Joycean observation that "Dog" is the reverse of "God."

The representation of Robin Vote as half-human, half-animal thus functions as an overt symbol of the emergence of the abject side of human existence. As such, it participates in a common literary motif. As I noted in Chapter 2, such transgressions of the boundary between human and animal are a standard technique of Menippean satire, dating back to Apuleius. In modern literature they are seen strikingly in Kafka's "The Metamorphosis." More recently Salman Rushdie has used such images effectively, and Carter's *Nights at the Circus* centers on Sophie Fevvers, a human-animal hybrid. Fevvers is a clear literary descendent of Barnes's Frau Mann with hints of Dr. O'Connor and Robin Vote thrown in as well, a trapeze artist who is ostensibly half-human, half-swan, but who may simply be a charlatan. In fact, Carter's text echoes *Nightwood* in numerous ways, but her comic tone gives *Nights at the Circus* a rather different "feel" than Barnes's text, a difference that might be symbolized by that between the graceful swan and the sinister dog. Yet Fevvers's status as half-animal is abject as well, and linked directly to the dog and wolf images of Barnes. Thus we are told that during a performance Fevvers's "teeth are big and carnivorous as those of Red Riding Hood's grandmother" (18).[14]

THE CIRCUS AS CARNIVAL IN
NIGHTS AT THE CIRCUS

Paulina Palmer notes the relevance of Bakhtin's concept of the carnival to *Nights at the Circus*, but suggests that "unlike Bakhtin, Carter takes the unusual step of giving a feminist critique of certain carnivalistic images and values" (198). In this undertaking, Carter is heir to the project begun by Woolf in *Orlando*, although Carter places more emphasis on the dark, abject side of certain types of ritual violence often associated with the carnival. As Mary Russo points out, real historical carnivals have often been sites not of emancipation, but of brutal violence directed against women, Jews, and other marginal groups, because "in the everyday indicative world, women and their bodies . . . are always already transgressive—dangerous, and in danger" (217). The adventures of Carter's dual-natured heroine present an excellent space for the exploration of the dual nature of the carnival as celebration of diversity and oppression of marginality.

Fevvers's swan's wings make her a star attraction among aerialists, despite her large bulk, and she joins a circus headed by the entrepreneur extraordinaire Colonel Kearney—a sort of cartoon composite of P. T. Barnum, Uncle Sam, and Colonel Tom Parker. This circus undertakes a monumental mission: to work its way across the vastness of turn-of-the-century czarist Russia, then to Japan, and on to the United States. Fevvers is followed on the trip by Jack Walser, a journalist who at first sets out to expose Fevvers as a fraud, but falls in love and joins the circus as a clown so that he can be with her on the long journey to America.

But the trip is beset with one misfortune after another, culminating in a train wreck in the midst of the frozen tundra of Siberia.[15] Various adventures ensue, but by the end Walser and Fevvers are back together in suitable romance fashion. However, this ending masks more uncertainties than it resolves. The two lovers are still stranded among primitive tribesmen in the Siberian wilderness at the end, and the exact status of their relationship remains unclear. Fevvers, an independent woman/bird, is not at all comfortable with the standard marriage ending, as she discusses with her old nurse, Lizzie:

> "Orlando takes his Rosalind. She says: 'To you I give myself, for I am yours.' And that," she [Lizzie] added, a low thrust, "goes for a girl's bank account, too."
> "But it is impossible that I should give myself," said Fevvers. Her diction was exceedingly precise. "My being, my me-ness, is unique and indivisible. To sell the use of myself for the enjoyment of another is one thing; I might even offer freely, out of gratitude or in the expectation of pleasure—and pleasure alone is my expectation from the young American. But the essence of myself may not be given or taken, or what would there be left of me?"
> "Precisely," said Lizzie, with mournful satisfaction. (280–81)

The feminist implications here at first seem rather heavy-handed. For the woman the standard romance ending is not the beginning of perpetual bliss, but of perpetual servitude—not exactly a novel observation. Yet the last few pages of the book avoid banality by maintaining an extreme hermeneutic instability. Fevvers, independent or not, pursues (and catches) Walser, expressing doubt whether she can live without him or whether she even exists except as he sees her. They may even be married (if only by a native Shaman), as Walser is referred to as her "husband" on the last page. Yet Fevvers gets the last laugh as Walser discovers her claim to virginity to have been somewhat of an exaggeration. In fact, this laugh is so powerful that it spreads across the entire globe, recalling (and perhaps parodying) the comments of Kristeva and Bakhtin on laughter and the carnival and of Cixous on the power of woman's laughter.[16] Marriage ending or not, Fevvers winds up on top—quite literally, as her wings render only that position comfortable for her.

The exact status of this ending is ultimately undecidable; it is both a romance ending and a mockery of romance endings.[17] This indeterminacy is typical of the entire text, which is informed by a fundamental carnivalesque ambivalence and destabilization of boundaries of all kinds. For example, one motif that runs throughout the text is that the action occurs in the waning hours of the nineteenth century. Indeed, the turn of the century occurs as midnight strikes during the climactic lovemaking of Walser and Fevvers. Veiled hints at the allegorical significance of this turning point are scattered throughout the text, much in the way that Pynchon makes his lady V. an allegorical representation of the progress of the twentieth century. But Carter's allegory (like Pynchon's) is parodic. Fevvers and Walser, otherwise occupied, do not even notice the momentous, long-awaited boundary between the centuries when it is finally crossed. It is, like all man-made (or woman-made) boundaries, an artificial one, lacking the real significance that Carter sees in the experience of love.[18]

Carter's highly allusive text also frequently transgresses the artificial boundary between "high" and "low" culture, freely intermixing allusions to authors such as Shakespeare, Byron, Swift, Yeats, and Joyce with references to prostitutes, con men, and the circus. I have discussed elsewhere the way in which such dialogic uses of allusion in Joyce can lead to explosions of signification, including an unpredictable proliferation of meaning through a variety of texts in a phenomenon I refer to as serendipitous intertextuality ("Works in Progress"). *Nights at the Circus* achieves this same kind of effect, as a brief look at some examples from Carter's extensive dialogue with Yeats illustrates. Fevvers's parentage implies an allusion to Yeats's "Leda and the Swan," with the rape imagery of that poem resonating with the current of violence that runs throughout Carter's text. And the differences between Fevvers and Helen[19] initiate a dialogue with "No Second Troy," in which allusions to the beauty, theatricality, and political involvement of Maud Gonne provide an interesting supplement to the roles of Fevvers and Lizzie in *Nights*. The strain of violence in Carter's text reinforces the apocalyptic intonations of the coming turn of the century, which in turn echoes Yeats's "The Second Coming." Indeed, this poem is directly referred to in Carter's description of the hint of doom in the clowning of Buffo: "Things fall apart at the very shiver of his tread on the ground. He is himself the centre that does not hold" (117). Finally, Fevvers describes Madame Schreck's museum as a home for "dispossessed creatures," as a "rag-and-bone shop of the heart" (69), in a reference (appropriately enough) to Yeats's "The Circus Animals' Desertion." And just to show how these things can propagate and link together, note that Gilbert and Gubar, in their discussion of *Nightwood*, argue that "Robin represents the wild reality beyond gender, the pure potency to be found in what Yeats called 'the rag and bone [sic] shop of the heart'" (*No Man's Land* 361).

One of Carter's favorite techniques is to introduce an image from high culture, and then immediately undercut its pretensions to seriousness through juxtaposition with a deflating image of more base origins. For example, we are told that a brothel run by "Ma Nelson" was decorated with original paintings by Old Masters such as Titian.[20] And if this conflation of art with the bordello were not enough, we are also told how the madam got these paintings: " 'Some bloke whose name I misremember give 'er the pictures,' said Lizzie. 'He liked her on account of how she shaved her pubes'" (28).

Similarly, we learn that Ma Nelson had an extensive library, willed to her by a client "[o]n account of she was the only woman in London who could get it up for him" (40). And later, we find Walser quoting Shakespeare in counterpoint to the animalistic copulation of the circus's Strong Man with Mignon, the wife of the Ape Man:

Walser hesitantly began:
    "What a piece of work is man! How noble in reason! How
infinite in faculty!"
    The Strong Man accomplished his orgasm in a torrent of brutish
shrieks, such a hullabaloo that Walser stumbled over his recitation.
(111)[21]

These starkly contrasting images contribute to an atmosphere of indeterminacy most directly represented by the uncertain legitimacy of Fevvers as a transgressive wonder of nature. Fevvers's own status partakes of the hesitancy in meaning traditionally associated with the genre of the fantastic, as do various other aspects of the book, such as the numerous hints of Lizzie's mysterious magical powers. Indeed, a radical indeterminacy is Fevvers's primary characteristic, as noted by the address directed to her by the sinister Mr. Rosencreutz:

"Queen of ambiguities, goddess of in-between states, being on the
borderline of species. . . . Lady of the hub of the celestial wheel,
creature half of earth and half of air, virgin and whore, reconciler of
fundament and firmament, reconciler of opposing states through
the mediation of your ambivalent body, reconciler of the grand
opposites of death and life." (81)

Fevvers straddles all sorts of fundamental boundaries. In addition to her challenge to the distinction between human and animal, she also destabilizes the boundary between the animate and the inanimate, at one point in her career posing as a sculpture of Cupid, thus becoming "half-woman, half-statue" (38).[22] But Cupid is traditionally male, so in this role Fevvers challenges the boundaries of gender as well. In fact, *Nights at the Circus* is filled with images of uncertain gender. For example, when Fevvers is forced to become an exhibit in Madame Schreck's museum of female freaks, one of her fellow exhibits is "Albert/Albertina, who was bipartite, that is to say, half and half and neither of either" (59).[23] And Fevvers spends her childhood in Ma Nelson's brothel, the madam of which is a cross-dresser who got her name because she "always dressed in the full dress uniform of an Admiral of the Fleet" (32).[24]

Fevvers herself displays a number of stereotypically masculine characteristics. In his first interview with her, Walser is attracted, but at the same time her large size and the sheer forcefulness of her presence lead him to wonder: "Is she really a man?" (35).[25] Of course, the entire relationship between Fevvers and Walser challenges a number of gender-role stereotypes, and it is particularly interesting to note the "feminization" of Walser late in the book. He begins the book as a walking masculine stereotype, a "man of action" who knows no fear, and who is out of touch with his feelings in general (10). But his reaction to Fevvers gradually erodes his masculine position. Then, after the train wreck, he is found unconscious by a band of migrating lesbian insurgents, who might have stepped right out of the pages of Wittig. One of them sardonically suggests that a kiss is generally the way to awaken a sleeping beauty, and the maternal Olga follows through, waking Walser with a kiss to the forehead that inverts the standard fairy-tale situation. Walser's mind has been scrambled by his injuries, but because he is a man, the lesbians abandon him. So he begins to wander aimlessly through the Siberian wilderness, now having become a virtual composite of stereotypical feminine characteristics:

The empty centre of a lost horizon, Walser flutters across the snowy wastes. He is a sentient being, still, but no longer a rational one; indeed, now he is all sensibility, without a grain of sense, and sense impressions alone have the power to shock and to ravish him. In his elevated state, he harkens to the rhythm of the drum. (236)

Transgressions of gender are probably the most important of the many transgressions in Carter's text. As the above passage indicates, these transgressions take the form not only of literal confusions between traditional masculine and feminine roles, but also of the direct confrontation and parody of a variety of sexual stereotypes. Many of these stereotypes involve the interrogation of objectionable masculine fantasies of the feminine that have been identified in recent feminist discourse. However, Carter's technique is far more sophisticated than a mere replication of standard feminist arguments. After all, feminist descriptions of masculine fantasies of the feminine are themselves mediated; they are, in fact, feminine fantasies of masculine fantasies of the feminine. The regression of such fantasies continues to infinity, never coming to rest in "reality" or in a "true" perspective. Carter shows her appreciation for this *mise en abîme* effect by including images of infinite regression in her book, such as Walser's comparison of Fevvers's eyes to Chinese boxes (30), or the worlds within worlds of the Rousselesque artificial eggs of the Grand Duke (189).

Obviously, Fevvers's status as half-woman, half-bird makes her a particularly entrancing visual object, which has its advantages in her line of work, but also its limitations. As Lizzie reminds her, "All you can do to earn a living is to make a show of yourself" (185). Yet freak of nature or not, Fevvers' plight here is perhaps not that different from the one women have traditionally suffered throughout Western history. Fevvers herself is pure spectacle, a showwoman extraordinaire, greatly narcissistic, but at times dependent upon the attentions of her audience for her own sense of self-worth. As such, she participates in a complex network of images and motifs that have been prominent in recent feminist discourse. Early in the book, we see her presented on stage in her flashy show costume:

Look at me! With a grand, proud, ironic grace, she exhibited herself before the eyes of the audience as if she were a marvellous present too good to be played with. Look, not touch.

She was twice as large as life and as succinctly finite as any object that is intended to be seen, not handled. Look! Hands off! LOOK AT ME! (15)

Similar descriptions follow Fevvers throughout the book. She herself tells Walser, for example, that while playing Cupid as a child "I served my apprenticeship in being looked at—at being the object of the eye of the beholder" (23). And she explains that, during her later performances as "Winged Victory" in Ma Nelson's parlor, "I existed only as an object in men's eyes" (39).

Fevvers's status as object of the male gaze invites a number of obvious interpretations. One thinks, for example, of John Berger's suggestion that

men act and women appear. Men look at women. Women watch themselves being looked at. This determines not only most relations between men and women but also the relation of women to themselves. The surveyor of woman in herself is male: the surveyed female. Thus she turns herself into an object—and most particularly an object of vision: a sight. (47)

This dynamic has been widely discussed in feminist film theory, especially that done from a Lacanian perspective. It also invokes the extensive feminist interrogations of the visual orientation of psychoanalytic theory performed by Luce Irigaray. In the particular case of Fevvers, however, there is more involved than the ordinary visual relationship between the sexes; she is specifically a performer in a public spectacle, and thus actively invites her own treatment as the object of the male gaze. In short, she appropriates her status as visual object and uses it to her own advantage, "acting" as well as "appearing," to use Berger's terms.

But a woman is supposed to be quiet and discreet. She is specifically supposed to avoid making a spectacle of herself, even though she is constantly in danger of doing so because of her status as visual object. By appropriating the male stereotype of the woman as object of the gaze and driving it to its extreme in spectacle, Fevvers is able to undercut the original stereotype by carnivalizing it. Russo has discussed the notion of woman as spectacle within the framework of the Bakhtinian carnival. Though noting the problematic nature of the carnival metaphor, Russo concludes that the "figure of the female transgressor as public spectacle is still powerfully resonant, and the possibilities of redeploying this representation as a demystifying or utopian model have not been exhausted" (217).

In particular, Russo notes the carnivalesque potential of the female body, based on Bakhtin's discussion of the role of the grotesque body in Rabelais. The grotesque image of the body emphasizes physicality by highlighting bodily functions and specific body parts, as opposed to the classical image of the body as a seamless whole. As Bakhtin notes, the "unfinished and open body (dying, bringing forth and being born) is not separated from the world by clearly defined boundaries; it is blended with the world, with animals, with objects" (*Rabelais* 26–27).[26] Fevvers's body, of course, is quite grotesque in this sense; the hybrid nature of her anatomy calls attention to her body as hybrid and undercuts any attempt to view it as a classical whole.[27]

Bakhtin's discussions of the importance of the "lower bodily strata" in Rabelais point to the specifically social and political implications of his description of the grotesque body. To Bakhtin, attempts to taxonomize the body into "high" and "low" segments stand as a figure for the oppression of marginal social groups by dominant ones in class society. Attempts to view the body as a classical whole by denying excremental and other processes that emphasize the dynamic interaction between body and world represent a denial of history. But the dynamic nature of this blending and of the carnivalesque representation of bodily functions thrusts the subject directly into the contemporaneous flow of history: "The material bodily lower stratum and the entire system of degradation, turnovers, and travesties presented this essential relation to time and to social and historical transformation" (*Rabelais* 81).[28]

I have already noted (in Chapter 5) Carter's highly carnivalesque treatment of the male body in her "dance of the buffoons" (123–25). Her treatment of the physical reality of Fevvers's body is at times highly carnivalesque as well. We first meet Fevvers as she is being interviewed by Walser in her dressing room, a "mistresspiece of exquisitely feminine squalor" (9). Fevvers's room echoes both the "reeking falsification" of the dressing rooms of the circus performers in *Nightwood* and the feminine squalor of the room of Dr. O'Connor, with its swill-pail "brimming with abominations" (*Nightwood* 79). Fevvers's room is filled with the detritus of femininity, including an assortment of soiled undergarments and "a powerful note of stale feet, final ingredient in the highly personal aroma, 'essence of Fevvers', that clogged the room" (9). Fevvers is intensely physical, a fact we witness when we are treated to a description of her decidedly unladylike eating habits (22) and of how she "shifted from one buttock to the other and—'better out than in, sir'—let a ripping fart ring around the room" (11).[29]

Of course, the notion of women as being linked especially to the physical has been promulgated in various forms not only by men, but by feminists such as Cixous and Irigaray as well. Here again, Fevvers at first seems to be conforming to a stereotype of the feminine only to push that stereotype into parody. For example, the particular "feminine squalor" of Fevvers's room can be read as a parody of such literary predecessors as Swift's Celia and Eliot's Fresca. But perhaps the most enlightening literary referent is Joyce's intensely physical Molly Bloom, who has been both praised as a representative image of genuine femininity and reviled as an insidious example of male fantasies of the feminine. Molly, like Fevvers, is somewhat sloppy in her eating and with her discarded clothing, and she is also similarly flatulent, emitting a fart of her own and explaining (à la Fevvers): "that was a relief wherever you be let your wind go free" (628).[30]

But while Bakhtin's reading emphasizes the positive and celebratory implications of Rabelais's overt treatment of physicality, the traditional notion of woman as figure of the physical aspect of life has often been associated with the revulsion of abjection: woman implies the physical, implies the mortal, implies death. This tendency is summarized in Felicity Nussbaum's suggestion that "Swift's despicable women forecast the end of man's time. A memento mori not only predicts man's death—she may contribute to it" (102). Actually, Swift's rampant irony makes interpretation of his passage highly contestable.[31] More straightforward is Eliot's anticipation of the "essence of Fevvers" in a deleted passage from the manuscript version of *The Waste Land*, in which he depicts the lady Fresca making her toilet:

This ended, to the steaming bath she moves,
Her tresses fanned by little flutt'ring Loves;

Odours, confected by the cunning French,
Disguise the good old hearty female stench.
>   (*The Waste Land: Facsimile* 39)

A few lines later in the manuscript Eliot shows the true horror
that inheres in these lines, linking (like Swift, at least per
Nussbaum) woman's physicality with death:

But at my back from time to time I hear
The rattle of the bones, and chuckle spread from ear to ear.
>   (41)[32]

The difference between Eliot and Carter is clear: Fresca's physicality is linked to death, while Fevvers's physicality (like that
of Molly Bloom, according to most readings) is linked to life.
Carter overturns society's strictures against the lower bodily
stratum with carnivalesque exuberance, using the tremendous
leveling power of excremental functions to undercut preten-
tiousness.[33] Or, as we learn when Walser avails himself of Fevvers's chamber pot: "The act of engaging in this most human of
activities brought him down to earth again, for there is no element of the metaphysical about pissing, not, at least, in our
culture" (52).

In Swift's "The Lady's Dressing Room," the hypersensitive
Strephon is appalled by the revelations he finds therein (such as
the fact that "Celia shits") because of the excessively idealized
way in which he views the divine Celia. Indeed, the stereotypical views of woman as physical being and of woman as ideal
ethereal creature, though apparent polar opposites, are quite intimately related, both having to do with the repression of abjection. One of the standard manifestations of this latter stereotype
is the myth of woman as angel, to which the winged Fevvers
seems to invite connection, especially since this myth was especially prevalent in the turn-of-the-century milieu in which the
Nights takes place.[34] Gilbert and Gubar have discussed this image of woman in some detail in *The Madwoman in the Attic*,
noting in particular how this view of the feminine is often
closely linked to a hidden view of the woman as monster. They
themselves attribute much of their diagnosis of the symptoms
of woman as angel to Virginia Woolf, who described the figure of

the "Angel in the House" as a stereotype that prevented women from fulfilling their potentials:

She was intensely sympathetic. She was immensely charming. She was utterly unselfish. She excelled in the difficult arts of family life. She sacrificed herself daily. If there was chicken, she took the leg; if there was a draught she sat in it—in short she was so constituted that she never had a mind or a wish of her own, but preferred to sympathize always with the minds and wishes of others. ("Professions" 237)

Fevvers is explicitly linked to the angel metaphor at numerous points in *Nights*, though as usual she becomes a parody of the stereotype by overliteralizing it. For example, late in her career at Ma Nelson's she plays the angel of that house. Having become too large to be Cupid, Fevvers (still playing statue) assumes the role of "Winged Victory," standing in the parlor of the brothel holding Ma Nelson's sword for added effect, "as if a virgin with a weapon was the fittest guardian angel for a houseful of whores" (38). But here Fevvers triggers the fear of women that Gilbert and Gubar see as a part of the notion of woman as angel. Her weaponry evokes an additional stock male fantasy, the castrating female, and her presence in this role turns out to be bad for business, as "it may be that a large woman with a sword is not the best advertisement for a brothel" (38).[35]

When Fevvers performs in Paris her fans refer to her as l'Ange Anglaise, and later, when she goes to the home of the evil Rosencreutz, he greets her as an angel: " 'Welcome, Azrael,' he says. 'Azrael, Azrail, Ashriel, Azriel, Azaril, Gabriel; dark angel of many names' " (75). Indeed, Rosencreutz has plans to sacrifice Fevvers as part of an occult ritual designed to give him everlasting life—a literal enactment of the feminist suggestion that the myth of woman as angel is intended to shore up men at the expense of women.

But Fevvers flies out the window and escapes, eluding the stereotypical angel role by utilizing precisely the characteristic that links her most strongly to that role. In *Nights at the Circus* Carter consistently interrogates feminine myths not by seeking to evade them, but by meeting them head-on in a mode of parody. For example, in confronting the myth of feminine physicality, Carter presents us with a blatantly physical Fevvers, not denying that women are physical creatures, but in fact emphasizing it. This strategy is somewhat analogous to that of Cixous, but is even more similar to that employed by Wittig in *The Lesbian Body*. Similarly, Carter endows Fevvers with a number of characteristics that recall Woolf's description of the Angel of the House. After all, such traits as compassion and selflessness are not in themselves necessarily negative; they become insidious only when they are imposed upon women as exclusive reactions regardless of the situation. But Fevvers consistently exceeds this limitation, displaying many other characteristics (such as independence, strength, and courage) as circumstances demand.

From a feminist perspective one notes how Carter's depiction of Fevvers indicates the interrelationship of various myths of the feminine: images of woman as spectacle, as physical being, and as angel are all closely related and all arise from similar sources. None of this is news, though Carter's instantiation of these myths in the character of Fevvers has a richness that purely theoretical discussions often lack. In particular, the indeterminacy of Carter's text prevents it from descending into the monologism of a one-sided attack that would simply reverse normal hierarchies and privilege the feminine over the masculine. She is thus (in a textual dynamic similar to the one I discussed in Chapter 4) able to critique traditional patriarchal values while at the same time maintaining an ironically self-conscious perspective on feminist values as well. Patrick Kinmonth summarizes Carter's evenhanded tactics: "Carter is not a feminist, in the embattled sense of the word; she is a femalist, exposing both wolf-men and literary lionesses" (224).

On the other hand, Carter's refusal to affirm categorically any single position makes the exact orientation of her fiction highly complex. Her heavy emphasis on parody partakes of the paradoxical politics that Linda Hutcheon has seen to be at the heart of postmodernism, which "at once inscribes and subverts the conventions and ideologies of the dominant cultural and social forces of the twentieth-century western world" (*Politics* 11). But there is in this kind of politics a fine line between complicity and critique. Robert Clark, for example, argues that Carter simply reinscribes patriarchal values in a way that is dangerous for all but the most enlightened feminist reader, who can deconstruct the ideologies she presents (159). This criticism is quite similar to that levied against Fowles by Michael (see Chapter 4), and my response is the same. Even if Clark's charge is true (and I don't think it is), all it means is that enlightened critics (like Clark) have a responsibility to aid in this deconstruction, not that they should reject Carter's work, which has great feminist potential. Moreover, unlike Fowles, Carter does include a strong element of positive feminist statement in *Nights*, and elsewhere she makes her own feminist position quite clear: "The Women's Movement has been of immense importance to me personally and I would regard myself as a feminist writer, because I'm a feminist in everything else and one can't compartmentalize these things in one's life" ("Notes" 69).

Note also that Clark is speaking principally of Carter's work prior to *Nights at the Circus*. Palmer suggests that Carter's earlier work concentrates on demythologizing male myths, while her later work (like *Nights*) concentrates more on the production and celebration of positive feminist alternatives (179). This change of emphasis might allay some of Clark's criticism. However, Carter herself claims to see no such dramatic dualism in her career, which all has fundamentally to do with the deconstruction of dominant cultural myths: "I'm in the demythologising business" ("Notes" 71).

This critical strain in Carter's feminism leads her to distrust dogma of all kinds, whether they be produced by patriarchal society or by feminists. For example, Walser's attraction to rhythm when he becomes prototypical woman parodies the privileging of rhythm as an aspect of feminine language in the work of writers ranging from Woolf to Cixous and Kristeva. And *Nights* contains two separate instances of parodic feminine utopias. The first involves the bordello of Ma Nelson, who is not only a madam, but also an active feminist and suffragette. Fevvers describes the feminine paradise of Ma Nelson's establishment:

"Let me tell you it was a wholly female world within Ma Nelson's door. Even the dog who guarded it was a bitch and all the cats were females, one or the other of 'em always in kitten, or newly given birth, so that a sub-text of fertility underwrote the glittering sterility of the pleasure of the flesh available within the academy. Life within those walls was governed by a sweet and loving reason.

I never saw a single blow exchanged between any of the sisterhood who reared me, nor heard a cross word or a voice raised in anger." (38–39)

The parallel between this "wholly female world" and the island of Wittig's *The Lesbian Body*, where even the animals are all female, is quite strong. In a sense there is a special power to be derived from the situation of this feminist utopia in a brothel, with all its attendant reminders both of the sexual subjugation of women and of the nature of capitalist society.[36] One might compare, for example, the similar use of prostitutes as feminist symbols in *Orlando*. But there is also an obvious irony in Carter's brothel utopia, where every night the feminine solidarity is penetrated by the entrance of their masculine clientele. The constant pregnancy of the household cats bespeaks a masculine presence as well, and the whole episode acts to suggest that a feminist utopia does not necessarily require complete sexual separatism.

An even more radical instance of such separatism occurs later in the book in the story of the "panopticon," a prison founded by the Countess P. to assuage her guilt over poisoning her husband. All of the inmates of the prison, in fact, are women who have killed their husbands. The prison is designed "on the most scientific lines available," consisting of a circular arrangement of cells facing toward a central room in which the Countess sits, viewing the inmates, who are cut off from all contact with one another or with their guards (210). The direct referent of the "scientific lines" upon which this prison is constructed is the program of prison reform expounded early in the nineteenth century by Jeremy Bentham, who proposed precisely this panopticon model as the ideal prison design. But in Carter's immensely rich text there are often multiple layers of reference, many of them openly political. For example, the total separation of the inmates in the Countess P.'s prison literalizes the isolation that Marxist analysis sees as being forced upon individuals by bourgeois society. Moreover, the use of the panopticon motif invokes the work of Foucault, who sees this model as representative of the way in which the modern state tends to define all of its institutions and power structures in direct relation to a central authority, with no interactions among themselves.

Foucault's description of the effect of this system provides (except for the gender of the pronouns) an extremely precise portrait of Carter's panopticon:

Each individual, in his place, is securely confined to a cell from which he is seen from the front by the supervisor; but the side walls prevent him from coming in to contact with his companions. He is seen, but he does not see; he is the object of information, never a subject in communication. The arrangement of his room, opposite the central tower, imposes on him an axial visibility; but the divisions of the ring, those separated cells, imply a lateral invisibility. And this invisibility is a guarantee of order. (*Discipline and Punish* 200)[37]

To Foucault, this system is designed specifically to enforce discursive conformity and to homogenize the mechanisms of power in society. Because in Carter's case this discursive conformity is being imposed on women, one might expect various feminist discussions of ways in which women can oppose dominant discourses to be highly relevant here. One of the common strategies for such opposition, an integral part of *l'écriture féminine* of Cixous and *le parler femme* of Irigaray, involves the notion of writing from a woman's special relation to her body. So when inmate Olga Alexandrovna receives a forbidden note from her guard, she replies by writing her response quite literally from the female body:

There was not a pencil nor pen in the cell, of course, but, as it happened, her courses were upon her and—ingenious stratagem only a woman could execute—she dipped her finger in the flow, wrote a brief answer on the back of the note she had received and delivered it up to those brown eyes that now she could have identified amongst a thousand. (216)

Writing from the body is supposed to generate great subversive energy, so it comes as no surprise that this initial contact spreads, and all of the guards begin to communicate with all of the inmates via secret notes, again writing from the body

on all manner of substances, on rags of clothing if paper was not available, in blood, both menstrual and veinous, even in excrement, for none of the juices of the bodies that had been so long denied were alien to them. (217)

An obvious literary referent here is Joyce's Shem, who in *Finnegans Wake* alchemically produces ink from his own excrement and then writes on his own skin (185.14–186.1). But of course Joyce (according to Cixous) is a prime practitioner of *l'écriture féminine*, so this reference does not diminish the feminist orientation of Carter's parody.

All of this feminine discourse gives rise to a tremendous outburst of love and camaraderie. The inmates and the guards unanimously fall in love with each other, then band together as "an army of lovers" (217)—that greatly resembles Wittig's les guérillères—to overthrow the Countess P. They lock the Countess in her own prison, then "set off hand in hand, and soon started to sing, for joy" (218). Again, song is a mode of speech consistently privileged by both Cixous and Kristeva as a feminine form of communication harking back to the pre-linguistic rapport between mother and infant. Moreover, Wittig's women do a great deal of singing as well, and Carter's women intend to found a feminist utopia that would do Wittig proud.[38]

The singing of these women mirrors the earlier development of lesbian communication between Mignon and the Princess of Abyssinia, the tiger-tamer: "They would cherish in loving privacy the music that was their language, in which they'd found the way to one another" (168). And earlier, Mignon sings a memorized song from Byron, though she doesn't understand the words because she speaks no English. Yet this lack of verbal understanding seems to make the song all the more powerful: "she sang her song, which contained the anguish of a continent" (134).

But again the demythologizing Carter complicates the picture. We later find a band of primitive tribesmen who come upon two members of the wrecked circus troupe playing classical music, but are rather unaffected:

they scarcely recognized the Schubert lied as music, for it had little in common with the scales and modes of the music they themselves, at the infrequent request of spirits, made on the skin drums, flutes fashioned from the femur of elk and xylophones of stone. (268)

In short, music does not necessarily represent some primal appeal to a pre-linguistic realm. Though certain rhythmic elements may provoke universal reactions, music in general is highly conventionalized and culturally coded, perhaps every bit as Symbolic (in Kristeva's terms) as is language.[39] And if Carter's feminist prison escapees cannot thus escape the realm of masculine discourse through their use of musical language, they also find that other masculine contributions are necessary for the survival of their clan. They encounter the sleeping beauty Walser and leave him in the wilderness, but we learn that they later "regretted having abandoned such a fine repository of semen" (241). Indeed, when they meet a male prison escapee they ask him to "deliver 'em up a pint or two of sperm" that they can take with them for purposes of propagating their tribe (240). They will have no further need of men in their new utopia (at least for a while), though the ever-incisive Lizzie spots a potential flaw in the plan, asking "What'll they do with the boy babies? Feed 'em to the polar bears? To the female polar bears?" (240–41).

The point is not that women cannot live without men, but that they don't necessarily have to live without men in order to be happy. Carter's simultaneous parodies of patriarchal and feminist stereotypes contribute to the complex Menippean logic of the carnival that forms the fabric of her text. This logic is fundamentally informed by ambivalence, by a disruption of the Aristotelian "either-or" principle of noncontradiction. In particular, the denial of Aristotelian logic problematizes the usually firm boundary between "*A*" and "not *A*," or between truth and fiction.

 Bakhtin emphasizes the way in which the carnival calls into question the distinction between reality and performance, to the way in which "carnival knows neither stage nor footlights" (*Problems* 128). Fevvers again serves as personification of this concept, and the boundary between her stage persona and her "real" self is extremely tenuous. Her personal slogan—"Is she fact or is she fiction?"—resonates throughout the text, applying to almost every person, thing, and event in the book. Carter enhances this effect by building an atmosphere of ontological uncertainty in her text, liberally sprinkling it with images of trickery and illusion, including the Indian rope trick (16), a fake medium at a seance (43), a confidence man who makes and sells fake photographs of the dead to grieving relatives (134–38), and a native Shaman who works miracles through no other power than the confidence of his constituents (263). This effect is further enhanced by allusions to works that similarly question the boundaries between reality and illusion. Thus, late in the book Fevvers asks: "Is my fate to be a female Quixote, with Liz my Sancho Panza?" (245).

All of these images contribute to the atmosphere of ontological uncertainty that builds throughout the text, posing to Carter's reader the question posed to Walser by an Indian fakir: "[I]s not this whole world an illusion?" (16). But the central image of uncertainty and illusion in the book is Fevvers herself. She may or may not be a fake bird-woman, but she is almost surely a fake virgin, and images of artificiality linger around her like cheap perfume. When we first meet her on the initial page of the book she is in the process of removing her false eyelashes after a performance. Later we learn that she is a peroxide blonde and that her wings get their bright purple and red colors from synthetic dyes. Indeed, she is surrounded by so much artifice that one begins to wonder where (or if) the illusion stops and the "real" Fevvers begins.

This fundamental indeterminacy, so crucial to carnivalesque logic, is also crucial to Fevvers's success as a performer. It is, Walser surmises, precisely the possibility that she is a sham that creates the fascination with which she is viewed by the public, since "in a secular age, an authentic miracle must purport to be a hoax, in order to gain credit in the world" (17). This air of potential chicanery is fundamental to the modern circus, as indicated by P. T. Barnum's notorious (though apparently apocryphal) declaration concerning the frequent birth of gullible persons. Indeed, the circus itself makes a vital contribution to the carnivalesque flavor of Carter's text, as is forcefully brought home in her description of the contradictory mixture of sensory perceptions arising from their performance before the Russian aristocracy in St. Petersburg, where

the aroma of horse dung and lion piss permeated every inch of the building's fabric, so that the titillating contradiction between the soft, white shoulders of the lovely ladies whom young army officers escorted there and the hairy pelts of the beasts in the ring resolved in the night-time intermingling of French perfume and the essence of steppe and jungle in which musk and civet revealed themselves as common elements. (105)[40]

The circus in which Fevvers performs is headed by the indomitable Colonel Kearney (which, not coincidentally, can be pronounced "Carney"), who "presides over the carnival-like proceedings" (146), and who is himself a sort of carnivalization of the American entrepreneurial spirit.[41] He is constantly accompanied by a sentient pig, who gives him advice on various matters—thus "Sybil," her Petronian name. The intelligence of this pig, like that of the circus's trained chimps, participates in the same transgression of the boundary between human and animal as does Fevvers.[42] These chimps, for example, produce in Walser a "dizzy uncertainty about what was human and what was not" (110). Moreover, pigs have historically had a special association with both the carnivalesque and the abject. Stallybrass and White discuss the importance of pigs as "symbolically base and abject animals," much like rats (5). They cite examples of carnivalesque literature (such as Ben Jonson's *Bartholemew Fair*) that feature pigs as central images, such that "[i]deological combat is enjoined around the pig which becomes the site of competing definitions and desires" (63). And, interestingly, they cite the case of "Toby the Real Learned Pig," who appeared at the real Bartholomew Fair in 1833:

He will spell, read, and cast accounts, tell the points of the sun's rising and setting, discover the four grand divisions of the Earth, kneel at command, perform blindfold with twenty handkerchiefs over his eyes, tell the hour to a minute by a watch, tell a card, and the age of any party. He is in colour the most beautiful of his race, in symmetry the most perfect, in temper the most docile. And when asked a question he will give an immediate answer. (Morley 480, cited in Stallybrass and White 58).

The parallels between the abilities of Colonel Kearney's Sybil and those of "Toby" are striking. Sybil, for example,

could spell out your fate and fortune with the aid of the alphabet written on cards—yes indeed! could truffle the future out of four-and-twenty Roman capitals if they were laid out in order before her and that wasn't half of her talents. (98)

The humanlike characteristics of Sybil provide a mirror image of the traditional association of animal-like persons with pigs. Those who display transgressive behavior, especially behavior that suggests the kind of filth from which polite society seeks to distance itself, are frequently described as "pigs."[43] Stallybrass and White discuss a modern circus act in which a tramplike clown, or "August" plays the role of mother, with a pig playing the role of baby. This act, according to Stallybrass and White, is transgressive because it forces the audience to recognize its own repressed knowledge of the animal side of humanity: pigs and babies are similar in many ways, and "the squealing, urinating baby is, in the language of praise-and-abuse, a little pig" (59).[44] There is also a carnivalesque element in pig imagery, as when police or other figures of authority are referred to as "pigs." Allon White, reviewing the uses of pigs as symbols in modern literature by authors such as Pynchon, concludes that "[w]henever we find people described as pigs, something of this carnivalesque inversion, a world turned upside-down, is being re-used and applied" ("Pigs and Pierrots" 56–57).

As I indicated in Chapter 5, Carter makes good use of circus clowns as representatives of the carnivalesque, especially in the episode of the "dance of the buffoons."[45] Buffo the Great (a.k.a. George Buffins), leader of the clowns, consistently appears as a travesty of Christ, and he specifically acts out a carnivalized version of the resurrection of Christ (and of rebirth myths in general) in the circus routine known as "The Clown's Funeral."[46] After Buffo's apparent death, his fellow clowns, after much comic difficulty, place him in a coffin, and prepare to carry him out of the ring, "[a]t which Buffo burst through the coffin lid! Right through. With a great, rending crash, leaving behind a huge, ragged hole, the silhouette of himself" (118).

Buffo also provides a striking enactment of the grotesque body in his clown costume:

he wears a wig that does not simulate hair. It is, in fact, a bladder. Think of that. He wears his insides on his outside, and a portion of his most obscene and intimate insides, at that; so that you might think he is bald, he stores his brains in the organ which, conventionally, stores piss. (116)

This conflation of the intellectual with the excremental is quintessential carnival. It also points to the dark side of carnivalesque exuberance, to the fact that carnivalesque images often effect (à la Barnes) a return of the socially repressed, loudly proclaiming the existence of factors (such as excrement) that polite society would just as soon forget. There is potential for great humor here, but beneath the humor there is also potential for considerable terror as these abject images come to the fore.

Michael André Bernstein has noted the current of abjection that constantly runs through the carnival, countering proclamations of the power of joyous carnivalesque celebration with reminders of the "negative and bitter strand at the core" of the carnival (100). Similarly, there is a consistent undertone of abjection in Carter's treatment of her clowns. A young boy, Ivan, who has never seen a circus, at first finds the clowns terrifying (though fascinating),[47] and Carter describes them as marginal figures with a disturbing potential:

A band of irregulars, permitted the most ferocious piracies as long as, just so long as, they maintain the bizarrerie of their appearance, so that their violent exposition of manners stays on the safe side of terror, even if we need to learn to laugh at them, and part, at least, of this laughter comes from the successful suppression of fear. (151)

The dark side of clowning is shown most forcefully when Buffo goes insane during a performance and attempts to murder Walser. Buffo is finally subdued (to the uproarious laughter of the crowd, which thinks it is all part of the act) and taken away to an asylum, whence he will never return. Near the end of the book, the remaining clowns perform one last abject dance, to "eldritch music," in honor of their fallen leader and for marginal persons everywhere:

Didn't clowns always summon to your mind disintegration, disaster, chaos?
    This dance was the dance of death, and they danced it for George Buffins, that they might be as him. They danced it for the wretched of the earth, that they might witness their own wretchedness. They danced the dance for the outcasts who watched them. (242)

Again, Carter's book is highly authentic; there is much historical precedent for linking clowns to madness. For example, Stallybrass and White note the relation between "clownism" and hysteria drawn by Freud (175) and suggest that in general the "showman and the circus" are charged images for the hysterical patient.[48] From a feminist perspective it is also useful to note the discussion of the relationship between hysteria and the transgressive energies of the "festival" as discussed by Catherine Clément (22–26). Indeed, Clément succinctly summarizes the emergence of the abject in Carter's clowns when she states that "[a]ll laughter is allied with the monstrous" (33). This same insight inheres in Eliot's image of the "rattle of the bones, and chuckle spread from ear to ear," clearly linking laughter to abjection.

ABJECTION AND THE CARNIVALESQUE

Clément describes the inverted logic of the festival as follows: "Social life is "right side up" (not real social life but whatever the era's mythical image of it is). The festival is "upside down." Everything happens backward, and even bodies find a way to turn upside down" (22).

This description is in close accord with Bakhtin's discussions of the carnival, as one might expect. However, it is also strikingly similar to the description of the abject "night" by Barnes's Dr. O'Connor: "The very constitution of twilight is a fabulous reconstruction of fear, fear bottom-out and wrong side up. Every day is thought upon and calculated, but the night is not premeditated" (80). Much of the transgressive power of *Nights at the Circus* arises from the way in which its comic exuberance is always shaded by threatening hints of the monstrous and the abject. As such, Carter's work resonates with that of Barnes in interesting and productive ways, despite the differences in tone. The combination of these two works, one so informed by darkness and abjection (with hints of exuberance) and the other so informed by laughter and celebration (with hints of darkness) strikingly illustrates the frequent complicity between seemingly opposed sets of imagery. This situation is fundamental to the carnival, according to Bakhtin:

All the images of the carnival are dualistic; they unite within themselves both poles of change and crisis: birth and death . . . blessing and curse . . . praise and abuse, youth and old age, top and bottom, face and backside, stupidity and wisdom. (*Problems* 126)

Such duality is also central to abjection, because, according to Kristeva, "abjection is above all ambiguity" (*Powers of Horror* 9).

It comes as no surprise, then, that abjection and the carnival should turn out to be closely related. But the close relationship between carnival and abjection poses a difficult quandary for readers of literary texts that are informed by these principles. One might read a text of abjection, such as *Nightwood*, as being largely in complicity with official society, as it, too, recognizes the terror and disgust associated with sexuality, mortality, and all of the physical aspects of human life that are contained within the realm of the abject. On the other hand, *Nightwood* can be read as radically oppositional, as it insists on highlighting these abject realities, while official society seeks to keep them safely hidden away. Similarly, a highly carnivalesque text like *Nights at the Circus* can be read as highly subversive because it celebrates the things that society repudiates as abject. Or it can be read as being a mere strategy for the containment of the subversive energies of abjection by making it into a joke.

It is possible to adopt any of these reading strategies. I read Barnes's abject text as subversive because of the tone of transgression given it by its many carnivalesque images of inversion. These images demonstrate the unreliability of all hierarchical oppositions, thus making it impossible simply to reject the book's images of the abject. Likewise, I read Carter's carnivalesque text as subversive because of the tone of transgression given it by its many images of abjection. The book is filled with instances of rape, murder, insanity, castration, and death; it cannot be read merely as comedy. Finally, both *Nightwood* and *Nights at the Circus* are saturated with a fundamental ambiguity that renders it impossible to settle comfortably into any one interpretation of or attitude toward the texts. This ambiguity, combined with the political specificity of both books (especially in the case of gender) makes it difficult to read either as a simple support for existing dominant ideologies, which rest on closure and fixed meaning.

The availability of widely different reading strategies for these texts indicates how important the reader is in activating the transgressive energies of any text. At the same time, the texts' resistance to finalized interpretation stands as a reminder that the truly transgressive reader must not seek merely to impose her own political agenda upon her reading. Instead, reader and text should collaborate in an ongoing and never-ending dialogic exchange. Granted, closure has its pleasures, but it also threatens simply to replace one authoritarian ideology with another. As I come to the close of my own book I have no mighty parting words. I can only suggest that the transgressive reader might do well to eschew closure and to adopt the motto suggested for Fevvers by Lizzie near the end of *Nights at the Circus*: "to travel hopefully is better than to arrive" (279).

POSTSCRIPT

The essays presented in this study are intended to explore a range of transgressive strategies of both reading and writing, and to do so in a way that resists the kind of totalizing summary that would seem to be inimical to the centrifugal energies embodied in these strategies. One of the most important effects of transgressive literature is simply the indication of alternatives, the suggestion that things need not necessarily be as they are. It is thus essential that the transgressive critic resist totalizing and impoverishing systems of interpretation that would limit the availability of alternative readings. There is no cookbook formula for writing—or reading—transgressive texts. However, it is still useful to observe certain trends that arise from these essays as long as that observation does not become overrigid. I have emphasized that transgressive energies arise from the reader as well as from the text: almost any sufficiently complex work contains some transgressive elements, given a sufficiently subtle critic, and almost any text can be reduced to banality by a sufficiently narrow-minded one. Still, some texts provide more convenient entry points for transgressive critical interventions than do others. Certain strategies are central to the repertoire of the transgressive, and understanding these strategies is a great aid to the critic who seeks to read transgressively. In this volume I have emphasized the way in which many of these strategies can be grouped according to their relationship to the dual concepts of abjection and the carnivalesque.

My opening essay on Chaucer, Pynchon, and Joyce indicates how language itself can be used in ways that create an atmosphere of linguistic turbulence that resists interpretive closure. Moreover, in these authors, this transgressive use of language is combined with a rich mixture of social voices that injects a decidedly political charge into the polysemic proliferation of meaning, a charge that undercuts the kind of systematization and hierarchization upon which oppressive political regimes are based. A similar process occurs in the attacks on dualistic oppositions in Rushdie, in the parodic dialogues of Woolf, Wittig, and Carter with the literary tradition, and in the rich ambiguity of Fowles. All of these activities can be roughly associated with the Bakhtinian notion of the carnivalesque.

However, in order to effect the kinds of changes in attitudes that can lead to genuine social and political change, such carnivalesque images must not be too easily recuperable as mere amusements (even though one effect of carnivalization is to challenge an oversimplistic privileging of the serious over the playful). The sorts of troubling effects that can lead to the unsettling of long-held opinions and attitudes often arise from the horror related to images of abjection. Abject images are centrally associated with the kind of filth, degradation, and animality with which dominant social groups traditionally seek to identify marginal groups, so again these images can take on a specifically political flavor. Abjection is also closely related to the Lacanian experience of *jouissance*, and the link here to sexuality indicates how abject images can be particularly transgressive, as demonstrated in my discussions of Fowles and Barnes, and of the use of the castration motif in transgressive literature.

Abjection and the carnivalesque are not mutually exclusive strategies, but can be used together with excellent effect. Indeed, the exclusion of marginal groups performed by dominant groups in associating them with images of abjection is precisely the sort of hierarchical social distinction that carnivalesque literature most powerfully undercuts. Moreover, any transgressive strategy is in danger of being recuperated as a merely formal technique, so that texts and readings of texts that employ multiple—even contradictory—strategies are often in the best position to maintain a genuinely transgressive force.

Finally, transgression in literature must involve more than mere technical and formal experimentation in order to take on a legitimate political force. As I argue in my reading of Sorrentino's *Mulligan Stew*, transgression in literature is politically effective only when that transgression has specific social and political targets. This kind of targeting might involve the identification of particular real-world adversaries, as in Rushdie's dialogue with Islam and with Pakistan; or it might simply involve the carving out of especially well-defined political perspectives and orientations, as in Woolf and Wittig. Various strategies are possible, but it is important that these targets be legitimate political ones, with social implications that go beyond exclusively individual experience.

The essays in this volume demonstrate ways in which a number of texts can be read to emphasize transgressive political energies. Still, it is by no means simple to convert these kinds of transgressive readings into concrete political action. For example, books are almost always read silently, in private, by one reader alone with her thoughts and the text, a situation that would seem at odds with the necessity for a strong communal element in the transgressions that literature undertakes. Moreover, relatively few members either of the oppressed masses or of the power structures which effect that oppression actually read literature (much less literary criticism), individually or otherwise. Such things being the case, the ability of literature (or of critical readings of literature) to effect social and political change is called into question. Martha Nussbaum, calling for ethical responsibility in literary criticism, recognizes such problems and produces an answer to this difficulty that is as good as any, however unsatisfactory it may be:

Well, what can we do but try? Some major choices affecting our lives—say, Supreme Court decisions—are made in effect by one or two complex reflective processes in the minds of one or two reading, thinking, feeling beings. An eloquent piece of writing (say, about James on the moral value of privacy) might possibly alter the course of that reflection. (85)

Given the alternative, politically committed writers and critics seem to have little choice but to pursue the Beckettian option of going on with dogged determination despite the apparent futility of going on. Nussbaum's suggestion provides some encouragement that literature might be a privileged place for transgression to occur. It is true that literary transgression is far easier than "real-world" transgression, and this difference should not be taken lightly. At the same time, the increased ease with which authoritarian ideals and received opinions can be challenged in literature suggests that the literary genre might serve as a sort of kindling to ignite genuine social and political change. We should not forget, amid all this political commitment, that literary critics have one tremendous advantage over workers in the social sciences and other fields that might seem more directly related to concrete events: as René Girard points out, "We have the greatest texts in the world" (254).

Following this suggestion, I have focused on literary texts in this study, outlining some of the ways in which these texts lend themselves to reading in more or less transgressive ways. But there is much more to be done. A great deal of attention also needs to be paid to the specific relationship of literary texts to their historical and political contexts and to the dynamics by which literary transgression might be converted into real-world action. Much of this project is already under way in the burgeoning interest in cultural studies in literary criticism, of which the highly visible "new historicism" is only one aspect. These sorts of studies, especially as derived from the theoretical work of Foucault, already show signs of being the trend in literary criticism in the 1990s. But in all of this we should not lose sight of the specificity of literature. More work also needs to be done in exploring the ways in which literature differs from the nonliterary, allowing it to serve a special and valuable social function not available in other realms of discourse.

Pedagogy will also play an important role in this project. Forced to admit that many of the most transgressive texts in literature will never have a wide audience, English professors are increasingly coming to recognize the tremendous opportunity that inheres in their efforts to teach literature in socially and politically responsible ways. As a bare minimum, this recognition will lead politically committed teachers to reexamine their own classroom strategies in the coming years as they seek to make the best of the captive audience of a dozen or several dozen students handed them each term. At best, it will lead to sweeping changes in the academic institution itself that will increase the viability of the university as an instrument of political change.

I would like, in my book, to have done all of these things, just as I would like for the world to be a beautiful garden in which everyone is kind and the beasts have no claws. But we do what we can. One book can only do so much, and I hope that this book is a step, however small, in the right direction. Perhaps Carter provides the best summary of the situation with her picture of the elephants in Colonel Kearney's circus who incessantly pull at their chains on the off-chance that they might someday break free:

since, in their millennial and long-lived patience they knew quite well how, in a hundred years, or a thousand years' time, or else, perhaps, tomorrow, in an hour's time, for it was all a gamble, a million to one chance, but all the same there was a chance that if they kept on shaking their chains, one day, some day, the clasps upon the shackles would part. (*Nights* 106)

NOTES

INTRODUCTION

1. The reference is to the youthful service of Malcolm X as a shoe-shine boy.

2. There is, however, a great deal of potential for transgressive readings of Shakespeare as well. Some of my own thoughts on Shakespeare and transgression have been transferred to another upcoming book ("Works in Progress") and to a forthcoming paper (" 'Nothing That Is So Is So.' ")

CHAPTER 1

1. Because of the dense nature of the text, citations of *Finnegans Wake* generally give both page and line numbers, separated by a period. I have followed that practice throughout.

2. In her comparison of Chaucer and Joyce, Cooper identifies three principal areas of similarity: an extreme naturalism, self-conscious emphasis on language, and effective use of the literary tradition. The last two fit in well with Jordan's parallel between Chaucer and postmodernism. As for the first, *Finnegans Wake* (which is probably the most "medieval" of Joyce's works but which Cooper curiously ignores) demonstrates that naturalism is not central to Joyce's overall project. In fact, I have argued elsewhere that even the extreme naturalism of *Ulysses* is in fact a parody of naturalism ("Joyce"). Chaucer would not seem to be parodying naturalism (as he had no naturalistic tradition to oppose), but many modern commentators have begun to recognize that it is lan-

guage itself that is at the heart of Chaucer's work, not the representation of "reality."

3. Cooper rightly suggests that one parallel between Joyce and Chaucer is the way both anticipate recent developments in modern critical theory (153). Along this line, Vance presents a discussion of medieval theories of language and signs, showing strong similarities to modern semiology and linguistics. He suggests: "There is scarcely a term, practice, or concept in contemporary theory that does not have some rich antecedent in medieval thought" (xii). Note also that Shoaf has demonstrated the relevance of modern literary theory for medieval studies ("Literary Theory"), as well as showing special parallels between medieval thought and the work of Heidegger and Derrida ("Medieval Studies"). Similarly, McClellan discusses a variety of parallels between the work of Bakhtin and medieval rhetorical theory.

4. See Fokkema, Lyotard, McHale, Spanos, and Wilde for representative discussions of the nature of postmodernism.

5. The "Strange Loop" is a system that infinitely resists the establishment of a single meaning because of its own self-referential nature. The famous "liar paradox" is a simple example. See Hofstadter (15–24 and passim). The relationship between metaphor and metonymy is a Strange Loop because metaphor depends upon metonymy, while metonymy depends upon metaphor. Jakobson himself moves toward recognizing this fact, admitting that his model is complicated by poetic language. He suggests that in poetry "every metonymy is slightly metaphoric, and every metaphor has a metonymic tinge" (370).

6. Maria Ruegg presents a useful discussion of the inadequacies of Jakobson's bipolar model of metaphor and metonymy. Moreover, she argues that Jacques Lacan's problematization of Jakobson's dichotomy is itself based on fundamentally conservative dualistic thinking, and therefore not so radical as it might appear. Still, it is clear that Lacan's view of the workings of language depends upon a mutual implication of metaphor and metonymy, and in this respect it is interesting to note Lacan's dependence on puns in his own discourse. In fact, Meltzer specifically relates Lacan's "metonymized" view of metaphor to his use of puns (162–63).

7. See Ahl for a useful discussion of this Latin pun (39).

8. The way in which O'Brien calls attention to his pun is similar to the way in which Pynchon explicitly discusses his play on the term "dt." One difference between Chaucer and postmodernist writers is that the latter tend to be more explicitly self-conscious about the devices they employ, but this is a difference of degree, not of kind.

9. One might note that Meltzer curiously (and no doubt unintentionally) echoes Pynchon in noting that, throughout Lacan's writing, the "pun trembles like an orgasm" (163).

10. See Freccero for a discussion of the Ugolino episode as an allegory of the damaging effects of overliteral interpretation, and note that, when Ugolino and his sons are locked in the tower, the Count says "sì dentro impetrai" ["I turned to stone"] (line 49).

11. It is no accident that Jonathan Culler, discussing Shoaf's work, refers to Joyce as the "supreme juxtologist" (9).

12. Moreover, I would even argue that this connection then inevitably extends to the "coillons" of the Pardoner. In this case, the astonishment of Dorigen and the sexual ambiguity of the Pardoner are parallel cases of confusion. The corruption of the Pardoner thus adds a special taint to "The Franklin's Tale." In any case, the problematic "gender" of the Pardoner can be seen as another case of the transgression of category boundaries that pervades *The Canterbury Tales*. See Dinshaw for a discussion of the ways in which gender transgression in the case of the Pardoner is related to Chaucer's general concern with linguistic transgressions. The falseness of the Pardoner's language is thus related to his corrupted sexuality: "The breakdown of language and determinate sexuality are of a piece" (39).

13. In fact, one might argue that Bakhtin's "double-voiced" word is always a sort of "social" pun. Moreover, in a dialogic discourse, virtually all words are more or less double-voiced. Therefore, all words are at least potentially puns of this sort.

14. The potential political force of deconstruction has gained increasing recognition in recent years. Michael Ryan, for example, offers an "articulation" of deconstruction with Marxism, noting that the philosophical difference between Marxism and deconstruction "does not mean that deconstruction does not have radical political implications and uses" (9). Such uses, of course, have been little explored by American formalist-deconstructionist critics. See Dunn for a discussion of the opposing views of the Marxist and the formalist views of deconstruction.

15. See *Paradiso* XXVI, line 117, in which Adam's sin is referred to as "il trapassar del segno"—literally, "going beyond the boundary marker."

16. For example, see Engle for a discussion of the ways in which the inflections of the Bakhtinian double-voiced word can be used to gain a considerably enriched understanding of "The Clerk's Tale" quite apart from the idea of the carnival.

17. Jill Mann is among those who have emphasized the status of the various pilgrims as representatives of groups rather than as true individuals. She argues that, although Chaucer gives the impression of individuality in the Canterbury pilgrims, the portraits of them in the "General Prologue" are composed largely of conventional details from the tradition of describing various estates. Even when he invents new details,

they are largely intended to emphasize conventional aspects of the portrait (15–16).

18. However, Chaucer's technique is far more complex than a simple association with a particular style or social attitude with each individual tale. Many tales include extensive internal dialogue as well. "The Nun's Priest's Tale," for example, includes within its dazzling verbal complexity "practically every literary genre in medieval England" (Knight 208). Moreover, there is often an extensive dialogic relationship among the teller of a tale, the characters in the tale, Chaucer as author, Chaucer's sources (such as Petrarch and Boccaccio) and the listeners of the tale, particularly Harry Bailly as host.

19. The Monk is the second most prominent representative of the prevailing order. It is significant, then, that he is first supplanted by the Miller, then later interrupted by the Knight. Authority is questioned in the Tales not only by "cherls," but also by itself.

20. Pynchon's concern with the opposition between chance (freedom) and determinism is quite common in postmodernist literature. One might compare, for example, John Fowles's The French Lieutenant's Woman, which has two endings, the order of which is ostensibly determined by a coin toss on the part of the narrator. As a result, a deterministic ending comes first, followed by an aleatory one. Fowles's coin toss parallels Chaucer's drawing of lots quite closely.

21. Interestingly, the narrator of The French Lieutenant's Woman makes this same connection: "We can trace the Victorian gentleman's best qualities back to the parfit knights and preux chevaliers of the Middle Ages; and trace them forward into the modern gentleman, that breed we call scientists" (233).

22. One might compare here the obvious fascination with violence demonstrated in "The Knight's Tale" as a similar indication of the dark side of social power.

23. The debate between "modern" and "medieval" readings of Chaucer has of course long been central to Chaucer scholarship. See Ferster for a recent brief summary of the debate (148–51). Ferster, incidentally, implies that the dichotomy may not be absolute, and that the methods of modern phenomenological hermeneutics she eventually employs for her reading of Chaucer have clear medieval antecedents.

24. See Straus for a useful discussion of the way in which the Wife's language "articulates the phallocentric conditions of the discourse within which she and her readership are constituted, and provides a critique of these patriarchal foundations of language" (527).

25. Moreover, this closure is highly problematic and unstable. By being allowed to make the choice, the new bride is ostensibly granted the "sovereynetee" that women supposedly so desire. Yet it is the knight (a convicted rapist who epitomizes sexual exploitation) whose

wishes are actually granted: "And she obeyed hym in every thyng" (line 1255). As Straus points out, "the choice the knight's wife asks him to make is set up in terms that can do nothing but fulfill the knight's desire" (544).

26. This technique is one of the ways in which postmodernism raises ontological issues by mixing different ontological levels within the same text. See McHale for an extensive discussion of this aspect of postmodernism. Note that *The Canterbury Tales*, with its embedded narrative and its narrator who is also a tale-teller, is structured around a similar mixture of ontological levels.

27. Joyce's writing is highly palinodic as well. See my extensive discussion of this point in "Works in Progress."

CHAPTER 2

1. For a brief review of some of the parallels between *Midnight's Children* and *Tristram Shandy*, see Keith Wilson (34). The most important parallel that Wilson does not list concerns the theme of questionable parentage that permeates both books.

2. In this regard, and in keeping with my interest in gender transgressions, I would be remiss if I did not note the Rushdie joke now in circulation: "What famous writer is blond, buxom, and living in Sweden?"

3. Rushdie's work echoes Joyce's in a number of interesting ways. I discuss certain aspects of this relationship in my "*Finnegans Wake* and *The Satanic Verses*: Two Modern Myths of the Fall."

4. The name of this character may refer to the Zenobia who appears in Hawthorne's *Blithedale Romance*. Indeed, Rushdie's character names are often highly allusive, and often with important implications. Thus, the "Ayesha" who appears in *The Satanic Verses* evokes the powerful African queen of the same name in Rider Haggard's *She*. This link to Haggard's work opens up a whole dialogue with the ideology of British imperialism and with the complicity between the imperialism and the patriarchal domination of women. On *She* see Gilbert and Gubar, who accurately describe *She* as a "dramatization of the notion that women and colonized peoples were analogically a single group (*No Man's Land* 41).

5. An emphasis on the significance of naming is a standard feature of Rushdie's fiction. In *Midnight's Children*, Saleem Sinai, himself meaningfully (if illegitimately) named, explains this emphasis as a part of his Indian heritage: "Our names contain our fates; living as we do in a place where names have not acquired the meaninglessness of the West, and are still more than mere sounds, we are also victims of our titles" (364).

6. The deconstruction of dualism inherent in Sinai's status as

"man-dog" is further emphasized by the fact that he is referred to by his "trainers" as "buddha," which is not only Urdu for "old man," but also evokes the image of Gautama the Buddha, of whom it was characteristic to be "capable of not-living-in-the-world as well as living in it; he was present, but also absent" (*Midnight's Children* 418).

7. In *Shame* Rushdie emphasizes the many changes that can occur in the course of a life through the repeated use of the motif, "Life is long."

8. I shall discuss this topic in much more detail in Chapter 8 in relation to the work of Djuna Barnes and Angela Carter. Note that Rushdie emphasizes the political dimension of this phenomenon: dominant groups associate abject traits with marginal groups as an excuse for political oppression. In *The Satanic Verses* the half-goat Chamcha enters a surrealistic hospital filled with similarly hybrid creatures. One of them, a "Manticore" (a half-man–half-tiger creature borrowed from Borges), explains how such transformations into animality come about: "They describe us. . . . That's all. They have the power of description, and we succumb to the pictures they construct" (*Satanic Verses* 168). This statement has a special resonance for Chamcha, who has accepted the definitions of Indianness brought about by British Orientalism and has sought to reject all characteristics associated with his homeland.

9. Such challenges to this traditional notion of the self are by now hardly news. However, the political force of Rushdie's challenge and the way in which it places the multiplicity of the self within the context of the multiplicity of Indian culture give his challenge a special vitality. In particular, the breakdown of the Us–Them dichotomy problematizes the kind of distinctions necessary to oppressive political regimes.

10. I have noted elsewhere the way in which Rushdie's treatment of the multiplicity of the self resonates with Jameson's discussions of postmodernism and schizophrenia ("Works in Progress"). Of course, in Rushdie these images of the self as a teeming multitude of sometimes contradictory elements also have much to do with the complexity and multiplicity of his Bombay and London cultural backgrounds.

11. Saladin Chamcha's name is itself an oxymoronic opposition with strong political connotations. "Saladin" refers to the great Egyptian Muslim sultan and warrior who successfully opposed the imperialism of the Crusaders in the twelfth century. "Chamcha," on the other hand, is literally Urdu for "spoon," but also has a second meaning with important resonances concerning Saladin's Anglophilia. "Colloquially, a chamcha is a person who sucks up to powerful people, a yes-man, a sycophant. The British Empire would not have lasted a week without such collaborators among its colonized people" (Rushdie, "The Empire" 8). Rushdie also notes this idiomatic meaning of "chamcha" in *Midnight's Children* (467).

12. As does Joyce. See Leopold Bloom's attempts to decipher the confused maternity of Corley in *Ulysses* (504).

13. There are many fairy-tale-like elements in the fiction of Rushdie, a characteristic he shares with other practitioners of what has been come to be known as "magic realism," most notably Gabriel García Márquez, an important Rushdie predecessor. Rushdie particularly shares with García Márquez a tendency to combine fairy-tale elements with an intense engagement in real-world political issues.

14. This episode has a particular political charge for Islamic fundamentalists because it grows out of actual accounts in Arabic history, accounts that have been rejected by later commentators on the Koran as apocryphal.

15. Calling Muhammad "Mahound" has apparently also been a major source of the violent reactions of Islamic fundamentalists to Rushdie's book. A. G. Mojtabai indicates that this naming is shocking indeed to Muslims, but notes that the name is to be attributed to Gibreel (who is either insane or at least highly unstable), not to Rushdie himself (3). Actually, the narration of *The Satanic Verses* is so complex that it is not even possible to attribute this usage to Gibreel in a nonproblematic way, as it may also come from the narrator. Another source of offense in Rushdie's text involves the repeated suggestion that Mahound was primarily a businessman, for whom the prophet-motive was decidedly punlike. Note, finally, that Saleem Sinai also mentions Mahound as a common alternative appellation for Muhammad (*Midnight's Children* 192).

16. This mode of narration is frequently used in the work of authors such as Beckett and Joyce, as I noted in Chapter 1. Rushdie himself lists Beckett, Joyce, and Flann O'Brien as important predecessors of contemporary writing in what was once the British Empire ("The Empire" 8).

17. *The Satanic Verses* itself is filled with such chillingly prophetic passages; e.g., this description of the sacrifice of the artist: "the writer agrees to the ruination of his life, and gains (but only if he's lucky) maybe not eternity, but posterity, at least" (459).

18. These similarities are not entirely coincidental. Rushdie directly alludes to the philosophy of Nietzsche. For example, Mirza Saeed Akhtar in *The Satanic Verses* experiences apocalyptic nightmares after having read Nietzsche the night before (*Satanic Verses* 216).

19. I trace the history of attacks on dualistic thinking in Western culture, especially as they relate to the work of Joyce, in "Western Culture in the Wake of Joyce."

20. Rushdie's technique here (as in many other places) is reminiscent of that of Joyce. Late in *Ulysses*, for example, as the boundaries between different characters become more and more diffuse, as characters freely begin to share thoughts and memories, they begin to share

names as well, with Stephen and Bloom at one point being supplanted by "Blephen and Stoom" (558). Joyce employs a similar strategy in *Finnegans Wake*, with (for example) Butt and Taff becoming Tuff and Batt (349.8–9).

21. Nietzsche and Derrida both have much in common with the Menippean tradition as well, and Bakhtin has been its most important modern theorist. Note the suggestion by Kristeva that the Bakhtinian carnival "calls to mind Nietzsche's Dionysianism" ("Word" 78). Allon White makes a connection between Menippean satire and Derrida, comparing Derrida and the deconstructionists to Bakhtin's clowns, parodying and carnivalizing Western philosophy ("Bakhtin" 139). White apparently means this comparison as a criticism, but, as I noted in Chapter 1, Derrida himself has suggested that the genre of *Glas* is Menippean satire.

22. For an extensive discussion of the parallels between *Midnight's Children* and Grass's *The Tin Drum*, see Bader. Also note that Wilson compares *Midnight's Children* to Robert Burton's *Anatomy of Melancholy*, a work very much in this same tradition (35).

23. Note Rushdie's own contention that "*The Satanic Verses* is not, in my view, an antireligious novel" ("The Book Burning" 26).

24. Rushdie conjectures that his attempts to deal with the treatment of women in Islamic society and in the Koran constitute a major reason for the violent reaction to *The Satanic Verses* ("The Book Burning" 26).

25. Curiously enough, Barthes's comments on the loss of authority of the author (and his relating that loss to the loss of theological authority) is highly relevant to Rushdie's work. To Barthes this challenging of traditional authority shifts much of the responsibility for the creation of meaning in a text from the author to the reader. Note that Keith Wilson (while not appealing to Barthes) has noted the tendency of Rushdie's work to demand active reader involvement: "the reader himself has entered the tussle and the novelist seems more than willing to share with an ally his assault on the intransigence of both art and life" (23).

CHAPTER 3

1. There is some question whether *The Formal Method* was authored by Bakhtin or by his associate P. N. Medvedev. The English translation of the book proposes a compromise, listing the authorship as Bakhtin/Medvedev. For simplicity I refer to the book as Bakhtin's in my text, but I take no position on the actual authorship of the book.

2. McHale notes that the term was first transferred from heraldry to literature by André Gide in a journal entry (124).

3. Bakhtin, of course, has demonstrated the subversive power of

laughter. However, in *Mulligan Stew* we laugh not at traditional modes of characterization, but at the characterization in *Mulligan Stew* itself.

4. Thielemans, however, presents a different view, arguing that Sorrentino's imitation of "varieties of debased language" leads to a questioning of the normal hierarchies of what is valuable and what is trash (124).

5. It may be that the distinction I make here is that between parody and pastiche, where pastiche is a mere imitation of style, not involving a true dialogic encounter with the text being imitated. However, the confusion over such terms in the critical literature is so extensive that there is probably little to be gained by employing them here.

6. Critics who have made this point include Huyssen and Modleski.

CHAPTER 4

1. It is only as a convenience that I speak of this trend as "beginning" with the Romantics. As J. Hillis Miller points out, the "gradual disappearance of God from the world" is a major trend of all postmedieval literature (*Disappearance* 1). In fact, that disappearance was well under way even within the medieval period, as the relatively tenuous presence of God in the texts of Chaucer as compared to the much stronger presence in the works of Dante amply demonstrates. Miller's argument that Victorian literature is so fundamentally informed by this disappearance of God supports my argument in this chapter.

2. Linda Hutcheon notes within a Bakhtinian perspective how writers such as Burroughs and Leonard Cohen employ pornographic sexual imagery in ways that achieve carnivalesque effects ("Carnivalesque" 89–94).

3. Deborah Byrd, for example, argues that *The French Lieutenant's Woman* is "an almost ideal feminist fictional work" because of the development of a genuine feminist consciousness in Sarah Woodruff (306). Magali Cornier Michael, on the other hand, argues that the book fails as a feminist statement because the figure of Sarah is never able to transcend the boundaries of male fantasy. Thus, "the male perspective . . . brings to the novel all sorts of preconceptions and myths about women" which are never finally denied by the text (225).

4. It should be kept in mind that "Victorian," in *The French Lieutenant's Woman*, is not so much a property of the late nineteenth century as a way in which the twentieth century views its predecessor. Fowles both problematizes and utilizes various stereotypes of Victorianism to construct his novel, which is not about the Victorian era per se, but about how we view that era and how we construct the past in

general. Throughout the remainder of this chapter, "Victorian" should probably be visualized as appearing within quotation marks, though I have chosen to avoid the intrusiveness of literally using such indications. That the actual Victorian era was far more complex than many of our notions of it is recognized by Fowles and indicated at several points in his text. For a study of this complexity, see Steven Marcus. And for an especially important problematization of the role of sexuality in Victorian society, see Foucault (*History of Sexuality*).

5. The incredibility of the notion of lesbianism for the typical Victorian mind is underscored by the earlier scene in which Sarah sleeps with Millie, described with the suggestion that "we many ascribe this very common Victorian phenomenon of women sleeping together far more to the desolating arrogance of contemporary man than to a more suspect motive" (130).

6. Tony Tanner, in fact, notes the centrality of adultery as a theme in so much of nineteenth-century literature. Tanner recognizes that adultery is employed as a symbol of transgression, and suggests that the novel itself is a "transgressive mode" (3).

7. It is in connection with the inadequacy of translating "*jouissance*" as "bliss" that Howard makes the comments about Sterne that I mentioned in the beginning of this chapter. This extra unsettling dimension of *jouissance* is precisely what separates the "text of bliss" from the mere "text of pleasure," and can be associated with the abject.

8. This implied maleness of the reader would appear to indicate Fetterley's remarks about gender positioning in literature, perhaps indicting another failure of Fowles's novel to make a positive feminist statement. However, the book here calls attention to an important feminist issue and creates an opportunity for feminist critics to intervene by reading against the grain.

9. See, for example, Barthes's reading of Balzac in *S/Z* and J. Hillis Miller's reading of George Eliot in "Narrative and History."

10. Questions of boundaries and of the relationship between art and the external world have occupied an important position in recent critical discourse, especially in rereadings of Kant as performed by critics such as Derrida and de Man. Of particular interest for my purposes here is Derrida's discussion of Kant in *The Truth in Painting*, especially because Derrida here specifically relates the problematization of frames and boundaries to the Kantian sublime. David Carroll summarizes Derrida's argument: "For Derrida, the Kantian sublime is not the simple transcendence of all borders. Without borders the overflow itself cannot be measured, the almost-unpresentable cannot be presented. The sublime differs, for him, from the aesthetic in that the movement across the border or frame is an explicit element of its excessive nature and that the unpresentable is a basic component of the dynamics of its

presentations" (142). Derrida, like Fowles, does not seek to do away with boundaries. He recognizes that the crossing of boundaries leads to exciting effects, but of course such crossing requires that boundaries exist.

11. It should be obvious that if both modernism and postmodernism are concerned with the questioning of boundaries, then the boundary between modernism and postmodernism itself must be problematic. Indeed, it is not clear if this sort of categorization is useful as more than a terminological convenience. More important are the mechanisms of transgression activated in individual texts, in dynamic interaction with the social, historical, and political contexts in which those texts are produced. Thus, literature of any era can enact many of the transgressive features that I have here associated with the twentieth century, as my reading of Chaucer in Chapter 1 shows.

12. I discuss this point in some detail in relation to the work of Joyce in "Works in Progress."

13. Sandra Gilbert has attacked Joyce's representation of gender issues in "Circe" as antifeminine (see "Costumes of the Mind"). But also see my detailed reply to Gilbert in "The Baby in the Bathwater."

CHAPTER 5

1. Compare Pynchon's neo-Shandean discussion in *V.* of interpretations of the significance of the nose in the pop-culture figure of Kilroy: "Hinting perhaps at a precarious virility, a flirting with castration, though ideas like this are inevitable in a latrine-oriented (as well as Freudian) psychology" (436).

2. De Lauretis acknowledges the availability of an "aberrant" reading of Lotaria as "the representative of a postmodernism of resistance," but opts against emphasizing that reading (80).

3. The term "castration" itself becomes somewhat slippery in a Lacanian framework, since "castration" is the name given by Lacan to the symbolic process of loss associated with the entry into language. As a result, for a male "castration" is paradoxically the rite of passage into phallic authority.

4. As Dinshaw points out, the Church never officially approved of self-mutilation, and Abelard (whose castration was not voluntary) condemns Origen for his self-emasculation (45n). The Christian opposition to castration is based on a belief that nature as God created it should not be defaced. On the other hand, the Church never officially opposed the ritual of circumcision, which has obvious resonances of a symbolic castration, in a quasi-Lacanian submission to the Law of the Father. Many founders of the Church even argued that Judaic law should be maintained in the new religion and that circumcision should be required.

5. Medieval "relics" were themselves images of fragmentation, consisting of bits and pieces of consecrated objects divided up in order to allow wider distribution. Popular among these relics were parts of the bodies of saints. Indeed, one of the more popular relics was the foreskin of Christ (presumably the only part recoverable), which was so popular that at least five or six of them were on display in various places (Dinshaw 31). This phenomenon has interesting implications in light of Lacan's view of the phallus as a perceptually detachable *objet a*.

6. There are certain biographical reasons to suspect that this motif of male sexual insecurity is influenced by factors in Sterne's own life. Such interpretations may even be interesting if pursued with subtlety, but they should not be allowed to obscure other aspects, such as Sterne's relation to the Menippean tradition.

7. Incidentally, Macksey posits that Parson Yorick is actually Tristram's father (1010). My money is on Uncle Toby (which seems suitably ironic), but unfortunately a defense of that argument is beyond the scope of my purposes here.

8. One thinks particularly of works such as the story "A Rose for Miss Emily." Note, however, that the Gothic aspect of Faulkner's work often takes on comic dimensions that are much more Menippean in orientation, as in *As I Lay Dying*. The Gothic can be related to the Romantic grotesque, which Bakhtin treats as a degraded form of carnival involving a retreat into individual subjectivity and a loss of social dimension. Other elements of Faulkner's work, however, act to restore this dimension.

9. Christmas himself is not reborn, but Lena Grove's baby is born on the day he dies, and the text shifts into a comic mode after his gruesome demise.

10. In *Problems of Dostoevsky's Poetics* Bakhtin states that "[t]he primary carnivalistic act is the *mock crowning and subsequent decrowning of the carnival king*" (124, Bakhtin's emphasis).

11. Sexual mutilation has long been seen as a means of exerting dominance, and the mutilation of Christmas resonates with real events in the grisly racial history of the American South. In literature, this symbolism goes back at least as far as Homer's *Odyssey* (Book XXII), in which the returning Odysseus demonstrates his triumph over the suitor Melanthios by having Melanthios's genitals torn off and thrown to the dogs.

12. Fischer, incidentally, is Jewish, thus his lack of interest in Christmas.

13. Significantly, *The Waste Land* takes its epigraph from *The Satyricon*, and there are suggestions of Petronius's influence in the general theme of sexual impotence that pervades Eliot's poem. On Eliot and Petronius, see Lees, Soldo, Nänny, and Schmeling and Rebmann. Nänny

in particular urges that *The Waste Land* be considered a work of Menippean satire, and the identification with Petronius in general helps to reveal transgressive energies in the work of the conservative Eliot.

14. On the other hand, similarly shocking scenes do appear in earlier work, for example in the French texts of de Sade, Lautréamont, and Apollinaire. Perhaps here again we have a matter that is managed better in France. On the other hand, one could argue that these French texts participate in the turn toward the Romantic grotesque that Bakhtin decried in modern literature and that they are less avowedly political and carnivalesque in orientation than is the work of Burroughs.

15. Joyce's "play" in fact has a number of similarities to the cinema; see Briggs.

16. In psychoanalytic lore, of course, the fear of being blinded is closely aligned to the fear of castration. It is interesting to note, however, that this "castration substitute" occurs to the son, not the father, evoking the biblical dictum that the sons shall suffer for the sins of the fathers. Perhaps a more literal reading of this link between blinding and castration would occur in the taking of Gloucester's eyes in *King Lear*.

17. Compare the story related by Felix Volkbein in Djuna Barnes's *Nightwood* of "the prince who was reading a book when the executioner touched him on the shoulder telling him that it was time, and he, arising, laid a paper-cutter between the pages to keep his place and closed the book" (21).

18. The lack of differentiation between the sexes in this procedure is emphasized by the fact that one Midnight's Child is a hermaphrodite who must therefore undergo two operations.

19. This scission contributes to the atmosphere of sterility that permeates Rushdie's novel. This atmosphere is again related to the motif of the sexual wound of the Fisher King in the Grail legend, which is echoed in various ways throughout the book.

20. Pigs are commonly associated with the carnival, and Slothrop first acquires the costume so that he can participate in a carnival as Plechazunga the Pig Hero. See Chapter 8 for more discussion of pigs as carnivalesque images.

21. There is still transgressive potential in such works, however, because they demonstrate the difficulty of overcoming existing gender stereotypes.

22. Berger's book nicely illustrates Luce Irigaray's comment on feminists: "if their aim were simply to reverse the order of things, even supposing this to be possible, history would repeat itself in the long run, would revert to sameness: to phallocratism" (33). The ending of Berger's book seems to take a recuperative turn as the hero gets the girl and begins to reassert his male dominance: "If he was going to be builder and killer, he could be boss once in a while. Also, he was the one

with the protuberant organ" (317). However, this overblatant ending can also be read as a reminder of the fatuousness of all systems of dominance of one gender by the other.

23. On the other hand, when the central character, Bron Helstrom, undergoes an operation to become a woman, he experiences considerable psychic difficulty, very unlike the anxiety-free gender change of Woolf's *Orlando*. The problem, his counselor tells him, is that "you are a woman made by a man—specifically by the man you were" (299).

24. By "retroactive" I mean that *Orlando* was read relatively little until recently. Now that it has been discovered, it appears to have been a predecessor to numerous other texts, even if the authors of those texts had not read it. Of course Woolf's text itself has numerous predecessors, particularly the comedies of Shakespeare, which virtually everyone has read.

CHAPTER 6

1. For a discussion of the way in which Shakespeare's gravedigger scene is based on the macabre humor of Lucian's *Dialogues of the Dead*, see W. Sherwood Fox.

2. For a brief discussion of Bakhtin's theories of genre, see Thomson.

3. Frye admits that *Tristram Shandy* can be considered a novel, but suggests that its central features all belong to the tradition of the anatomy (312).

4. Note, however, that Schlack's list of generic components actually describes a typical anatomy rather well.

5. The same, of course, might be said for *Tristram Shandy*, and one is here clearly reminded of the notorious suggestion by Viktor Shklovsky that "*Tristram Shandy* is the most typical novel in world literature" (57). It is interesting to note that Lucio Ruotolo agrees that Woolf's "aesthetic of the novel invites comparison with Bakhtin's" (10). But Ruotolo then curiously omits *Orlando* from his study of Woolf's novels, because "I take seriously Woolf's designation of *Orlando* as 'A Biography'" (2n).

6. Minow-Pinkney, for example, emphasizes the carnivalesque elements of *Orlando* in her discussion of the role of the fantastic in the novel. Minow-Pinkney specifically discusses *Orlando* in the light of Rosemary Jackson's work on fantasy, but acknowledges that Jackson's discussions of the role of carnival in the fantasy rely on Bakhtin (123).

7. See also Yaeger for an extensive treatment of the "emancipatory" potential of laughter and play in women's discourse.

8. This extra terminology is, however, quite unnecessary. Bakhtin's concept of dialogism does not require that there be merely two partici-

pants in the exchange; dialogism can in fact accomodate any number of speakers and listeners.

9. Richter notes that in *Orlando* "Each chapter of the novel contains parodies of literary genres or specific works belonging to the period with which the chapter deals" (155n). This method of construction leads Bonnie Kime Scott to compare *Orlando* to the "Oxen of the Sun" chapter of Joyce's *Ulysses*, concluding in fact that *Orlando* is a more worthy effort (36).

10. See, for example, her dialogue with Professor Trevelyan's *History of England*, a book in which references to women in English history are limited to such things as a mention of the fact that wife-beating was once considered acceptable behavior (*Room* 44).

11. Meisel sees a dialogue with Pater in this scene as well, suggesting that "[i]n many ways, too, the Tube woman is even a radical deidealization—a common-ing down—of a figure like Pater's Mona Lisa" (175).

12. For an extensive compilation of many of Woolf's allusions, see Schlack.

13. For an excellent discussion of Woolf's feminist appropriation of Shakespeare as a literary predecessor, see Schwartz.

14. Herrmann suggests that this kind of salon setting bears certain similarities to the Bakhtinian carnival (127).

15. Among other things, this scene emphasizes the authorized nature of carnival, as in this case the entire operation is personally supervised by King James himself.

16. For a discussion of the significance of "Anon" in Woolf's work, see Schwartz.

17. One might compare the "two friends" meeting in this passage to the man and woman getting in the taxi in the famous scene in *Room* (100). The confluence of the latter two leads Woolf to a meditation on androgyny, and there is clearly a way in which androgyny, by seeking to heal the rift between the sexes, can be seen as a general recuperative force that might combat the modern tendency toward schizophrenia.

18. See Minow-Pinkney for a discussion of this setting in terms of Said's concept of Orientalism (124).

19. Orlando here echoes Ovid's Tiresias (via Eliot), whose advice on love is sought by Juno and Jove because he has been first a man and then a woman and thus knows both sides of the picture. Note, however, that Tiresias finally manages to turn back into a man, while Orlando sees no need to do so, though she does continue occasionally to disguise herself as a man for fun.

20. See my " 'Nothing That Is So Is So' " for a discussion of a similar phenomenon in Shakespeare and Chaucer.

CHAPTER 7

1. The comment of Wenzel is typical: "I would argue that, far from being a subversive discourse as Cixous would have us believe, *écriture féminine* perpetuates and recreates long-held stereotypes and myths about woman as natural, sexual, biological, and corporal by celebrating her essences" (272).

2. Wenzel, in fact, makes precisely this argument, suggesting that in Wittig's texts patriarchal authority has always already been previously displaced: "Having no necessity to describe the rupture or emphasize the conversion, the resulting text is perforce more unsettling in its complacency" (279).

3. Compare here the suggestion by Barthes that "there is no language site outside bourgeois ideology. . . . The only possible rejoinder is neither confrontation nor destruction, but only theft: fragment the old text of culture, science, literature, and change its features according to formulae of disguise, as one disguises stolen goods" (*Sade* 10).

4. Lynn Higgins notes this relationship, arguing that in *The Lesbian Body* "[t]he text itself is a body in several ways. Like Osiris, it is dismembered" (161). Marthe Rosenfeld agrees, noting the "the segments of about fourteen pages corresponding to the number of pieces of which Osiris was reconstructed" (236).

5. Namascar Shaktini discusses some of the implications of this version of the Isis–Osiris myth for Wittig's text (33–34).

6. Both Cixous and Irigaray emphasize the importance of treating the body as an integrated unity. However, Diane Griffin Crowder suggests that although Cixous affirms the unity of the body, her bodily references are most often to pieces, such as the breast, abdomen, mouth, vagina, or head (133). Similarly, the glorification of the vulva is obvious in works of Irigaray such as "This Sex Which Is Not One" (23–33). Such emphases have led Irigaray, like Cixous, to be accused of being a "patriarchal wolf in sheep's clothing," to use the phrase of Toril Moi (146).

7. Durand calls the feminaries the "guides and histories" of the women" (72). Suleiman calls the feminary the "sacred book" of the women warriors (20). Crowder, meanwhile, notes that the feminaries, as opposed to male texts, contain "accurate descriptions of the vulva" (120). One might note, however, that there is a decidedly patriarchal cast to the entire notion of a sacred text, which might explain Wittig's parody: feminists do not need new sacred texts, but to do away with sacred texts altogether.

8. The quotation from *Les Guérillères* appears on p. 44.

9. Note that Foucault, in *The History of Sexuality*, also links the sex drive and the research drive, though he inverts the priority, suggest-

ing that sexuality is merely one aspect of a more fundamental will to knowledge, rather than vice versa.

10. However, where Joyce and Nabokov initiate dialogues with Freud, Wittig's main psychoanalytical target is Lacan, as Suleiman notes (20).

11. See Haller for a discussion of Woolf's use of Egyptian myth.

12. See Norris (37), and Scott (*Joyce and Feminism* 198–99).

13. Collage-like techniques have always played a large part in the construction of the multigeneric texts in the tradition of Menippean satire. In addition, such techniques were quite central to the composition of medieval texts in general, as the example of Chaucer's *Canterbury Tales* clearly demonstrates. Collage, in fact, has much in common with the medieval technique of textual construction that Shoaf has referred to as "juxtology" ("Play of Puns").

14. Ironic echoes of *The Waste Land* can be found throughout Reed's book. For example, the "Jes Grew epidemic" that forms the central subject of the book can be read as an inversion of the plague that sweeps Eliot's mythic landscape. This epidemic, in fact, is referred to in the text as an "anti-plague" (6). Note also that most of the action in Reed's book is set in the early 1920s, and that he makes extensive use both of the atmosphere of that historical period and of various mythic structures, especially those based on the quest and on death-rebirth. For example, he specifically mentions the Grail legend (15) and the debilitating psychic effects of World War I (63), both of which figure strongly in Eliot's poem. The generally fragmented nature of Reed's text also recalls Eliot's poem, but it is important to keep in mind the significant ironic distance that is maintained between the two texts.

15. This connection has been made, for example by Frank D. McConnell (196–97). David Cowart, meanwhile, relates Slothrop's fate both to that of Osiris and to that of Orpheus (47).

16. Indeed, "Oedipa" appears in one of the lists (à la the Homeric catalogue) of the names of Wittig's women warriors in *Les Guérillères* (101). Note also that Calvino's "Lotaria" can be read as a feminized version of "Lothario," which might account for her rapaciousness.

17. Rosemary Jackson indicates that Lacan forms a particularly valuable intertext for understanding the implications of Pynchon's treatment of Oedipa Maas. Though she does not suggest a parodic relationship, she does note that Pynchon's book "needs extensive relation to Lacan's theoretical model" (169).

18. Durand suggests that Wittig's use of present tense gives it the "timelessness and universality" of "a time outside of time" (72–73). My interpretation here is precisely the opposite, that the use of present tense projects the action of the text directly and immediately into the

flow of time that characterizes any contemporary moment. My interpretation is heavily informed by Bakhtin's concept of the "contemporary," which is far different from the mere "present." Juliet Flower McConnell notes the way in which Bakhtin rejects the traditional notion of the present as "presence," seeing it rather in terms of the "contemporary," a zone not oriented toward the past, but toward open-endedness: "it re-evaluates the past, and it thereby re-evaluates the present, for the emphasis in the present is no longer on full, immediate reality, but on disintegration—dissolving epic wholeness" (970). Also see Kumkum Sangari's argument for the political force of the lack of linear chronology in Gabriel García Márquez, where he notes that "the absence of a single linear time need not be read as the absence of a historical consciousness but rather as the operation of a different kind of historical consciousness" (172).

19. Wittig's great lesbian predecessor, Sappho, employs a similar mode of conflation of the epic and the lyric mode in poems such as "To Anaktoria."

20. There is a narrator in the book, but note that, in the book's final paragraph she joins this community as well, shifting into a first person plural mode of narration, a move that Durand calls a "really stunning effect" (77).

21. See the relevant argument by Joel Fineman from a Lacanian perspective that practitioners of the poetry of praise prior to Shakespeare create a poetry in which the poet is drawn to the loved one not as a separate individual, but as an idealized image of unity that contributes to the poet's own sense of psychic wholeness. It is also relevant to note the centrality of this rejection of the physical (and of women) in the Christian tradition, which makes Marks's comments on the anti-Christian force of Wittig's project all the more meaningful.

22. Clive Thomson discusses the relationship between the theories of genre of Bakhtin and those of Jameson. Note, however, that Thomson does not appear to afford sufficient appreciation to the importance of history and ideology in Bakhtin's theory.

23. Williams's "Portrait of a Lady" is especially relevant to the work of Wittig. In this poem he mocks the tradition of metaphorizing the various parts of the female body, parodically comparing the lady's thighs to apple trees and her knees to a southern breeze—or a gust of snow.

24. Compare here the suggestion by Alice Jardine that in general women writers "seem much less willing to experiment in a radical way with existing conventions. . . . Most feminist critics recognize women's 'respect for form' as the obvious cultural result of having always been closer to all possible transgressions: one fatal step outside of symbolic pre-scriptions and she is designated as 'mad'" (232–33).

25. Compare this emphasis on the need to redefine grammar before we can redefine our notions of gender to Nietzsche's famous declaration in *Twilight of the Idols* that "I fear we are not getting rid of God because we still believe in grammar" (38).

26. These lists (and many of the various other lists that Wittig employs) are presented without delimiting commas, which I interpret as a gesture against artificial compartmentalization through language. Both Ishmael Reed and Salman Rushdie frequently employ similarly undelimited lists and, I think, for similar reasons.

27. The following passage is typical of Cixous: "In women's speech, as in their writing, that element which never stops resonating, which, once we've been permeated by it, profoundly and imperceptibly touched by it, retains the power of moving us—that element is the song: first music from the first voice of love which is alive in every woman" ("Laugh" 251).

28. The English "I," of course, has no multiple letters to separate with a slash, so the English translation of *The Lesbian Body* uses an italicized "I" to indicate this effect. In a text with obvious relevance to the work of Wittig (especially *Les Guérillères*), Maxine Hong Kingston notes a similar problem with the simplicity of the English "I": "The Chinese 'I' has seven strokes, intricacies. How could the American 'I,' assuredly wearing a hat like the Chinese, have only three strokes, the middle so straight?" (193).

29. This point is clearer in the English translation than in Benveniste's original French: in French the genders of pronouns are governed by the genders of the nouns to which they refer. In English, where nouns are ungendered, the masculine prononun has generally been taken as the default, illustrating the feminist argument that the default gender is traditionally male.

30. Benveniste's theory of linguistic constitution of the subject bears many similarities to the model of subjectivity espoused by Lacan. However, Benveniste's subject is constituted dynamically and continually through the actual act of speech, whereas the Lacanian subject is stabilized by the continuing existence of an unconscious that transcends such constitutive moments. In this sense, Benveniste's notion of subjectivity is actually more similar to those proposed by Vygotsky and by Voloshinov and Bakhtin; the disposal of the unconscious in all three of these theories opens exciting possibilities for introducing a historical dimension into the constitution of the subject. For example, Kaja Silverman notes the way in which Benveniste's subject "has the capacity to occupy multiple and even contradictory sites. This descriptive model thus enables us to understand the subject in more culturally and historically specific ways than that provided by Lacan" (199).

31. On the other hand, it is clear that an emphasis on the self as a

stable entity has a distinctly male character to it. Norman Holland's work on "identity themes" among readers epitomizes this approach in the field of literature, and it is significant (given Wittig's treatment of pronouns) that Holland's most extensive study of the self is entitled *The I*. For a discussion of the way in which Holland's theories of identity are more applicable to male than to female subjects, see Judith Kegan Gardiner.

32. The quoted phrase is from Woolf's discussion of the intrusive presence of the author's self in Joyce and Dorothy Richardson (*Writer's Diary* 22).

33. Wittig's impatience with psychoanalysis, particularly Lacanian psychoanalysis, can be seen to arise from the difficulty of formulating any program for effective political action within that framework. As Michael Ryan points out, "Lacan's theory . . . offers little that would enable collective action to transform oppressive social institutions and relations" (107).

34. Compare the statement by de Lauretis that a sex-gender system is always intimately interconnected with political and economic factors in each society" (*Technologies* 5).

CHAPTER 8

1. One might also approach *Nightwood* from the point of view of metaphoric, as opposed to metonymic, form, per the discussions of David Lodge. Similarly, Eliot suggests in the introduction to the book that it should be read as poetry rather than prose (xii). However, these strategies involve the same attempt at imposing coherence as does Frank's notion of spatial form.

2. Also note Singer's discussion of Barnes's nontraditional use of metaphor in a way that defies the tenor and vehicle model, generating new meanings in the act of metaphor rather than simply transferring meaning from one image (48–49).

3. *Nightwood* echoes *The Waste Land* in numerous ways, and O'Connor is a clear descendent of Eliot's Tiresias. Eliot suggests in one of his notes to *The Waste Land* that "What Tiresias *sees*, in fact, is the substance of the poem" (*Collected Poems* 72, Eliot's emphasis). The same might be said of O'Connor, whose vision unites the various themes of *Nightwood*.

4. See Reizbaum for a discussion of Jewishness as an image of marginality in *Nightwood* and *Ulysses*.

5. Dolls function as rather sinister images throughout *Nightwood*, echoing in certain ways the emphasis on puppets in the early fiction of Carter, an emphasis Palmer relates to Cixous's notion of the "coded mannequin" as a symbol of the psychic state of repressed individuals (Palmer 180).

6. I explore this argument in some detail relative to the work of Joyce in my "Works in Progress."

7. Carter emphasizes the sexual basis of the encounter between Red Riding Hood and the wolf even more explicitly in "The Company of Wolves," a reinscription of the standard tale in *The Bloody Chamber*. After an elaborate seduction scene, we find the heroine indeed in bed with the wolf, as "sweet and sound she sleeps in granny's bed, between the paws of the tender wolf" (118).

8. Compare here the scene in Günter Grass's *The Tin Drum* in which a man fishes for eels using a horse's head as bait. He draws in the head and extracts "an enormous eel from the horse's ear, followed by a mess of white porridge from the horse's brain" (151).

9. This connection between abjection and love (summed up in the Lacanian notion of *jouissance*) is perhaps most clearly indicated by the declaration of Felix Volkbein that "[t]he unendurable is the beginning of the curve of joy" (117).

10. These marginal figures might be described as members of "muted" groups (see Chapter 6). Note that their symbol in *Lot 49* is a muted post horn, and that O'Connor describes the inhabitants of the night as giving off something "dark and muted" (94).

11. Barnes does, however, employ a number of other allusions to enhance the atmosphere of abjection in her book. Robin is found reading from the Marquis de Sade (47), O'Connor's abject inhabitants of the night are compared to Lady Macbeth (95), and O'Connor quotes Taylor on the necrophilia between Periander and Melissa (103). The reference to Sade particularly contributes to the note of abjection, and it is interesting to note that Carter has produced a book-length feminist study of the ideology of pornography based on the work of Sade (*Sadeian Woman*).

12. Moynihan suggests the connection between Eliot and Petronius, pointing out: "Given directions for the decoration of his monument at his grave, Trimalchio asks that 'At the feet of my effigy have my little bitch put . . .' —'bitch' here referring to his wife. Then, shortly after an argument with his wife, he cries, 'All right! I'll make you long yet to dig me up again with your fingernails'" (28–29). In this connection, Lees notes that when Encolpius and his companions enter Trimalchio's house they are startled by a wall-painting of a big dog on a chain, over which is written "BEWARE OF THE DOG" (352).

13. Melchiori was among the first to point out the parallel between Eliot's passage and this one from Joyce, suggesting that Eliot may have been directly influenced by Joyce here (74–75). See also Sultan for a detailed discussion of parallels between *Ulysses* and *The Waste Land*.

14. Also note that birds can have a sinister aspect in Barnes, as in her reference to "the drearful bird—*Turdus musicus*, or European singing

thrush" (137). Barnes's image gains energy through reference to *The Waste Land*, whose singing hermit-thrush is identified in Eliot's notes as *Turdus aonalaschkae pallasti*.

15. This wreck, in which all of the circus elephants die, illustrates the tremendous allusive richness of Carter's text. Train wrecks loom large in circus lore. In particular, Jumbo, the most famous circus elephant in history, was killed when hit by a train while being loaded into his boxcar.

16. Turner links the universality of this laughter to "folk" laughter, which has traditionally been seen to have a great unifying effect, expressing "a relationship to existence of all inclusive regeneration that is both mocking and triumphant" (57).

17. In point of fact, we are not exactly told that Fevvers is not a virgin, only that she is not a "fully-feathered intacta" (294). One could infer from this statement either that her virginity is fake, or that her feathers are (or both). The general tone of the text clearly favors the former alternative, though in reality virgins are more common than bird-women.

18. Midnight also functions as a symbol of the artificiality of boundaries in the first scene of the book, in which Lizzie and Fevvers apparently manipulate time so as to make midnight occur repeatedly throughout the night (see pp. 37, 42, 48).

19. A shameless punster, Carter refers to Fevvers as a Helen who "launched a thousand quips, mostly on the lewd side" (8).

20. The Titian painting, appropriately enough, is of Leda and the Swan. Carter employs a number of intertextual references to paintings in *Nights*. Palmer points out that the description of Fevvers's costume on page 14 echoes Max Ernst's *The Robing of the Bride* and that the bizarre scene in which the circus tigers become absorbed into shattered mirrors after the train wreck recalls Magritte's *Découverte* and *Le Faux Miroir* (204 n. 48). *Nightwood* can also be effectively read using paintings as intertexts. Kannenstine points out that the "visual dimension" of *Nightwood* suggests an analogy with painting, particularly with the works of such surrealists as Ernst, Magritte, or de Chirico (99–100).

21. This Strong Man himself is an interesting allegorical figure. He first appears as a caricature of the brutish, insensitive male who sees women only as collections of orifices. But later he has his consciousness raised and ends up as a caricature of the new sensitive male, selflessly acting as loyal servant to Mignon and her lesbian lover.

22. Walser refers to Fevvers as a "marvellous machine" (29); at another point a rumor arises that Fevvers is in fact "an automaton made up of whalebone, india-rubber and springs," again echoing Pynchon's *V.* (147). There is also here an interesting echo of Carter's earlier *The*

Magic Toyshop, in which the vile Philip orchestrates the rape of the heroine Melanie by a mechanical swan.

23. Private visitors to this museum can receive sexual favors from the exhibits (with the exception of Fevvers and the "Sleeping Beauty") for an extra fee. Customers have to pay double for Albert/Albertina, of course, and there is one regular whose fancy with the hermaphrodite resonates in interesting ways with Joyce's "Circe" and Burroughs's "Orgasm Death Gimmick" (see Chapter 5): "Albert/Albertina put a noose around his neck and give it a bit of a pull but not enough to hurt, whereupon he'd ejaculate and give him/her a fiver tip" (61).

24. She is linked specifically to Nelson because she has only one good eye, in a reference to Nelson's having lost one of his eyes.

25. This particular question echoes the relationship of Woolf's androgynous couple, Orlando and Shel, as indeed in many ways does the relationship of Fevvers and Walser in general: "'Are you positive you aren't a man?' he would ask anxiously, and she would echo, 'Can it be possible you're not a woman?'" (*Orlando* 258).

26. Wittig's anatomization of the female body in *The Lesbian Body* stands as a particularly striking grotesque/carnivalesque image.

27. Stallybrass and White note the transgressive potential of hybridization, suggesting that it "produces new combinations and strange instabilities in a given semiotic system" (58).

28. Compare here Dr. O'Connor's reference to the untidiness of history in *Nightwood* (118).

29. Carter specifically links Fevvers's dining habits to Rabelais, noting that she ate the "earthiest, coarsest cabbies' fare with gargantuan enthusiasm" (22).

30. Note, however, that Molly "utters" these words only in her own mind, whereas Fevvers proclaims her fart openly in the presence of Walser.

31. Swift's irony seems to be largely at the expense of Strephon, thus undercutting any interpretation of this poem as simple misogyny. Gubar essentially equates Swift with Strephon, arguing that Swift shows an inability to "accept the ambiguities and contradictions of the human condition" (381). But one could just as easily read the poem as a jibe at those (such as Strephon) who have such an inability. Thus Donald Siebert proposes the diametrically opposed view that Swift is demonstrating that men "must be familiar with the flaws of womankind—and of *man*kind—but should accept human limitations with full knowledge and with good humor" (38, his emphasis).

32. Eliot's allusion is to Marvell's "To His Coy Mistress": "But at my back I always hear / Time's wingèd chariot hurrying near." Compare Fevvers's description of the time she perched on the mantelpiece in Ma

Nelson's parlor about to attempt her first flight: "And behind me, truly, sir, upon the wall, I could have sworn I heard, caught in time's cobweb but, all the same, audible, the strenuous beating of great, white wings" (30).

33. Barnes uses this same strategy in *Nightwood* when O'Connor relates the story of how Catherine the Great "took old Poniatovsky's throne for a water-closet" (104).

34. Note also that one of the most prominent images of the ideal woman in all of literature occurs in the "bird-girl" of Stephen Dedalus's famous epiphany in *A Portrait of the Artist as a Young Man*. Interestingly, this girl is described not only in terms of bird imagery, but also as a "wild angel" (172).

35. Later, in Madame Schreck's museum, Fevvers continues this role, playing the Angel of Death to discourage clients from taking liberties with the Sleeping Beauty (70).

36. See Carter's interesting discussion of prostitution in *The Sadeian Woman*. Here, she argues that "in a world organised by contractual obligations, the whore represents the only possible type of honest woman. . . . At least the girl who sells herself with her eyes open is not a hypocrite and, in a world with a cash-sale ideology, that is a positive, even a heroic virtue" (57–58).

37. The situation of the inmates in the panopticon, who can be seen but who cannot see, parallels Berger's comments noted above on the visual position of women in general.

38. Music is also a prominent motif in *Nightwood*. Kannenstine suggests that "*Nightwood*'s structure is far from rigidly bound to the form of the fugue. . . . But *Nightwood* does to an extent specifically imply the texture and inevitability of movement of a fugue, and its musical nature is enhanced by numerous references to music in the text (98).

39. Or, as Joyce's Leopold Bloom puts it: "Numbers it is. All music when you come to think" (*Ulysses* 228).

40. Compare here the scene in Shakespeare's *As You Like It* in which the shephered Corin privileges courtiers over shepherds because the former have hands perfumed with civet, while the hands of the latter are often soiled with tar. The clown Touchstone then reminds him that "civet is of a baser birth than tar, the very uncleanly flux of a cat" (III.ii.59–65).

41. Carter's treatment of the circus is too rich to be treated exhaustively here. For example, she adds such touches as a family of acrobats, the "Charivari," who function as Fevvers's enemies in the circus. But "charivari," Stallybrass and White tell us, is a traditional carnivalesque ritual, "a rowdy form of crowd behavior often used

against 'unruly women,' and . . . an overt reminder of patriarchal domination" (24).

42. Compare Kafka's "A Report to an Academy," in which an educated, articulate ape explains his training in human ways to a group of scholars. The blurred boundary between human and animal is made clear by Kafka in numerous ways, such as the ape's suggestion that the scholars retain a bit of their simian ancestry: "Yet everyone on earth feels a tickling at the heels; the small chimpanzee and the great Achilles alike" (250).

43. Thus, in Henry Miller's *Tropic of Cancer*, a Hindu who is new to Paris fails to understand the proper uses of a bidet while visiting a brothel, receiving a predictably porcine reprimand: "The five of us are standing there looking at the bidet. There are two enormous turds floating in the water. The madam bends down and puts a towel over it. 'Frightful! Frightful!' she wails. 'Never have I seen anything like this! A pig! A dirty little pig!'" (96).

44. Compare the episode in Carroll's *Alice's Adventures in Wonderland* in which Alice tends a recalcitrant baby, which is rebuked for its piglike behavior. The baby responds by literally transforming into a pig, whereupon Alice muses on the fact that a number of children she knows would make better pigs than people (66–68).

45. As Walser serves in the circus as a clown he participates in Fevvers's transgression of the boundary between human and bird by playing the role of the "Human Chicken."

46. Compare the similar carnivalesque relation between clowns and kings that inheres in Barnes's "King Buffo," an obvious predecessor of Carter's head clown.

47. Stallybrass and White suggest that the disgust felt for images of filth and degradation is generally accompanied by "nostalgia, longing, and fascination" (191)

48. Turner suggests that Carter's clowns can be productively viewed as representatives of what Bakhtin calls the "romantic grotesque" (49). The romantic grotesque is a debased form of carnival that has lost its communal power due to Romanticism's emphasis on individualism. Bakhtin notes that in the romantic grotesque "madness acquires a somber, tragic aspect of individual isolation" (*Rabelais* 39).

WORKS CITED

Ahl, Frederick. "Ars Est Caelare Artem (Art in Puns and Anagrams Engraved)." In *On Puns: The Foundation of Letters*. Ed. Jonathan Culler. London: Basil Blackwell, 1988, 17–43.

Dante Alighieri. *Paradiso*. Trans. Allen Mandelbaum. Berkeley and Los Angeles: University of California Press, 1984.

Altieri, Charles. *Enlarging the Temple: New Directions in American Poetry During the 1960s*. Lewisburg, Penn.: Bucknell University Press, 1979.

———. "Why Stevens Must Be Abstract." In *Wallace Stevens: The Poetics of Modernism*. Ed. Albert Gelpi. Cambridge: Cambridge University Press, 1985, 86–118.

Arthur, K. "Bakhtin, Kristeva and Carnival." Diss. Melbourne, Australia, 1982.

Attridge, Derek. "Joyce and the Ideology of Character." In *James Joyce: The Augmented Ninth*. Ed. Bernard Benstock. Syracuse, N.Y.: Syracuse University Press, 1988, 152–57.

———. *Peculiar Language: Literature as Difference from the Renaissance to James Joyce*. Ithaca, N.Y.: Cornell University Press, 1988.

Bader, Rudolph. "Indian Tin Drum." *International Fiction Review* 11 (1984): 75–83.

Baker, Carlos, ed., *Hemingway: Selected Letters, 1917–61*. New York: Charles Scribner's Sons, 1981.

Bakhtin, M. M. *The Dialogic Imagination*. Trans. Caryl Emerson and

Michael Holquist. Ed. Michael Holquist. Austin: University of Texas Press, 1981.

———. *Problems of Dostoevsky's Poetics*. Trans. and ed. Caryl Emerson. Minneapolis: University of Minnesota Press, 1984.

———. *Rabelais and His World*. Trans. Helene Iswolsky. Bloomington: Indiana University Press, 1984.

———. *Speech Genres and Other Late Essays*. Trans. Vern W. McGhee. Ed. Caryl Emerson and Michael Holquist. Austin: University of Texas Press, 1986.

Bakhtin M. M., and P. N. Medvedev. *The Formal Method in Literary Scholarship: A Critical Introduction to Sociological Poetics*. Trans. Albert J. Wehrle. Cambridge: Harvard University Press, 1985.

Barnes, Djuna. *Nightwood*. New York: Harcourt, Brace, 1937.

Barthelme, Donald. *The Dead Father*. 1975. New York: Pocket Books, 1978.

Barthes, Roland. "The Death of the Author." In *Image—Music—Text*. Trans. Stephen Heath. London: Collins, 1977, 142–48.

———. *Mythologies*. Trans. Annette Lavers. New York: Hill and Wang, 1970.

———. *The Pleasure of the Text*. Trans. Richard Miller. New York: Hill and Wang, 1975.

———. *Sade, Fourier, Loyola*. Trans. Richard Miller. Berkeley and Los Angeles: University of California Press, 1989.

———. *Système de la mode*. Paris: Seuil, 1967.

———. *S/Z*. Trans. Richard Miller. New York: Hill and Wang, 1974.

Beckett, Samuel. *Murphy*. New York: Grove, 1957.

———. *Three Novels: Molloy, Malone Dies, and The Unnameable*. New York: Grove, 1965.

Bennett, Tony. *Formalism and Marxism*. London and New York: Methuen, 1979.

Benson, C. David. *Chaucer's Drama of Style: Poetic Variety and Contrast in the Canterbury Tales*. Chapel Hill: University of North Carolina Press, 1986.

Benveniste, Emile. *Problems in General Linguistics*. Trans. Mary Elizabeth Meek. Coral Gables, Fl.: University of Miami Press, 1971.

Berger, John. *Ways of Seeing*. London: Penguin, 1972.

Berger, Thomas. *Regiment of Women*. New York: Popular Library, 1973.

Bernstein, Michael André. "When the Carnival Turns Bitter: Preliminary Reflections Upon the Abject Hero." In *Bakhtin: Essays and Dialogues on His Work*. Ed. Gary Saul Morson. Chicago: University of Chicago Press, 1986, 99–121.

Booker, M. Keith. "The Baby in the Bathwater: Joyce, Gilbert, and Feminist Criticism." *Texas Studies in Literature and Language*, 32 (1990): 446–67.

———. "*Finnegans Wake* and *The Satanic Verses*: Two Modern Myths of the Fall." *Critique*, forthcoming.

———. "Joyce, Planck, Einstein, and Heisenberg: A Relativistic Quantum Mechanical Discussion of *Ulysses*." *James Joyce Quarterly*, 27 (1990): 577–86.

———. "'Nothing That Is So Is So': Dialogic Discourse and the Voice of the Woman in *The Clerk's Tale* and *Twelfth Night*." *Exemplaria*, forthcoming.

———. "Western Culture in the Wake of Joyce: From Egypt to Derrida (by Way of Nietzsche)." *College English* 53 (1991): 19–33.

———. "Works in Progress: History, Subjectivity, and Textuality in the Fiction of James Joyce." Manuscript in preparation.

Booth, Wayne C. "Freedom of Interpretation: Bakhtin and the Challenge of Feminist Criticism." In *Bakhtin: Essays and Dialogues on His Work*. Ed. Gary Saul Morson. Chicago: University of Chicago Press, 1986, 145–76.

Borges, Jorge Luis. *Labyrinths*. Ed. Donald A. Yates and James E. Irby. New York: New Directions, 1964.

Brewer, Derek. "Gothic Chaucer." In *Geoffrey Chaucer*. Ed. Derek Brewer. Athens: Ohio University Press, 1975, 1–32.

Briggs, Austin. "'Roll Away the Reel World, the Reel World': 'Circe' and Cinema." In *Coping With Joyce*. Ed. Morris Beja and Shari Benstock. Columbus: Ohio State University Press, 1989, 145–56.

Bruns, Gerald L. "A Short Defense of Plagiary." *Review of Contemporary Fiction* 1 (1981): 96–103.

Burroughs, William S. *Naked Lunch*. New York: Grove, 1966.

Byrd, Deborah. "The Evolution and Emancipation of Sarah Woodruff: The French Lieutenant's Woman as a Feminist Novel." *International Journal of Women's Studies* 7 (1984): 306–21.

Caesar, Terry. "Joycing Parody." *James Joyce Quarterly* 26 (1989): 227–37.

Calinescu, Matei. *Five Faces of Modernity*. Durham, N.C.: Duke University Press, 1987.

Calvino, Italo. *If on a winter's night a traveler*. Trans. William Weaver. San Diego, Calif.: Harcourt Brace Jovanovich, 1981.

Carroll, David. *Paraesthetics: Foucault, Lyotard, Derrida*. New York: Methuen, 1987.

Carroll, Lewis. "*Alice's Adventures in Wonderland*" and "*Through the Looking-Glass*." New York: Magnum Books, 1968.

Carter, Angela. *The Bloody Chamber*. London: Penguin, 1981.

———. *The Magic Toyshop*. London: Virago, 1981.

———. *Nights at the Circus*. New York: Penguin, 1986.

———. "Notes from the Front Line." In *On Gender and Writing*. Ed. Michelene Wandor. London: Pandora, 1983, 69–77.

————. *The Passion of New Eve*. London: Virago, 1977.

————. *The Sadeian Woman and the Ideology of Pornography*. New York: Pantheon, 1978.

Chaucer, Geoffrey. *The Riverside Chaucer*. 3rd ed. Ed. Larry D. Benson, et al. Boston: Houghton Mifflin, 1987.

Cixous, Hélène. "Castration or Decapitation?" Trans. Annette Kuhn. *Signs* 7 (1981): 41–55.

————. "The Character of 'Character.'" *New Literary History* 5 (1974): 383–402.

————. "The Laugh of the Medusa." In *New French Feminisms*. Ed. Elaine Marks and Isabelle de Coutivron. New York: Schocken, 1981, 245–64.

Clark, Robert. "Angela Carter's Desire Machine." *Women's Studies* 14 (1987): 147–61.

Clément, Catherine. "The Guilty One." In *The Newly Born Woman*, by Hélène Cixous and Catherine Clément. Trans. Betsy Wing. Minneapolis: University of Minnesota Press, 1986.

Collins, Jim. *Uncommon Cultures: Popular Culture and Post-Modernism*. New York and London: Routledge, 1989.

Cook, Jon. "Carnival and The Canterbury Tales." In *Medieval Literature: Criticism, Ideology, and History*. Ed. David Aers. Brighton, England: Harvester, 1986, 169–91.

Cooper, Helen. "Chaucer and Joyce." *Chaucer Review* 21 (1986): 142–54.

Coover, Robert. *Pricksongs and Descants*. New York: New American Library, 1969.

Couto, Maria. "Midnight's Children and Parents." *Encounter* 58 (1982), 61–66.

Cowart, David. *Thomas Pynchon: The Art of Allusion*. Carbondale: Southern Illinois University Press, 1980.

Crowder, Diane Griffin. "Amazons and Mothers? Monique Wittig, Hélène Cixous and Theories of Women's Writing." *Contemporary Literature* 24 (1983): 117–44.

Culler, Jonathan. "The Call of the Phoneme: Introduction." In *On Puns: The Foundation of Letters*. Ed. Jonathan Culler. London: Basil Blackwell, 1988, 1–16.

Davidson, Cathy N. "Oedipa as Androgyne in Thomas Pynchon's *The Crying of Lot 49*." *Contemporary Literature* 18 (1977): 38–50.

Delany, Samuel R. *Triton*. New York: Bantam Books, 1976.

de Lauretis, Teresa. *Technologies of Gender: Essays on Theory, Film, and Fiction*. Bloomington: Indiana University Press, 1987.

de Lorris, Guillaume, and Jean de Meun. *The Romance of the Rose*. Trans. Charles Dahlberg. Hanover, N.H.: University Press of New England, 1986.

Derrida, Jacques. *Speech and Phenomena*. Trans. David B. Allison. Evanston, Ill.: Northwestern University Press, 1973.

——. "Structure, Sign, and Play in the Discourse of the Human Sciences." In *The Languages of Criticism and the Sciences of Man*. Ed. Richard Macksey and Eugenio Donato. Baltimore, Md.: Johns Hopkins University Press, 1970, 247–65. (Published discussion, 265–72.)

——. *The Truth in Painting*. Trans. Geoff Bennington and Ian McLeod. Chicago: University of Chicago Press, 1987.

——. "Ulysses Gramophone: Hear say yes in Joyce." In *James Joyce: The Augmented Ninth*. Ed. Bernard Benstock. Syracuse, N.Y.: Syracuse University Press, 1988, 27–76.

Dinshaw, Carolyn. "Eunuch Hermeneutics." *ELH* 55 (1988): 27–51.

Donaldson, E. Talbot. "The Ending of Troilus." In his *Speaking of Chaucer*. Durham, N.C.: Labyrinth, 1983, 84–101.

Dunn, Allen. "Derrida at Work and Play: Morality and the Appropriation of Deconstruction." *Boundary 2* 14 (1985–86): 237–59.

Durand, Laura G. "Heroic Feminism as Art." *Novel* 8 (1974): 71–77.

Eagleton, Terry. *Walter Benjamin: Towards a Revolutionary Criticism*. London: Verso, 1981.

Eco, Umberto. *The Role of the Reader: Explorations in the Semiotics of Texts*. Bloomington: Indiana University Press, 1979.

Eliot, T. S. *Collected Poems 1909–1962*. New York: Harcourt, Brace, and World, 1963.

——. Introduction to *Nightwood*, by Djuna Barnes. New York: Harcourt, Brace, 1937, xi–xvi.

——. *The Waste Land: A Facsimile and Transcript of the Original Drafts Including the Annotations of Ezra Pound*. Ed. Valerie Eliot. New York: Harcourt Brace Jovanovich, 1971.

Engle, Lars. "Chaucer, Bakhtin, and Griselda." *Exemplaria* 1 (1989): 429–59.

Faulkner, William. *Light in August*. New York: Random House, 1972. Originally published by Harrison Smith and Robert Haas, 1932.

Felman, Shoshana. "Turning the Screw of Interpretation." In *Literature and Psychoanalysis: The Question of Reading: Otherwise*. Ed. Shoshana Felman. Baltimore, Md.: Johns Hopkins University Press, 1982, 94–207.

Ferster, Judith. "Interpretation and Imitation in Chaucer's Franklin's Tale." In *Medieval Literature: Criticism, Ideology, and History*. Ed. David Aers. Brighton, England: Harvester, 1986, 148–68.

Fetterley, Judith. *The Resisting Reader: A Feminist Approach to American Fiction*. Bloomington: Indiana University Press, 1981.

Fineman, Joel. *Shakespeare's Perjured Eye: The Invention of Poetic Subjectivity in the Sonnets*. Berkeley and Los Angeles: University of California Press, 1986.

Flaubert, Gustave. *Bouvard and Pécuchet*. Trans. T. W. Earp and G. W. Stoner. New York: New Directions, 1954.

Fleischman, Avrom. *Virginia Woolf: A Critical Reading*. Baltimore, Md.: Johns Hopkins University Press, 1975.

Fokkema, Douwe. *Literary History, Modernism, and Postmodernism*. Amsterdam: John Benjamins, 1984.

Foster, Hal. "Postmodernism: A Preface." In *The Anti-Aesthetic: Essays on Postmodern Culture*. Port Townsend, Wash.: Bay Press, 1983, ix–xvi.

Foucault, Michel. *Discipline and Punish: The Birth of the Prison*. New York: Vintage, 1979.

———. *The History of Sexuality, Volume I: An Introduction*. Trans. Robert Hurley. New York: Vintage, 1980.

———. "A Preface to Transgression." In his *Language, Counter-Memory, Practice: Selected Essays and Interviews*. Trans. Donald F. Bouchard and Sherry Simon. Ed. Donald F. Bouchard. Ithaca, N.Y.: Cornell University Press, 1977, 29–52.

Fowler, Alastair. "The Future of Genre Theory: Functions and Constructional Types." In *The Future of Literary Theory*. Ed. Ralph Cohen. New York: Routledge, 1989, 291–303.

———. *Kinds of Literature: An Introduction to the Theory of Genres and Modes*. Cambridge: Harvard University Press, 1982.

Fowles, John. *The French Lieutenant's Woman*. New York: New American Library, 1969.

Fox, Alice. "Literary Allusion as Feminist Criticism in *A Room of One's Own*." *Philological Quarterly* 63 (1984): 145–61.

Fox, W. Sherwood. "Lucian in the Grave-scene of Hamlet." *Philological Quarterly* 2 (1923): 132–41.

Frank, Joseph. "Spatial Form in Modern Literature." In his *The Widening Gyre*. Bloomington: Indiana University Press, 1963, 3–62.

Frazer, Sir James George. *The Golden Bough: A Study in Magic and Religion*. Abridged ed. New York: Macmillan, 1922.

Freccero, John. "Bestial Sign and Bread of Angels: Inferno XXXII and XXXIII." In his *Dante: The Poetics of Conversion*. Ed. Rachel Jacoff. Cambridge: Harvard University Press, 1986, 152–66.

Freud, Sigmund. *Leonardo da Vinci and a Memory of his Childhood*. Trans. Alan Tyson. New York: Norton, 1964.

Frye, Northrop. *Anatomy of Criticism*. Princeton, N.J.: Princeton University Press, 1957.

Gardiner, Judith Kegan. "On Female Identity and Writing by Women." In *Writing and Sexual Difference*. Ed. Elizabeth Abel. Chicago: University of Chicago Press, 1982, 177–91.

Gass, William. *Willie Masters' Lonesome Wife*. Evanston, Ill.: Northwestern University Press, 1968.

Gilbert, Sandra M. "Costumes of the Mind: Transvestitism as Metaphor in Modern Literature." In *Writing and Sexual Difference*. Ed. Elizabeth Abel. Chicago: University of Chicago Press, 1982, 193–219.

———. "Introduction: A Tarantella of Theory." In *The Newly Born Woman*, by Hélène Cixous and Catherine Clément. Trans. Betsy Wing. Minneapolis: University of Minnesota Press, 1986.

———. "Woman's Sentence, Man's Sentencing: Linguistic Fantasies in Woolf and Joyce." In *Virginia Woolf and Bloomsbury: A Centenary Celebration*. Ed. Jane Marcus. Bloomington: Indiana University Press, 1987, 208–24.

Gilbert, Sandra M., and Susan Gubar. *The Madwoman in the Attic: The Woman Writer and the Nineteenth-Century Literary Imagination*. New Haven: Yale University Press, 1979.

———. *No Man's Land. Volume 2: Sexchanges*. New Haven and London: Yale University Press, 1989.

Gilbert, Stuart, ed. *Letters of James Joyce. Vol. I*. New York, Viking, 1966.

Girard, René. "Theory and Its Terrors." In *The Limits of Theory*. Ed. Thomas M. Kavanaugh. Stanford, Calif.: Stanford University Press, 1989, 225–54.

Gluck, Barbara Reich. *Beckett and Joyce: Friendship and Fiction*. Lewisburg, Pa.: Bucknell University Press, 1979.

Graff, Gerald. *Literature Against Itself: Literary Ideas in Modern Society*. Chicago: University of Chicago Press, 1979.

Graham, John. "The 'Caricature Value' of Parody and Fantasy in Orlando." In *Virginia Woolf: A Collection of Critical Essays*. Englewood Cliffs, N.J.: Prentice-Hall, 1971, 101–16.

Grass, Günter. *The Tin Drum*. Trans. Ralph Manheim. New York: Pantheon, 1962.

Greiner, Donald J. "Antony Lamont in Search of Gilbert Sorrentino: Character and *Mulligan Stew*." *Review of Contemporary Fiction* 1 (1981): 104–12.

Gubar, Susan. "The Female Monster in Augustan Satire." *Signs* 3 (1977): 380–94.

Haller, Evelyn. "Isis Unveiled: Virginia Woolf's Use of Egyptian Myth." In *Virginia Woolf: A Feminist Slant*. Ed. Jane Marcus. Lincoln: University of Nebraska Press, 1983, 109–31.

Hannah, Barry. *Airships*. New York: Vintage Books, 1985.

Hart, Clive. *Structure and Motif in Finnegans Wake*. Evanston, Ill.: Northwestern University Press, 1962.

Hayman, David. *Re-Forming the Narrative: Toward a Mechanics of Modernist Fiction*. Ithaca, N.Y.: Cornell University Press, 1987.

———. "Some Writers in the Wake of the Wake." In *The Avant-Garde*

Tradition in Literature. Ed. Richard Kostelanetz. Buffalo, New York: Prometheus Books, 1982, 176–203.

————. *"Ulysses": The Mechanics of Meaning*. Rev. ed. Madison: University of Wisconsin Press, 1982.

Hemingway, Ernest. *The Short Stories of Ernest Hemingway*. New York: Macmillan, 1986.

Herr, Cheryl. *Joyce's Anatomy of Culture*. Urbana: University of Illinois Press, 1986.

Herrmann, Anne. *The Dialogic and Difference: "An/Other Woman" in Virginia Woolf and Christa Wolf*. New York: Columbia University Press, 1989.

Higgins, Lynn. "Nouvelle Nouvelle Autobiographie: Monique Wittig's *Les Corps lesbien*." *Sub-Stance* 14 (1976): 160–66.

Hill, Christopher. *Milton and the English Revolution*. New York: Viking, 1978.

Hofstadter, Douglas R. *Gödel, Escher, Bach: An Eternal Golden Braid*. New York: Vintage, 1980.

Holland, Norman N. *The I*. New Haven: Yale University Press, 1985.

Holquist, Michael. "Whodunit and Other Questions: Metaphysical Detective Stories in Post-War Fiction." *New Literary History* 3 (1971): 135–56.

Howard, Richard. "A Note on the Text." In *The Pleasure of the Text*, by Roland Barthes. Trans. Richard Miller. New York: Hill and Wang, 1975, v–viii.

Howe, Irving. *William Faulkner: A Critical Study*. 3rd ed. Chicago: University of Chicago Press, 1975.

Hume, Kathryn. "Calvino's Framed Narrations: Writers, Readers, and Reality." *Review of Contemporary Fiction* 6 (1986): 71–80.

Hutcheon, Linda. "The Carnivalesque and Contemporary Narrative: Popular Culture and the Erotic." *University of Ottawa Quarterly* 53 (1983): 83–94.

————. "Modern Parody and Bakhtin." In *Rethinking Bakhtin: Extensions and Challenges*. Ed. Gary Saul Morson and Caryl Emerson. Evanston, Ill.: Northwestern University Press, 1989, 87–103.

————. *A Poetics of Postmodernism: History, Theory, Fiction*. New York: Routledge, 1988.

————. *The Politics of Postmodernism*. New York: Routledge, 1989.

Huyssen, Andreas. *After the Great Divide: Modernism, Mass Culture, Postmodernism*. Bloomington: Indiana University Press, 1986.

Irigaray, Luce. *This Sex Which Is Not One*. Trans. Catherine Porter with Carolyn Burke. Ithaca, N.Y.: Cornell University Press, 1985.

Irving, John. *The World According to Garp*. New York: E. P. Dutton, 1978.

Iser, Wolfgang. *The Implied Reader: Patterns in Communication in*

Prose Fiction from Bunyan to Beckett. Baltimore, Md.: Johns Hopkins University Press, 1974.

Jackson, Rosemary. *Fantasy: The Literature of Subversion*. London: Methuen, 1981.

Jakobson, Roman. "Linguistics and Poetics." In *Style in Language*. Ed. Thomas A. Sebeok. Cambridge: MIT Press, 1960, 350–77.

Jameson, Fredric. "Marxism and Postmodernism." In *Postmodernism/Jameson/Critique*. Ed. Douglas Kellner. Washington, D.C.: Maisonneuve, 1989, 369–87.

———. *The Political Unconscious: Narrative as a Socially Symbolic Act*. Ithaca, New York: Cornell University Press, 1981.

———. "Postmodernism and Consumer Society." In *The Anti-Aesthetic: Essays on Postmodern Culture*. Ed. Hal Foster. Port Townsend, Wash.: Bay Press, 1983, 111–26.

Jardine, Alice. "Pre-Texts for the Transatlantic Feminist." *Yale French Studies* 62 (1981): 220–36.

Jordan, Robert M. *Chaucer's Poetics and the Modern Reader*. Berkeley and Los Angeles: University of California Press, 1987.

Joyce, James. *Finnegans Wake*. New York: Viking, 1939.

———. *"A Portrait of the Artist as a Young Man": Text, Criticism, and Notes*. Ed. Chester G. Anderson. New York: Viking, 1968.

———. *"Ulysses": The Corrected Text*. Ed. Hans Walter Gabler with Wolfhard Steppe and Claus Melchior. New York: Random House, 1986.

Kafka, Franz. "The Metamorphosis." In *Franz Kafka: The Complete Stories*. Trans. Willa and Edwin Muir. Ed. Nahum N. Glatzer. New York: Schocken, 1946, 89–139.

———. "A Report to an Academy." In *Franz Kafka: The Complete Stories*. Trans. Willa and Edwin Muir. Ed. Nahum N. Glatzer. New York: Schocken, 1946, 250–58.

Kannenstine, Louis. *The Art of Djuna Barnes: Duality and Damnation*. New York: New York University Press, 1977.

Katz, Steve. *The Exaggerations of Peter Prince*. New York: Holt, Rinehart, and Winston, 1968.

Kearney, Richard. *The Wake of Imagination: Toward a Postmodern Culture*. Minneapolis: University of Minnesota Press, 1988.

Kenner, Hugh. "The Traffic in Words." *Harper's* 258 (June 1979): 89.

Kermode, Frank. "Nabokov's *Bend Sinister*". In his collection *Puzzles and Epiphanies*. London: Routledge and Kegan Paul, 1962, 228–34.

Kingston, Maxine Hong. *The Woman Warrior: Memoirs of a Childhood Among Ghosts*. New York: Vintage, 1977.

Kinmonth, Patrick. "Step into My Cauldron: A Chat with Angela Carter." *Vogue* (February 1985): 224.

Knight, Stephen. *Ryming craftily: Meaning in Chaucer's Poetry*. Sydney, Australia: Angus and Robertson, 1973.

Kreiswirth, Martin. "Plots and Counterplots: The Structure of *Light in August*." In *New Essays on Light in August*. Ed. Michael Millgate. New York: Cambridge University Press, 1987, 55–79.

Kristeva, Julia. *Powers of Horror*. Trans. Leon S. Roudiez. New York: Columbia University Press, 1982.

———. "Word, Dialogue, and Novel." In *Desire in Language: A Semiotic Approach to Literature and Art*. Trans. Thomas Gora, Alice Jardine, and Leon S. Roudiez. Ed. Leon S. Roudiez. New York: Columbia University Press, 1980, 64–91.

Lacan, Jacques. *Écrits: A Selection*. Trans. Alan Sheridan. New York: Norton, 1977.

———. *Feminine Sexuality*. Trans. Jacqueline Rose. Ed. Juliet Mitchell and Jacqueline Rose. New York: Norton, 1982.

Langbaum, Robert. "The Mysteries of Identity: A Theme in Modern Literature." In his *The Modern Spirit*. New York: Oxford University Press, 1970, 164–84.

Lees, F. N. "Mr. Eliot's Sunday Morning Satura, Petronius, and *The Waste Land*." In *T. S. Eliot: The Man and His Work*. Ed. Allen Tate. New York: Delacorte, 1967, 345–54.

Leff, Gordon. *The Dissolution of the Medieval Outlook: An Essay on Intellectual and Spiritual Change in the Fourteenth Century*. New York: New York University Press, 1976.

Le Guin, Ursula K. *The Left Hand of Darkness*. New York: Ace Books, 1976.

Lévi-Strauss, Claude. *The Savage Mind*. Chicago: University of Chicago Press, 1969.

Little, Judy. "(En)gendering Laughter: Woolf's *Orlando* as Contraband in the Age of Joyce." *Women's Studies* 15 (1988): 179–91.

Lodge, David. *The Modes of Modern Writing*. Ithaca, N.Y.: Cornell University Press, 1977.

Lyotard, Jean-François. *The Postmodern Condition: A Report on Knowledge*. Trans. Geoff Bennington and Brian Massumi. Minneapolis: University of Minnesota Press, 1984.

McClellan, William. "Bakhtin's Theory of Dialogic Discourse, Medieval Rhetorical Theory, and the Multi-Voiced Structure of the *Clerk's Tale*." *Exemplaria* 1 (1989): 461–88.

McConnell, Frank D. *Four Postwar American Novelists: Bellow, Mailer, Barth, and Pynchon*. Chicago: University of Chicago Press, 1977.

McConnell, Juliet Flower. "The Temporality of Textuality: Bakhtin and Derrida." *Modern Language Notes* 100 (1985): 968–86.

McDonald, Christie V. "Roundtable on Translation." In *The Ear of the Other: Otobiography, Transference, Translation—Texts and Discussions with Jacques Derrida*. Trans. Peggy Kamuf. Ed. Christie V. McDonald. New York: Schocken, 1985, 93–161.

McHale, Brian. *Postmodernist Fiction*. New York: Methuen, 1987.

Macksey, Richard. "'Alas, Poor Yorick': Sterne Thoughts." In *Lacan and Narration: The Psychoanalytic Difference in Narrative Theory*. Ed. Robert Con Davis. Baltimore, Md.: Johns Hopkins University Press, 1983, 1006–20.

Mann, Jill. *Chaucer and Medieval Estates Satire*. Cambridge: Cambridge University Press, 1973.

Marcus, Jane. "'Taking the Bull by the Udders': Sexual Difference in Virginia Woolf—A Conspiracy Theory." In *Virginia Woolf and Bloomsbury: A Centenary Celebration*. Ed. Jane Marcus. Bloomington: Indiana University Press, 1987, 146–69.

Marcus, Steven. *The Other Victorians: A Study of Sexuality and Pornography in Mid-Nineteenth-Century England*. New York: Basic Books, 1966.

Marks, Elaine. "Lesbian Intertextuality." In *Homosexualities and French Literature*. Ed. George Stambolian and Elaine Marks. Ithaca, N.Y.: Cornell University Press, 1979, 353–77.

Martin, Stephen-Paul. *Open Form and the Feminine Imagination: The Politics of Reading in Twentieth-Century Innovative Writing*. Washington, D.C.: Maisonneuve, 1988.

Meisel, Perry. *The Absent Father: Virginia Woolf and Walter Pater*. New Haven: Yale University Press, 1980.

Melchiori, Giorgio. "Echoes in *The Waste Land*." In his *The Tightrope Walkers*. London: Routledge and Kegan Paul, 1956, 53–88.

Meltzer, Françoise. "Eat Your Dasein: Lacan's Self-Consuming Puns." In *On Puns: The Foundation of Letters*. Ed. Jonathan Culler. London: Basil Blackwell, 1988, 156–63.

Michael, Magali Cornier. "'Who is Sarah?': A Critique of The French Lieutenant's Woman's Feminism." *Critique* 28 (1987): 225–36.

Miller, Henry. *Tropic of Cancer*. New York: Grove, 1961.

Miller, J. Hillis. "Deconstructing the Deconstructors." *Diacritics* 5 (1975): 24–31.

———. *The Disappearance of God: Five Nineteenth-Century Writers*. New York: Schocken, 1965.

———. "*Mrs. Dalloway*: Repetition as the Raising of the Dead." In his *Fiction and Repetition*. Cambridge: Harvard University Press, 1982, 176–202.

———. "Narrative and History." *ELH* 41 (1974): 455–73.

Millgate, Michael. *The Achievement of William Faulkner*. New York: Random House, 1966.

Minow-Pinkney, Makiko. *Virginia Woolf and the Problem of the Subject*. New Brunswick, N.J.: Rutgers University Press, 1987.

Modleski, Tania. "The Terror of Pleasure: The Contemporary Horror Film and Postmodern Theory." In *Studies in Entertainment: Critical Approaches to Mass Culture*. Ed. Tania Modleski. Bloomington: Indiana University Press, 1986, 155–66.

Moffett, Judith. *James Merrill: An Introduction to the Poetry*. New York: Columbia University Press, 1984.

Moi, Toril. *Sexual/Textual Politics: Feminist Literary Theory*. London: Methuen, 1985.

Mojtabai, A. G. "Magical Mystery Pilgrimage." Review of *The Satanic Verses* by Salman Rushdie. *New York Times Book Review* (January 29, 1989): 3+.

Moody, Ernest. *Studies in Medieval Philosophy, Science, and Logic*. Berkeley and Los Angeles: University of California Press, 1975.

Morley, H. *Memoirs of Bartholomew Fair*. London: Chapman and Hall, 1859.

Moynihan, William T. "The Goal of the Waste Land Quest." In *A Collection of Critical Essays on "The Waste Land."* Ed. Jay Martin. Englewood Cliffs, N.J.: Prentice-Hall, 1968, 28–29.

Nabokov, Vladimir. *Lolita*. New York: Putnam's, 1958.

Nänny, Max. "*The Waste Land*: A Menippean Satire?" *English Studies* 66 (1985): 526–35.

Nietzsche, Friedrich. *Twilight of the Idols and the Anti-Christ*. Trans. R. J. Hollingdale. Harmondsworth: Penguin, 1968.

Norris, Margot. *The Decentered Universe of Finnegans Wake: A Structuralist Analysis*. Baltimore, Md.: Johns Hopkins University Press, 1976.

Nussbaum, Felicity. *The Brink of All We Hate: English Satires on Women, 1660–1750*. Lexington: University Press of Kentucky, 1984.

Nussbaum, Martha. "Perceptive Equilibrium: Literary Theory and Ethical Theory." In *The Future of Literary Theory*. Ed. Ralph Cohen. New York: Routledge, 1989, 58–87.

O'Brien, Flann. *At Swim-Two-Birds*. New York: New American Library, 1976. (Originally published 1939).

———. *The Dalkey Archive*. New York: Macmillan, 1965.

O'Brien, John. "Every Man His Voice." *Review of Contemporary Fiction* 1 (1981): 62–80.

Palmer, Paulina. "From 'Coded Mannequin' to Bird Woman: Angela Carter's Magic Flight." In *Women Reading Woman's Writing*. Ed. Sue Roe. New York: St. Martin's, 1987, 179–205.

Payne, F. Anne. *Chaucer and Menippean Satire*. Madison: University of Wisconsin Press, 1981.

Pearce, Richard. "Faulkner's One Ring Circus." *Wisconsin Studies in Contemporary Literature* 7 (1966): 270–83.

———. "Pynchon's Endings." *Novel* 18 (1985): 145–53.

———. "What Joyce After Pynchon?" In *James Joyce: The Centennial Symposium*. Ed. Morris Beja et al. Urbana: University of Illinois Press, 1986, 43–46.

Perec, Georges. *Life: A User's Manual*. Trans. David Bellos. Boston: David R. Godine, 1987. (Originally published in French, 1978).

———. *W, Or The Memory of a Childhood*. Trans. David Bellos. Boston: David R. Godine, 1988. (Originally published in French, 1975).

Petronius. *The Satyricon*. In *Petronius: "The Satyricon" and Seneca: "The Apocolocyntosis."* Trans. J. P. Sullivan. New York: Penguin, 1986, 37–160.

Porush, David. "Reading in the Servo-Mechanical Loop: The Machinery of Metaphor in Pynchon's Fictions." In his *The Soft Machine: Cybernetic Fiction*. New York: Methuen, 1985, 1–23.

Pynchon, Thomas. *The Crying of Lot 49*. New York: Harper and Row, 1986. (Originally published 1966.)

———. *Gravity's Rainbow*. New York: Viking, 1973.

———. *V.* New York: Harper and Row, 1986. (Originally published 1963.)

Rabelais, François. *Gargantua and Pantagruel*. Trans. Jacques Le Clerq. New York: Modern Library, 1944.

Reed, Ishmael. *Mumbo Jumbo*. New York: Doubleday, 1972.

Reizbaum, Marilyn. "A 'Modernism of Marginality': The Link between James Joyce and Djuna Barnes." In *New Alliances in Joyce Studies*. Ed. Bonnie Kime Scott. Newark: University of Delaware Press, 1988, 179–89.

Richter, Harvena. *Virginia Woolf: The Inward Voyage*. Princeton, N.J.: Princeton University Press, 1970.

Rosenfeld, Marthe. "The Linguistic Aspect of Sexual Conflict: Monique Wittig's *Le corps lesbien*." *Mosaic* 17 (1984): 235–41.

Ruegg, Maria. "Metaphor and Metonymy: The Logic of Structuralist Rhetoric." *Glyph* 6 (1979): 141–57.

Ruotolo, Lucio P. *The Interrupted Moment: A View of Virginia Woolf's Novels*. Stanford, Calif.: Stanford University Press, 1986.

Rushdie, Salman. "The Book Burning." *New York Review of Books* 26 (March 2, 1989): 26.

———. "The Empire Writes Back With a Vengeance." *London Times* (July 3, 1982): 8.

———. *Midnight's Children*. New York: Avon, 1982.

———. *The Satanic Verses*. New York: Viking, 1989.

———. *Shame*. London: Picador, 1983.

Russo, Mary. "Female Grotesques: Carnival and Theory." In *Feminist Studies/Critical Studies*. Ed. Teresa de Lauretis. Bloomington: Indiana University Press, 1986, 213–29.

Ryan, Michael. *Marxism and Deconstruction: A Critical Articulation*. Baltimore, Md.: Johns Hopkins University Press, 1982.

Sangari, Kumkum. "The Politics of the Possible." *Cultural Critique* 7 (1987): 157–86.

Scanlon, Larry. "The Authority of Fable: Allegory and Irony in the *Nun's Priest's Tale*." *Exemplaria* 1 (1989): 43–68.

Schlack, Beverly Ann. *Continuing Presences: Virginia Woolf's Use of Literary Allusion*. University Park: The Pennsylvania State University Press, 1979.

Schmeling, Gareth L., and David R. Rebmann. "T. S. Eliot and Petronius." *Comparative Literature Studies* 12 (1975): 393–410.

Schwartz, Beth C. "Thinking Back Through Our Mothers: Virginia Woolf Reads Shakespeare." Unpublished essay, University of Florida.

Scott, Bonnie Kime. *James Joyce*. Atlantic Highlands, N.J.: Humanities Press International, 1987.

———. *Joyce and Feminism*. Bloomington: Indiana University Press, 1984.

Shaktini, Namascar. "Displacing the Phallic Subject: Wittig's Lesbian Writing." *Signs* 8 (1982): 29–44.

Shklovsky, Viktor. "Sterne's *Tristram Shandy*: Stylistic Commentary." In *Russian Formalist Criticism: Four Essays*. Ed. Lee Lemon and Marion Reis. Lincoln: University of Nebraska Press, 1965, 25–57.

Shoaf, R. A. "Literary Theory, Medieval Studies, and the Crisis of Difference." In *Reorientations: Literary Theory, Pedagogy, and Social Change*. Ed. Bruce Henricksen and Thais Morgan. Urbana: University of Illinois Press, forthcoming.

———. "Medieval Studies After Derrida After Heidegger." In *Sign, Sentence, Discourse: Language in Medieval Thought and Literature*. Ed. Julian N. Wasserman and Lois Roney. Syracuse, N.Y.: Syracuse University Press, 1989, 9–30.

———. *Milton, Poet of Duality: A Study of Semiosis in the Poetry and the Prose*. New Haven: Yale University Press, 1985.

———. "The Play of Puns in Late Middle English Poetry: Concerning Juxtology." In *On Puns: The Foundation of Letters*. Ed. Jonathan Culler. London: Basil Blackwell, 1988, 44–61.

Showalter, Elaine. "A Criticism of Our Own." In *The Future of Literary Theory*. Ed. Ralph Cohen. New York: Routledge, 1989, 347–69.

Siebert, Donald T. "Swift's Fiat Odor: The Excremental Re-Vision." *Eighteenth Century Studies* 19 (1985): 21–38.

Siegle, Robert. *The Politics of Reflexivity: Narrative and Constitutive*

Poetics of Culture. Baltimore, Md.: Johns Hopkins University Press, 1986.

Silverman, Kaja. *The Subject of Semiotics.* New York: Oxford University Press, 1983.

Singer, Alan. *The Metaphorics of Fiction: Discontinuity and Discourse in the Modern Novel.* Tallahassee: University Presses of Florida, 1983.

Sklute, Larry. *Virtue of Necessity: Inconclusiveness and Narrative Form in Chaucer's Poetry.* Columbus: Ohio State University Press, 1984.

Slabey, Robert M. "Myth and Ritual in *Light in August.*" In *Studies in Light in August.* Ed. M. Thomas Inge. Columbus, Ohio: Charles E. Merrill, 1971, 75–98.

Smith, Barbara Herrnstein. *Poetic Closure: A Study of How Poems End.* Chicago: University of Chicago Press, 1968.

Soldo, John J. "T. S. Eliot and the Classics: The Influence of Petronius." *Markham Review* 11 (1982): 36–40.

Sorrentino, Gilbert. *Mulligan Stew.* New York: Grove, 1979.

Spanos, William V. "Postmodern Literature and Its Occasion: Retrieving the Preterite Middle." In his *Repetitions: The Postmodern Occasion in Literature and Culture.* Baton Rouge: Louisiana State University Press, 1987, 189–276.

Stallybrass, Peter, and Allon White. *The Politics and Poetics of Transgression.* Ithaca, N.Y.: Cornell University Press, 1986.

Sterne, Laurence. *The Life and Opinions of Tristram Shandy, Gentleman.* Norton Critical Edition. New York: Norton, 1980.

Sterne, Laurence. *A Sentimental Journey through France and Italy by Mr. Yorick.* New York: Oxford University Press, 1984.

Stevens, Wallace. *The Collected Poems.* New York: Alfred A. Knopf, 1954.

Straus, Barrie Ruth. "The Subversive Discourse of the Wife of Bath: Phallocentric Discourse and the Imprisonment of Criticism." *ELH* 55 (1988): 527–54.

Suleiman, Susan Rubin. "(Re)writing the Body: The Politics and Poetics of Female Eroticism." In *The Female Body in Western Culture.* Ed. Susan Rubin Suleiman. Cambridge: Harvard University Press, 1986, 7–29.

Sullivan, J. P. Introduction to *Petronius: "The Satyricon" and Seneca: "The Apocolocyntosis."* New York: Penguin, 1986, 11–32.

Sultan, Stanley. *Ulysses, The Waste Land, and Modernism: A Jubilee Study.* London: Kennikat, 1977.

Tambling, Jeremy. *Dante and Difference: Writing in the Commedia.* Cambridge: Cambridge University Press, 1988.

Tanner, Tony. *Adultery in the Novel: Contract and Transgression*. Baltimore, Md.: Johns Hopkins University Press, 1979.

Thielemans, John. "The Energy of an Absence: Perfection as Useful Fiction in the Novels of Gaddis and Sorrentino." In *Critical Angles: European Views of Contemporary American Literature*. Ed. Marc Chénetier. Carbondale: Southern Illinois University Press, 1986, 105–24.

Thomson, Clive. "Bakhtin's 'Theory' of Genre." *Twentieth-Century Literature* 9 (1984): 29–40.

Todorov, Tzvetan. *The Fantastic: A Structural Approach to a Literary Genre*. Trans. Richard Howard. Ithaca, N.Y.: Cornell University Press, 1975.

Turner, Rory R. B. "Subjects and Symbols: Transformations of Identity in *Nights at the Circus*." *Folklore Forum* 20 (1987): 39–60.

Ulmer, Gregory L. "The Object of Post-Criticism." In *The Anti-Aesthetic: Essays on Postmodern Culture*. Ed. Hal Foster. Port Townsend, Wash.: Bay Press, 1983, 83–110.

Vance, Eugene. *Mervelous Signals: Poetics and Sign Theory in the Middle Ages*. Lincoln: University of Nebraska Press, 1986.

Vidal, Gore. *Myra Breckenridge*. Boston: Little, Brown, 1968.

Wasson, Richard. "From Priest to Prometheus: Culture and Criticism in the Post-Modernist Period." *Journal of Modern Literature* 3 (1974): 1188–1202.

Wenzel, Hélène Vivienne. "The Text as Body/Politics: An Appreciation of Monique Wittig's Writings in Context." *Feminist Studies* 7 (1981): 264–87.

White, Allon. "Bakhtin, Sociolinguistics and Deconstruction." In *The Theory of Reading*. Ed. Frank Gloversmith. New York: Barnes and Noble, 1984, 123–46.

———. "Pigs and Pierrots: The Politics of Transgression in Modern Fiction." *Raritan* 11 (1982): 51–70.

Wilde, Alan. *Horizons of Assent: Modernism, Postmodernism, and the Ironic Imagination*. Baltimore, Md.: Johns Hopkins University Press, 1981.

Wilson, J. J. "Why is *Orlando* Difficult?" In *New Feminist Essays on Virginia Woolf*. Ed. Jane Marcus. Lincoln: University of Nebraska Press, 1981, 170–84.

Wilson, Keith. "*Midnight's Children* and Reader Responsibility." *Critical Quarterly* 26 (1984): 23–37.

Wittig, Monique. *Les Guérillères*. Trans. David Le Vay. Boston: Beacon, 1985.

———. *The Lesbian Body*. Trans. David Le Vay. Boston: Beacon, 1986.

———. "Paradigm." Trans. George Stambolian. In *Homosexualities* and *French Literature*. Ed. George Stambolian and Elaine Marks. Ithaca, N.Y.: Cornell University Press, 1979, 114–21.

Wittig, Monique, and Sande Zeig, *Lesbian Peoples: Material for a Dictionary*. New York: Avon, 1979.

Wolf, Christa. *Cassandra: A Novel and Four Essays*. Trans. Jan Van Heurck. New York: Farrar, Straus, and Giroux, 1984.

Woolf, Virginia. "'Anon' and 'The Reader': Virginia Woolf's Last Essays." Ed. Brenda R. Silver. *Twentieth-Century Literature* 25 (1979): 356–441.

———. *The Diary of Virginia Woolf*. 5 vols., 1915–41. Ed. Anne Olivier Bell. New York: Harcourt Brace Jovanovich, 1977–84.

———. *Mrs. Dalloway*. New York: Harcourt, Brace, 1925.

———. *Orlando*. New York: Harcourt Brace Jovanovich, 1956.

———. "Professions for Women." In her *The Death of the Moth and Other Essays*. San Diego: Harcourt Brace Jovanovich, 1942, 235–42.

———. *A Room of One's Own*. New York: Harcourt Brace Jovanovich, 1929.

———. *The Waves*. New York: Harcourt, Brace, Jovanovich, 1931.

———. *A Writer's Diary*. Ed. Leonard Woolf. New York: Harcourt, Brace, 1954.

Yaeger, Patricia. *Honey-Mad Women: Emancipatory Strategies in Women's Writing*. New York: Columbia University Press, 1988.

INDEX

Cixous, Hélène, 82, 163, 164, 169, 173, 180, 181, 187, 189, 191, 192, 203, 204, 206, 211, 221, 228, 231, 232, 234, 235, 264nn.1, 6, 267n.27, 268n.5
Clark, Robert, 231, 232
Clément, Catherine, 241
Collins, Jim, 11, 12
Cook, Jon, 46, 55
Cooper, Helen, 20, 35, 249n.2
Coover, Robert, 148–50, 156
Couto, Maria, 50
Cowart, David, 265
Crowder, Diane Griffin, 191, 194, 201, 203, 264n.7
Culler, Jonathan, 251n.11

Dante Alighieri, 1, 2, 31, 34, 43, 212, 257n.1
Davidson, Cathy N., 198
Delaney, Samuel R., 6, 12, 160
de Lauretis, Teresa, 132–34, 137, 138, 159, 187, 259n.2, 268n.34
Derrida, Jacques, 23–26, 33, 34, 47, 61, 66, 67, 86–88, 97, 102, 117, 250n.3, 256n.21, 258n.10, 259n.10
Dinshaw, Carolyn, 137, 138, 149, 251n.12, 259n.4, 260n.5
Donaldson, E. Talbot, 42
Dunn, Allen, 251n.14
Durand, Laura G., 190, 200, 266n.20

Eagleton, Terry, 6, 7, 128
Eco, Umberto, 26
Eliot, George, 258n.9
Eliot, T. S., 144, 165, 198, 211, 217–19, 228, 229, 241, 260n.13, 263n.19, 265n.14, 268n.3, 269n.12, 270n.14
Engle, Lars, 251n.16

Faulkner, William, 90, 141–43, 146, 156, 260n.8
Felman, Shoshana, 114, 121
Ferster, Judith, 252n.23
Fetterley, Judith, 11, 258n.8
Fineman, Joel, 266n.21
Flaubert, Gustave, 110–12
Fleischman, Avrom, 167
Fokkema, Douwe, 250n.4
Foster, Hal, 99
Foucault, Michel, 81, 102, 104–6, 116, 122, 209, 233, 234, 247, 258n.4, 264n.9
Fowler, Alastair, 81, 82, 165
Fowles, John, 14, 16, 17, 52, 100–131, 149, 231, 232, 245, 252n.20, 257n.4, 258n.8, 259n.10
Fox, Alice, 176
Fox, W. Sherwood, 262n.1
Frank, Joseph, 211, 215, 268n.1
Frazer, Sir James George, 137, 142
Freccero, John, 251n.10
Freud, Sigmund, 105, 133–36, 139, 140, 193, 194, 217, 241, 265n.10
Frye, Northrop, 167

Gardiner, Judith Kegan, 268n.31
Gass, William, 154, 155
Gilbert, Sandra M., 134, 158, 159, 164, 172, 173, 183, 197, 198, 218, 219, 222, 229, 230, 253n.4, 259n.13
Girard, René, 247
Gluck, Barbara Reich, 211
Graff, Gerald, 7
Graham, John, 166, 169, 172
Grass, Günter, 67, 178, 187, 256n.22, 269n.8
Greiner, Donald J., 82–85
Gubar, Susan, 134, 159, 164, 172, 183, 197, 218, 219, 222, 229, 230, 253n.4, 271n.31

Haller, Evelyn, 265
Hannah, Barry, 20
Hart, Clive, 97
Hayman, David, 31, 78, 147, 148
Hemingway, Ernest, 103, 143, 144, 146, 156
Herr, Cheryl, 158
Herrmann, Anne, 176
Higgins, Lynn, 195, 204–6, 264n.4
Hill, Christopher, 2
Hofstadter, Douglas, 250n.5
Holland, Norman N., 268n.31
Holquist, Michael, 91
Housman, A. E., 4, 5
Howard, Richard, 102, 258n.7
Howe, Irving, 143
Hume, Kathryn, 89
Hutcheon, Linda, 7, 197, 231, 257n.2
Huyssen, Andreas, 257n.6